THE SUBVERSIVE SCRIBE

Translating Latin American Fiction

1 9 9 1

BOOKS TRANSLATED BY

SUZANNE JILL LEVINE

THE
SUBVERSIVE
SCRIBE

Translating Latin American Fiction

by Suzanne Jill Levine

GRAYWOLF PRESS / SAINT PAUL

Copyright © 1991 by Suzanne Jill Levine

Publication of this volume is made possible in part by a grant provided by the Minnesota State Arts Board through an appropriation by the Minnesota State Legislature, and by a grant from the National Endowment for the Arts. Additional support has been provided by generous contributions from foundations, corporations, and individuals, and through a major grant from the Northwest Area Foundation. Graywolf Press is a member agency of United Arts, Saint Paul.

Published by
GRAYWOLF PRESS
2402 University Avenue, Saint Paul, Minnesota 55114
All rights reserved.

ISBN 1-55597-146-6

9 8 7 6 5 4 3 2
First Printing, 1991

Library of Congress Cataloging-in-Publication Data
Levine, Suzanne Jill.
    The subversive scribe : translating Latin American fiction / by
Suzanne Jill Levine.
        p.   cm.
    Includes index.
    ISBN 1-55597-146-6 (pbk.) : $12.00
    1. Spanish American fiction—20th century—Translations into
English.   2. Spanish language—Translating into English.
3. Translating and interpreting.   4. Levine, Suzanne Jill.
I. Title.
PQ6044.L48   1991
863—dc20   91-15298

To Alice and Ben,

to the memory of my mother and father,

and in memory of Manuel Puig, who died July 22, 1990

Acknowledgments

Many are the dear friends and colleagues who encouraged me and offered helpful suggestions as I shaped my observations of the translation process into a book. Among them I would like to thank John Alexander Coleman, Guillermo Cabrera Infante, Eliot Weinberger, Claudia Gorbman, Martine Loutfi, Lydia Rubio, Kathleen Agena, Jeffrey Peck, Lawrence Venuti, Ernest Volinn, and especially the late Emir Rodríguez Monegal, to whom I am indebted for his inspirational presence in my life. I am particularly grateful to Cecilia Vicuña for her aid in revising the final manuscript and her belief in the artist in me.

I would also like to acknowledge the support of the Graduate School Research Fund at the University of Washington in Seattle and of the Interdisciplinary Humanities Center (as well as director Paul Hernadi and assistant director Barbara Herr Harthorn) and a Regents' Humanities Faculty Fellowship at the University of California at Santa Barbara. Thanks, too, to the National Endowment for the Arts for facilitating my task as a translator.

Earlier versions of sections in this book have appeared in *Translation, Review, World Literature Today, SubStance,* and in *The Art of Translation: Voices from the Field,* edited by Rosanna Warren. I am grateful to the editors for permission to reprint.

Table of Contents

Preface

Look, you're not alone in your feeling . . . the cultural moment is discovered in a fragment of created relation . . . It's the poet's and translator's perception, not the cultural or literary historian's.

CHARLES TOMLINSON

YOU OFTEN seek in the foreign what you are drawn to, perhaps unknowingly, in the familiar. I was born and raised in New York City, in a culture within a culture, in an "assimilated" Jewish family in which my mother spoke Yiddish to my father when she didn't want me to understand the topic of conversation. I made my first entry at age twelve into another language, French. The teacher, a gentleman with a British accent who recalled Alastair Sim in the sinister comedy film *The Green Man,* would tease us constantly, threatening that we would become "a grease spot on Academy Street" if we didn't learn our conjugations "chop chop." He made French into a *jeu de mots* and I played the game with ease since I seemed to have what they called an aptitude. Maybe too, I wanted to have access to a mysterious code, like my mother. But most of all I was curious to be transported, not from the sixth–floor window to Academy Street, but into a foreign world. We translate to be translated.

My first journey abroad in 1965 was also my first sojourn, for a year during college, in Spain. This experience brought home the magnetism of the Spanish language and culture. Hispanic expressiveness was deliciously exotic and yet evoked my Jewish background, which had

v

been relegated to oblivion. Even the topography of Ronda de Segovia in the old part of Madrid where I resided – with its macaronic colorfulness, the cries of lottery ticket vendors, the smell of olive oil frying – recalled somehow the ethnic (then Jewish, Irish, and Italian) New York neighborhood of my childhood. I eagerly donned the linguistic mask of Castilian Spanish, expressing myself more emphatically in Spanish than in English. But wasn't this mask also a means of bringing to life parts of myself suppressed in English? By adopting this exotic yet strangely familiar culture I had strayed from Anglo-American culture and language, but I was following, in a veiled way, my mother's forked path to a promised land of Yiddish words from which, in my "own" language, I was exiled.

When I first thought of translating, in college, as a Spanish major who dabbled in French and English literature courses, it struck me that the fun part would be to take on the most uncompromising texts, to try to solve the most difficult puzzles. The first Spanish work I attempted to translate was the subject of my senior thesis: the Galician Ramón del Valle Inclán's expressionist poetic drama *Divinas palabras*. Someday I would learn that the opaque style of "Divine Words" could find its closest historical equivalent in English in the convoluted arabesques of the decadent poet Algernon Swinburne. In attempting to translate Valle Inclán I encountered a resistance in English that derived from diverging rhetorical traditions.

Baroque extravagance was suppressed officially in English in the late seventeenth century by the Royal Society. The following pronouncement from the Bishop Sprat in his *History of the Royal Society of London* (1667), cited by Northrop Frye, documents this censorship:

> They have therefore been most rigorous in putting in execution the only Remedy that can be found for this *extravagance,* and that has been a constant Resolution to reject all amplifications, digressions, and swellings of style; to return back to the primitive purity and shortness, when men deliver'd so many *things* almost in an equal number of *words.* They have exacted from all their members a close, naked, natural way of speaking, positive expressions, clear senses, a native easiness, bringing all things as near the Mathematical plainness as they can, and preferring the language of Artizans, Countrymen, and Merchants, before that of Wits and Scholars. (350)

The Spanish Royal Academy did not perform the same surgery. José Lezama Lima, modern master of the Cuban neobaroque, wrote in *"La curiosidad barroca"*:

> Our Baroque, which began to flourish toward the end of the XVIIth century and all through the XVIIIth, coincided with the Enlightenment. Indeed, often grounded in Cartesian scientifism, in a rigorous search for knowledge, our Baroque writers (notably Sor Juana Ines de la Cruz) even preceded neo-classicism. (37)

Could it be that those of us who translate between Spanish and English are unconsciously working our way back to that common ground, classical rhetoric? At age twenty, confronting Valle Inclán's divine words, I felt that my own were hopelessly mundane. I gave up in exasperation after two pages, but years later, translating the poetic prose of the Cuban Severo Sarduy, I sought ways to resurrect traces of the dormant baroque in our pragmatic language, perhaps reversing some of the progress praised in the Bishop's dictum.

In 1969 I was in graduate school at Columbia University, where I had evolved from Iberian to Latin American Studies and where one of my professors, the translator Gregory Rabassa, encouraged me to pursue my curiosity to translate. Not willing to abandon the protective walls of academe for the dog-eat-dog world of freelance writers and commercial publishing, I was at the same time not satisfied with the traditional scholarly course. That translation and research were mutually enriching rather than exclusive seemed obvious from the start, and was confirmed years later when my doctoral research on the works of the Argentine writer Adolfo Bioy Casares began inadvertently in the process of translating his novella *Plan de evasión* (1945).

The very first piece I translated was *"Blacamán el bueno, vendedor de milagros,"* a short story about a charlatan miracle-seller, by Gabriel García Márquez, the now world-famous Columbian writer who was then the relatively obscure subject of my master's thesis. Just as the miracle-seller had to hawk his goods, I had to produce a rhetoric to persuade the reader that I could translate. Greg later did a much better version of this story, but it was nonetheless exciting to publish my first translation in a small English journal, *The London Magazine*. Venturing into the literary circles of New York, I had the good fortune to become acquainted with a lively coterie of displaced Latin American intellectuals and literati, among them the late Uruguayan literary critic Emir Rodríguez Monegal, then a professor at Yale University. Previously the director of the Paris-based Latin American journal *Mundo Nuevo,* he had introduced a number of unknown writers to an international readership, helping to foment what has been called the Latin American "Boom." It was Emir who urged me to read Guillermo Cabrera Infante's *Tres tristes tigres* (1965) and Manuel Puig's *La traición de Rita Hayworth* (1967).

The first chapters of *Rita Hayworth* were daunting: One-sided dialogues and thick Argentine monologues in the first chapters made it impossible to know who the characters were. Puig's hyperrealist technique of recording spoken language was a mimetic tour de force, but only an Argentine could understand what he wrote, I thought. It wasn't until reading his second novel, the more accessible *Boquitas pintadas* (1968), laughing and emoting with a cast of soap opera characters whose pleasures and pains transcended the language barrier, that I could gain entrance to his fictive town of Colonel Vallejos, and attempt to translate the words uttered in Puig's unique voice(s).

Guillermo Cabrera Infante's *Tres tristes tigres* also seduced the reader by re-creating a spoken language so real that one's impulse was to read the book aloud to friends, or to bring that language to spoken life in yet another, in one's own. "Three sad tigers," exiled from their *triste tropique,* would soon be sacrificed to Pun, the god of alliteration, and translated into *Three Trapped Tigers.*

Scientists could come up with new inventions; astronauts could set foot on new planets; the only frontier adventure available to the translator seemed to be the crossing of language and cultural barriers, stepping through the Looking Glass to see what a presumably untranslatable Spanish text would look like on the other side, in English. I was challenged thus (and perhaps doomed to the fate of Borges's pathetic Pierre Menard or Flaubert's bumbling Bouvard and Pécuchet) by these Latin American fictions.

What gave me some hope of creating a bridge was a shared (though radically different) "American" experience. I have translated works mostly from Cuba and Argentina, two dominant, opposing poles marking the diverse continent south of the United States, the "Northern Colossus." Argentina, one of the first countries to obtain independence from Spain, is closer culturally and racially to France and Italy. Cuba, where African and indigenous races intermingle with Hispanic blood, was one of the last to break from Spanish dominion. These two countries have been among the most prolific and innovative sources of literature in Latin America, in part because their principal cities have been such dynamic cosmopolitan centers.

Havana and Buenos Aires evolved in the same way as sprawling American cities such as New York, as havens for exiles, or for the grandchildren of exiles, cities where immigrant and native or black and white mingled, inventing a common living language and culture. These cities assimilated the cultural products of Europe and North America; this bridge between North and South, with the negative cargo of economic and cultural imperialism but also the positive charge of a shared energy and sensibility, made it initially possible for me to cross over. Like the streetwise Cabrera Infante and Puig, I too was nourished on the words and images of the American movies of the Thirties, Forties, and Fifties. My childhood as the youngest in a family of much older siblings put me in touch with this recent past, its values, emotions, and motion pictures.

Friendship preceded my role as one of *Tres tristes tigres*'s translators. The same year I read the book, I was introduced by Emir Rodríguez Monegal to Guillermo Cabrera Infante in his home in exile in the then swinging London, on an island far away from his native Cuba. I entered the flat on Gloucester Road (tripping nervously over the hardwood English threshold) in the company of Emir, and we were escorted down a long hallway by Guillermo's tall, dark-haired wife, Miriam Gómez, to a tiger-skin wallpapered den. It was Guillermo's brown study and there he was, sitting squatly (his Smith-Corona handy on a nearby desk snug against the rear window), this short fellow with somewhat Oriental features cum mustache. On the desk was a detailed map of Havana, which – I discovered later – he would take with him on all extended journeys, invariably stationing it reverently on the temporary desk in a hotel or at a friend's home.

Poker-faced humor spilled forth with his first words and especially when we began bandying words over the translation he was grappling with. *Tres tristes tigres* was his homage to Havana nightlife on the eve of Batista's fall. This "open novel," as it has been called, a "collage" of interweaving narratives, mainly in Cuban or in a Joycean re-creation of Havanan spoken dialect, required an open translation. The English version of *TTT* (Cabrera Infante coined this abbreviation) had to be written, spoken rather, in American English, an idiom full of sounds more in tune with crude Cuban than bloody British, just as Havana was closer geographically, culturally, even racially to New York than to the island-city of Cabrera Infante's exile, exotic London.

"Ah Bartleby, ah humanity!" Like Melville's scribe, we are all one in a double sense—at once unique and similar to the next person. Both Cabrera Infante and I dropped out of kindergarten; our first literary passions were the comics. He began building his vocabulary on *Dick Tracy* and *Tarzan* and his first "literary love" was Dragon Lady, a silky Oriental in *Terry and the Pirates*. Another primal literary affinity was that liberating world of nonsense, Lewis Carroll's *Alice's Adventures in Wonderland*. I had read *Alice in Wonderland* (and *Through the Looking Glass*) over and over again in my childhood and early adolescence—to escape the harsh Bronx accents and realities of working-class life in New York but also because it was a book hanging around the house, and like all children I was a tinkerer, making use of what was at hand. Years later, on a subsequent trip to London and Cabrera Infante, I visited Oxford, ostensibly on an academic mission but really to see the mythic site of the rabbit hole down which I had fallen so often in childhood, into an imaginary adventure.

We both relate uneasily to the length of our full names, and to the choice of our first names—Guillermo (too ordinary he always felt), Suzanne (too formal I always felt). "GCI" signed his first stories Guillermo C. Infante. In a letter concerning the translation of *La habana para un infante difunto* (literally, *Havana for a Dead Infant*, 1979), the book that became *Infante's Inferno*, he wrote (Jan. 26, 1980),

> Title page: Please take a look at the book. Forget about my first name and substitute it for just a G(igolo). I want to forget my first name first. Besides, the whole of it is quite a mouthful.

The narrator in *Infante's Inferno* explicitly admits a distaste for his too ordinary long name:

I repeated my name to her! So that she wouldn't forget it I gave her what was really my pseudonym. I've always felt that my real name, long and disorderly, is also forgettable. (269)

The connoisseur of Cabrera Infante can safely presume that the above-mentioned pseudonym is the acronym "Caín," to whom we are introduced in *Un oficio del siglo XX* (*A Twentieth-Century Job,* 1963). Cabrera Infante constructed this novel-essay collage out of "Caín's" film reviews and chronicles for Havana magazines from 1954 to 1960, under the anarchic inspiration of "Citizen Kane" Orson Welles. The more primal, biblical allusion is not casual: There were deep-seated rivalries between Guillermo and his younger sibling Sabá, both aspiring artists.

Cabrera Infante, or Caín, true to his name, is an abuser, a subversive of language: No name is sacred to him, including his own; the word lost its logocentric value in his private world of Havana night-talk. As a prospective translator-collaborator of *TTT* I was at first fearing to tread in these treacherous Cuban waters (what did I know from Cuban, then?), and Guillermo's autograph on my copy of *TTT* would have served as a caveat to one more sensible—"For Jill, *Three Sad Tigers,* with the hope that they don't turn out to be too ferocious, Cuban, that is. . . London, March 19, 1969"—but the fact that I was going to be working with the author himself seemed, at least then, to be a great advantage. With Guillermo and his three tigers I would be learning a lot of Cuban—also a lot about writing—and I wouldn't be accused of profaning a sacred script, because the author himself would be the first *traditore*. I was the willing apprentice of Count Dracula Infante, ready to tread upon his dread Transylvania (without a cross upon my breast, only the author as albatross), to follow him unfaithfully (*traditora*) into that dimension of the Living Dead, the world of writing.

To write about translation is to write about one of writing's most conscious operations, the one that lays open the function of writing as a manipulation of words and not of realities.

E. RODRÍGUEZ MONEGAL,
Borges: A Literary Biography

WHY HAS the art of translating poetry eclipsed that of prose in the history of translation studies? The answer seems simple: We have commonly believed that the poetry translator must be a poet, and therefore that his technique or philosophy deserves our inquiry, but any somewhat bilingual individual with dictionary in hand can translate a prose text. Again, the common belief is that novels are easier to translate than poetry. The traditional virtue of translators, particularly prose translators, has been their invisibility as humble scribes, scribbling transparent texts in the cellar of the castle of Literature.

The formal and linguistic complexities of twentieth-century fiction obviously belie these feudal notions. Exposing the poetics of prose translation and the prose translator's role as creative writer and literary critic can provide invaluable insights, for translation is the most concrete form of the interpretive act performed by all readers, scholars, and teachers of foreign literatures. Translations and the practice of translating, says Gideon Toury, are *observational facts;* the description of these facts is not only essential but prior to any possible theory. Self-referential inquisitions by prose translators should provide useful models for translation studies as well as models of self-questioning for all interpreters.

Umberto Eco speaks of telling the process of writing as an activity apart from the writing itself:

> Telling how you wrote something does not mean proving it is "well" written. Poe said that the effect of the work is one thing and the knowledge of the process is another. . . . Sometimes the most illuminating pages on the artistic process have been written by minor artists, who achieved modest effects but knew how to ponder their own processes. (11–12)

With this *excusatio propter infirmitatem* in mind, I would like to explain briefly what motivated me to write a book about translation.

The project began as a collection of the various notes, articles, and essays I had written from 1971 to 1984. My first attempt to record the challenging process of my first two translations, *Three Trapped Tigers* and *Betrayed by Rita Hayworth,* was guilelessly called "Notes on Translation." What struck me almost immediately about these early translation experiences was how much richer the process was than the final product. Writing about translation made me even more keenly aware that the reader could gain a more intimate knowledge of the literary work, and of the languages and cultures involved in the dialogue between original and translation, if only he or she knew how translation decisions were made, and how possible choices were finally set aside for what were considered better solutions.

These early translations were also close collaborations, or "closelaborations," a neologism coined by Guillermo Cabrera Infante. As I worked with him, and later with Manuel Puig, I observed that the dilemma of one word versus another was not a problem unique to translation. The original writer constantly chooses words and phrases, compelled by intuitions and reasons that often have more to do with language than with his own intentions; as the composer Maurice Ravel once responded to a eulogizing critic, creativity is not a matter of inspiration but of choices, of decision-making. The original is one of many possible versions. When jotting down these first notes, I realized that not only did the reader "lose" the constant dilemmas and fugitive process of the translation but also my ongoing dialogue with the authors. Since their letters reveal tantalizing views of the relationship between original and translation – both as product and process – I have translated excerpts that will serve as primary material in my presentations of translation strategies.

Other reasons for writing such a study took shape as I made the transition from freelance translator to university professor. The academic community is still under the sway of the positivist prejudice against translation as an unimaginative and unscholarly activity, and as Carol Maier observes, it still sees translation as "a task that does not occur in the realms of thought but between the pages of a dictionary." (25) Especially the translation of contemporary fiction situates me in a sphere that is too "literary" in the eyes of more traditional colleagues. The translation of poetry, both classical and modern, and of classical drama, have been marginal scholarly concerns, but does contemporary fiction merit the same respect? So far only James Joyce, the genius of modernism: *Finnegans Wake,* paradigm of the modern, provides in fiction what Pound forged in poetry, a theoretical though controversial place for translation as interpretation and creation.

But what can we learn from the translation of contemporary fiction – most of it not yet canonized – and particularly of works from "marginal" countries such as Cuba and Argentina? Much of contemporary Latin American literature, beginning perhaps with the master fabulist Jorge Luis Borges, falls under the rubric of "postmodernism," a tendency that reflects (for some) exhaustion; John Barth describes Borges's originality and obsessive, implicit theme as the "difficulty, perhaps unnecessity of writing original works." (22) Postmodern writers such as those I've translated and am writing about – Cabrera Infante, Puig, Severo Sarduy – have attempted to revitalize Literature by turning to popular forms. Is such writing worthy of translation, and do the problems involved in translating it deserve our attention?

I attempt here to address and to redress these questions. In a world preoccupied more with present than past, English speakers today need to know the concerns expressed in other languages; North American readers need to hear the voices of that "other" America alienated from the United States by a torturous political history. But these readers also need to understand *how* Latin American writing is transmitted to them, and *how* differences and similarities between cultures and languages affect *what* is finally transmitted. Knowing the other and how we receive or hear the other is a fundamental step toward knowing ourselves.

Introduction

Perhaps the translator's craft is more subtle, more civilized than the writer's: the translator obviously comes after the writer. Translation is a more advanced stage.

JORGE LUIS BORGES

Between Language

Translators, upon escaping the mother tongue in order to serve another language, experience exile in their own language, and share with exiles an expanded cultural context that gives them a privileged view of their original language's limitations. One becomes more conscious of the mother tongue's mechanisms by experiencing it from without, and now finds something missing. "Kindred spirits" is not quite *almas afines; afin,* from "affinity," seems more intimate than "kindred," *alma* more personal than "spirit." Commenting on Walter Benjamin's seminal essay "The Task of the Translator," Maurice Blanchot writes:

> The translator is indeed a strange, nostalgic man: he experiences in his own language, but in the manner of something missing, everything promised him in the way of present affirmations by the original work (the work which remains moreover – he can't quite reach it since he's not at home, at rest in its language but is an eternal guest who doesn't live there). That's why, if we can believe the testimony of specialists, he is always in more difficulty as he translates with the language to which he belongs than at a loss with the one he doesn't possess. (155)

The special or private associations as well as standard societal implications of words in one language seem, like poetry, untranslatable.

I

The translator's fate dramatizes that of the writer caught between the language of writing and the Real, or the elusive past, a "foreign country" as L. P. Hartley prefaces his novel *The Go-Between*. "My" language (in which I am also a visitor) can never fully express the Spanish original, but now I must make mine "home" again, express as fully as possible the other in whatever is my version of American English, for we all have our own private lexicon, even grammar. Translating is a mode of writing that might enable one to find one's own language through another's, but then again all writing involves such a search. Perhaps a found style completes the search, but doesn't the original language, intention, or reality remain eternally elusive? How faithful can one be? And faithful to what?

The "impossible" task of translation has long been the subject of philosophical and linguistic inquiry: Translation inevitably, disturbingly divorces sign and sense. A given word has different connotations, as well as different relationships to other words in its language, than its closest equivalent (or equivalents) in another language.

Consider briefly the lacunae between Spanish and English. The pitfalls are many: the temptation to choose cognates, Latinate words whose effect in English is often archaic, or even vague, such as *amiable,* whereas the Spanish counterpart *amable* is a common, vivid word. Or the betrayal of gender-identified noun in Romance languages by the neuter noun in English: *La luna* is always more feminine than "the moon."

A provocative grammatical difference is the optional presence of the subject pronoun in Spanish: The subject can be ambiguously (un)designated, subsumed in the predicate verb unless the writer needs to emphasize or clarify the subject's identity. José Lezama Lima set syntax free by generating sentences with floating subjects and objects in his novels *Paradiso* and *Oppiano Licario*. Upon translating an excerpt from the posthumously published *Oppiano Licario* some years back, I came across numerous instances of pronominal ambiguity, such as

> *Yo creo que Licario, conocedor de ese secreto como muchos otros, lo hizo budista. Ha dominado el ansia nefasta¿ tuvo acaso que hacer ese esfuerzo? y en él, según el simbolo tan reiterado por los devotos de esa religión, el dolor resbala como una gota de agua en una hoja de loto.* (180)

In the following literal translation you can see my•doubts:

> I think Licario, knowing this secret among many others, made [it, him –
> Abatón, a previous subject in the paragraph] Buddhist. Nefarious desire
> prevailed: did [he] [Licario] have to make an effort? Upon [him, it], accord-
> ing to the symbol so worshipped by these devotees, pain slides like a dew
> drop down a lotus flower.

By the time Lezama places an explicit *él* the reader is floating in uncer-
tainty: Who or what produces and receives actions here? The question
is, does Lezama's ambiguity speak to the Buddhist dissipation of the
ego, favoring an identification and erotic intermingling of the bodies
and souls of a group of friends, or to hallucinated distraction?

Intentional ambiguity permeated the first pages of Chilean author
José Donoso's *El lugar sin límites,* which I translated as *Hell Has No
Limits,* misquoting the title's source phrase "hell hath no limits" from
Marlowe's *The Tragical History of Dr. Faustus.* The novella begins by
introducing the principal character, a homosexual nicknamed La Ma-
nuela. Spanish enabled Donoso to imply gender duplicity, to maintain
the ambivalence of the subject's gender until, on page two, a male
character is quoted unequivocally as saying: "I'll screw the two of
them, Japonesita and her fag of a father." (150) In English I had no
choice but to use "she" right from the beginning since the third-person
narrator and other characters address "her." The effect changes in English, making the transition from "her" to "him" more explicit
though still appropriate to the disruptive jolt produced in the original.

These grammatical differences subsume, again, an ideological
schism: Spanish did not suffer the purge that English sustained. The
Spanish language tolerates, even seeks polyvalence, while modern English demands straightforward clarity. Translations are judged – by
editors and critics – even more severely than originals in this light. Our
detractors would tend to attribute ambiguity to literalism on the translator's part whereas inaccessible originals, in this century of vanguard-
isms and postmodernism, can pass as great art.

A translation should be a critical act, however, creating doubt, posing questions to its reader, recontextualizing the ideology of the original text. Since a good translation, as with all rhetoric, aims to (re)pro-
duce an effect, to persuade a reader, it is, in the broadest terms, a politi-

3

cal act. The good translator performs a balancing act, then, attempting to push language beyond its limits while at the same time maintaining a common ground of dialogue between writer and reader, speaker and listener.

Some have argued that *languages* or systems of signs can be translated, equivalents can be found, but that texts or *discourse* (involving a particular dialogue between text and context) cannot. You don't translate texts but rather you attempt to re-create contexts – inevitably lost, of course. And then there's the tantalizing question, Where does the context end and the text begin? But then again, the supposedly sacred boundaries between languages are not absolute; there are secret bonds among all languages. The bilingual writer, the translator, the exile can all vouch for language's impurity, the fact that no language is an island unto itself, that every language contains other languages. The Arab poet Meddeb, who writes in French, for example, notes that his mother tongue, the language "underneath," organizes a poetics in the borrowed language.

History's perpetual cycling of empires, colonizations, and migrations confirms the problematic nature of languages's boundaries, allowing languages to invade one another, as is reflected in polyglot Latin America and its literatures. *Tres tristes tigres* is nearly a bilingual book, riddled with invasive English from the United States. And our American English version of *TTT* takes advantage of Cuban Spanish's invasion of American English, an invasion that began during the discovery and colonization of the Americas. The Spanish contribution to American English and Cabrera Infante's Cuban polyglotism provoked me to bring attention, for example, to the "Havana" motif lost in the English title of Cabrera Infante's *La habana para un infante difunto* by maintaining in English the narrator's frequently uttered word *habanera* – meaning "woman from Havana." The fact that habanera is accepted in English, even though only in its limited definition as a musical form, made possible this "invasion" of boundaries.

A Poetics of Translation

In 1932, in *"Las versiones homéricas,"* an essay that could be translated as "Some Versions of Homer," Jorge Luis Borges questioned the privi-

4

leged status of the original books we call the *Odyssey* and the *Iliad*. Which interpretation of the original is the "original"? he asked; only a Greek from the tenth century B.C. (according to Borges) might be able to tell us. Borges prefigured here Michel Foucault's challenge to the concept of authorship: What is an author? How can we determine intentionality? The only real difference between original and translation – Borges playfully specified – is that the translator's referent is a *visible* text against which the translation can be judged; the original escapes this sceptical scrutiny because its referent is unspoken, perhaps forgotten, and probably embarrassingly banal.

This meditation on translation contains the subversive seed of Borges's poetics of "reading as writing," which he articulated further in 1939 in his perverse parable "Pierre Menard, Author of Don Quixote," the piece that George Steiner, in *After Babel,* considers the summa of all translation theory. Here Cervantes's masterpiece becomes a tentative web of propositions that change with each new historical act of reading; each successive reading, rewriting, translating of a text enriches and ensures the original's survival anew. Every work enters into a dialogue with other texts, and with a context; texts are *relationships* that of necessity evolve in other contexts.

Borges has shown us how literary works already give us the theoretical models through which we may interpret them: "Some Versions of Homer" and "Pierre Menard" both prefigure reader-response and reception theories. These texts reveal not only the thin line between originals and their interpretations but the parallel and complementary nature of these interpretations. "Pierre Menard" in particular illuminates the related functions of translation, parody, and literary criticism.

"Pierre Menard" is a stylized parody of the laborious bibliographic homage an obscure French provincial writer pays to his mentor Pierre Menard, an obscure French symbolist whose most fantastic project is his attempt to rewrite word-for-word, in the language of Cervantes, *Don Quixote.* Our vertigo upon reading this *ficcion* is infinite. To begin with, *Don Quixote* – often labeled the first modern novel – was born both as a parody (of the chivalresque novel) and a "translation." The narrator suggests in an aside that the "original" is a found manuscript written by an Arab named Cide Hamete Benengeli (to wit, Sir Egg-

plant). That a French writer of the late nineteenth century would attempt to re-create (without plagiarizing) a seventeenth-century Spanish classic, and that an Argentine writer – Borges – would attempt to
write Menard's disciple's homage, produces a *mise en abîme*. Menard's
faithful rendition of a sentence from the *Quixote* turns out as different
as a parody, that is, an imitation with a critical difference, because the
same Spanish phrase becomes an affectation and takes on different,
even opposite meanings, reinscribed in another linguistic and historical context. Borges's Spanish "rendition" of a supposed French original (the invented disciple's homage to the invented mentor) is both a
"translation" and a parody (about the parody/translation of a par-
ody/translation) that makes us question the status of what appears to
be an ever-elusive original. Indeed, where does the French end and the
Spanish begin in this text? Here Borges conflates the modes of parody
or satirical imitation and translation or imitation in another language,
and also shows how they function as literary criticism with one important difference: Both translations and parodies attempt to repeat the
discourse of the original; the critical essay uses another rhetoric.

Borges has proposed, essentially, a tentative status for the original as
one of many possible versions. James Joyce, collaborative translator of
the "Anna Livia Plurabelle" section of *Finnegans Wake* into Italian, was
thinking along similar lines when he chose to call his original "work in
progress" – which he continued to complete in the next stage – translation. Joyce "transelaborated" aspects of the original, which became
more *explicit* in Italian. He took advantage of his relationship to what
he experienced as the earthy musicality of the target language to invent
a more slangy version, and different double, even triple puns. The poet
laureate Robert Penn Warren once observed, Dante's *Inferno* on his lap
in the original Italian, that those outside of the language, like himself,
could appreciate its musicality more than a native speaker – precisely
because the outside reader would tend to focus more on (exotic) sound
than sense.

In a sacred vein Walter Benjamin privileges the original, radiating an
infinity of versions, over translation, one limited version among
many, but he coincides with the profane Joyce in seeing the original
"embodiment" as, in George Steiner's words in *Antigones,* "an annun-
ciation, however well wrought, of forms of being yet to come." (74)

Steiner shows how Benjamin's theory of "absolute translation and of the confluence of all secular tongues towards a mythical *Ursprache,* a primal source of perfect unison and facsimile" was inspired, in part, by Hölderlin's journey to the source, seeking through his translations of Sophocles to bring forth "the 'Oriental' substratum and well-spring stifled in fifth century Greek art." (74)

The bringing forth of a "substratum" is implied in the concept of subversion, in which translation betrays in the traditional *traduttore, traditore* sense but also because it makes evident a version underneath that becomes explicit, a latent version implied in the original. In a sense this latent version is a *subtext,* a term borrowed from psychoanalytical theory, which Terry Eagleton has defined as

> a text running within a work, visible at certain "symptomatic" points of ambiguity, evasion or overemphasis and which we as readers are able to "write" even if the novel itself does not. All literary texts contain one or more such sub-texts... which can be called the "unconscious" of the work. The work's insights... deeply related to its blindness – that it does not say, and how it does not say it – may be as important as what it articulates; what seems absent, marginal or ambivalent about it may provide the central clue. (178)

Persuasive translations uncover subtexts, or underlying meanings, for, after all is said and done, translation's first and final function is to relate meaning.

(Sub)versions

Authorized geniuses such as Borges, James Joyce, Ezra Pound, Samuel Beckett, and Vladimir Nabokov command an *authority,* unlike most translators, to re-create, to "subvert" the original – particularly their own. They offer an ideal model, nonetheless, for what literary translation should be: creation. Having collaborated with such polyglots as Guillermo Cabrera Infante, Julio Cortázar, Carlos Fuentes, and Manuel Puig, I have been able to observe a symbiotic if not parasitic relationship between translation and original composition.

Far from the traditional view of translators as servile, nameless scribes, the literary translator can be considered a subversive scribe. Something is destroyed – the form of the original – but meaning is re-

7

produced through another form. A translation in this light becomes a continuation of the original, which already always alters the reality it intends to re-create.

But let's take this argument beyond the cliché about what gets lost in translation – from reality to original, as well as from original to translation. The disruptive effect of books such as *Tres tristes tigres* and *La traición de Rita Hayworth* occurs through the violation of usage, through a resistance to language as useful or usual. Proper names become puns in Cabrera Infante's books; the communicative function of spoken language is subverted when Puig and Cabrera Infante transform it, with all its grammatical violations, into writing. The translation of their "abuses" – a term Philip Lewis applies to creative translation – must also violate, and in doing so sustain, their comment about language, in ways that are not arbitrary but which make the reader aware of decisive linguistic or textual knots of signification. The translation of Cabrera Infante's title *La habana para un infante difunto* into *Infante's Inferno* offers a prime example of this both abusive and sustaining process. Cabrera Infante, Manuel Puig, Severo Sarduy – principal exemplars in this meditation on my work as a translator – see their originals already as translations of texts and traditions as well as of realities; each in his own way is a parodist, a creator-commentator. Dethroning language's dominion over meaning, touching upon the gaps between language and meaning, they have also in a sense dethroned the "author." As collaborators or self-translators they are self-subverters.

Cabrera Infante, Puig, and Sarduy form a generational group that blossomed in the 1960s. Their work carries forth the avant-garde spirit of an earlier generation that included Borges, Cortázar, and Lezama Lima. But they break new ground in exploring popular culture and in interpreting the modernist tradition with a more streetwise Latin American, or better, Argentine or Cuban idiom. Their writing and the spoken language they make literary rises out of a filial revolt against the paternal tyranny of Castilian Spanish.

Tres tristes tigres is perhaps the first work to turn "Cuban" into a literary language spiked with slang, wordplays, and dislocations, a Spanish enriched by a specific region but also by many cultural and literary references. "The Death of Trotsky" – a critical chapter of this vast and fragmentary *roman comique* – comprises both savage and affectionate parodies of a diverse canon of Cuban writers. But Petronius's *Satyricon, Alice in Wonderland,* and Hollywood movies also form part of the book's rich dialogue of texts. Severo Sarduy's witty, hallucinatory novels take us on tortuous journeys through civilizations, high and low, West and East, subsumed within the rich texture of a wildly variegated Cuban discourse. Manuel Puig's writings can be considered even more "pop," less "literary": Within the stylized, parodic structures of his novels such as *Betrayed by Rita Hayworth* and *Kiss of the Spider Woman* he reproduces and analyzes popular culture and the spoken Argentine language.

How to translate the irrevocable unicity of a particular slang like "Havanan"? How to restate the homage to and critique of a dominant culture by a "marginal" culture in the language of the dominant culture? These constitute some of the challenges facing the American translator of contemporary Latin American fiction.

Translation theory oscillates between what Roman Jakobson called the "dogma of untranslatability," the claim that art, above all, is formally and essentially untranslatable, and the "transcreational" practices of the likes of Pound and Joyce, whose motto would appear to be "There is nothing that cannot be translated." Both positions are valid.

In telling the process of translating several works of fiction, I would like to locate those literary elements that strike us as untranslatable, such as puns, slang, parodies, and allusions, progressing in zigzag motion toward the most difficult, toward what we never consider to be the most difficult: words themselves. Detours will be necessary to describe the texts translated, since how can the reader understand choices and strategies without knowledge of the text itself? The translator's critical reading of a text precedes and accompanies her re-creation.

Part I:

Puns: The Untranslatable

> *The call between different words of similar sounds resembles those elective affinities between sundered souls in Celtic myth or the sexual tugs between bodies.*
>
> WALTER REDFERN, *Puns*

Puns and Translation

LANGUAGE'S impulsive, compulsive force reigns over verbal humor, moving the speaker to express what is repressed. Puns discover a coincidence, a potential affinity, a homonymy already latent in language. They place sound above meaning, and yet point to hidden semantic bonds between words. While puns leap out spontaneously in (and especially between) languages, the suggestion of causality between pun and pain, half-hiding and half-revealing itself, seems, according to Walter Redfern, "like wit to wed the dissimilar." Freud made us see that jokes signal something censured, that witty and "ready repartees" are often acts of revenge. Puns hide (hence reveal) pain and, as Shakespeare proved, are seriously laughter-provoking; we wield puns in order to provoke outrage. "Crime and Puns," used by Nabokov in his own translation of his novel *Despair* (1966), and added to *Three Trapped Tigers,* is no joke: Puns are punishment. "Pun" has evolved from "pound," meaning "to mistreat words": Have we discovered here the etymology of Ezra's patronym?

Socrates pinpointed language's unstable polyvalence in his aporiae, exposing how words like *pharmakon* (meaning both "remedy" and "poison") undermine logic, subverting our complacent dependence on an inert relation between word and idea, language and thought. Puns and portmanteaus expose how words vary in meaning according to their usage in juxtaposition with other words; puns reveal how words make love, how conjugations lead to copulations. Puns bring to the surface a duplicity in language in which it looks at ideas but also at itself, diverting our attention from object to word. The punful destruction of language and meaning in the works of Nabokov and Cabrera Infante is not gratuitous heresy: Language is *already always* a betrayal, a translation of the object it intends, pretends to re-create. Mythology claims that Satan fell from grace because of his games with God's sacred words, as Borges claims in his venomous article "The Art of Verbal Abuse" (which I translated for *Borges: A Reader,* an anthology with a pun in its title):

> The particle ël was trimmed off the angel Satanaël, God's rebellious firstborn. . . . Without it, he lost his crown, splendor, and prophetic powers. . . . Inversely, the Cabalists tell that the seed of the remote Abraham was sterile until they interpolated in his name the letter *he,* which made him capable of begetting. (48)

The all-powerful word has a life of its own, beyond good and evil, according to Nietzsche, another punster. "In the beginning was the pun," quipped Beckett in *Murphy.* St. Augustine was perhaps the first to recognize the wordsmith in God, who incarnated the Word in the speech-less *(infans)* infant Jesus.

One of the first puns Freud ponders in *Wit and Its Relation to the Unconscious* is the well-worn *traduttore, traditore,* meaning "translator, traitor," the most oft-used cliché in translation debates, betrayed of course in translation. This pun is the meeting point not only of two meanings but of two intimately related linguistic processes, wordplaying and translating.

The wordplay, an identity in sound, a similarity in difference, forces the translator to transloot, to be a traitor. Translating forces the writer/translator to displace an original meaning, or effect, onto words other than the original term: Supplementary meanings are brought in, the focus of the original statement is somehow diverted. *Traditore* pushes toward *traduttore* in sound but pulls in the opposite direction in meaning. Translation intends fidelity but perpetrates infidelity. And yet, as with puns, where the accent falls on a rediscovered familiarity between two distant terms, so does good translation seek out, stress the common but hidden bonds that may exist between two languages, two cultures, two poems, two puns. Through its synonymous movement, translation too lays bare a potential of the original text in another language.

The translator of puns, a tinkerer with a musical ear, makes use of her language and its possible associations with the language of the source pun and, as Pound advised, selects the living part. Substitutions play with sounds and words in English and take advantage of English's flexible morphology, thanks to Anglo-Saxon's adoption of Norman words and to the Latinization of melting-pot English, which increased its volume of synonyms and homonyms. I often find that substitutions magically reiterate at least some of the senses, or related senses, of the original, creating unavoidably other associated meanings.

The most radical means of recuperating puns *perdus* and other dislocated dislocutions has been labeled "mimetic" or "iconic" translation, in which, as Paolo Valesio observes, morphophonemic and syntactic relationships between words in different languages are "privileged at the expense of, and in direct contrast with, lexical relationships." In mimetic translations such as the Zukovsky's Catullus the similarity of sounds takes precedence over the possible difference in meaning. The original meaning is radically altered but also enriched. In *Three Trapped Tigers* Cabrera Infante subversively translated from the Cuban folk song "Guantanamera"—a pop hit in the Sixties in the United States—the line *"Yo soy un hombre sincero"* ("I'm a sincere man") into "I'm a man without a zero," basing the English joke on the indistinguishable Cuban pronunciation of *z* and *c*. As always this joke was serious since Cabrera Infante, during both the writing and translating of *TTT*, was experiencing his lack of Cuba as a man without a country. He further elaborated this joke into "I am a man without a Xerox copy," introducing the technical trivia of our manuscript production.

Valesio writes that mimetic translation makes explicit

> what is to a certain extent present in every translation. It demystifies this ideology of faithfulness. . . . Above all, in showing how far it is possible to go in metamorphosing the semantic content of a text, this kind of translation shows that the text itself in the original is never clear, and that it is always remote from us. (59)

Mimetic translation radicalizes the hermeneutic function of translation; by favoring the graphic or phonetic aspects of Catullus's words, the Zukovskys sought other meanings suppressed in more traditional translations, and reached for, or, as Paul Mann claims, tried to make familiar the emotion conveyed in the alien tongue. Whatever we may think of this perhaps too-radical experiment, it makes us see how traditional translation practices reveal a fear of the other, a need to turn the alien into the familiar. We are reminded that translation is a manipulative political act, that language—always "scarred" by its politico-historical context—can be manipulated to censure the foreign. Mimetic translation allows the foreign to enter one's own language, obliging us to experience the foreignness in our "own" language, but also calls into question the possibility that any one translation suffices, or is independent of other translations of the same original.

The traditional authority of original over translation has prevented us, on the other hand, from seeing translation as a continuation of the original's distant yet interpretative relationship to an unspoken network of referents. The miraculous possibility and occasional recuperation of meaning in mimetic translation justifies the mythic belief in a possible primal source that would be the "confluence of all secular tongues" but, more to the point, places original and translation in an interdependent, relativist perspective. Translating the pun-filled *Tres tristes tigres* and Spanish writer Julián Ríos's novel *Larva* has led me to believe in the confluence of mimetic and semantic translation: Both "methods" can be felicitously fused or alternated.

Larva's "plot" very loosely follows the adventures of a modern-day Don Juan in swinging London—and the adventures of Spanish in the land of puns. Like Juan Goytisolo, Ríos has adopted the most daring innovations of contemporary Latin American fiction and poetry to renew Spain's prose tradition. "Larva," the immature state of an insect in its metamorphosis toward maturity, etymologically (in Neo-Latin) means "mask." If Joyce explored English's polyphony in its Irish subversion, Ríos's novel explores Spanish's metamorphosis as an infinite series of masks, sometimes disguised as English, other times as German, French, Italian. We become suddenly aware of how languages—like larvae—are in a perpetual state of metamorphosis, how languages evolve through mispronunciations and mistranslations. *Larva* requires a treasonous translation that transmits its multiplicity of tongues and senses, reinstating the play of sounds and meanings that strike the reader's outer and inner ear.

On a London bus, an old man stands up to get off: *"se abalanza balanceándose"*—an obvious alliteration meaning "he rushes forward swaying from side to side." "Balancing" in English was an immediate association, and so I (circum)invented with mimetic effects a portmanteau—one of the many Joycean devices recurring in *Larva*—"balanswaying," "swaying" evoking in the ear *ceándose* (the Spanish *ing* at the end of the verb). Though displaced, the referent surfaced elsewhere in the sentence: "tripping downstairs as the bus took off, and balanswaying strangerously toward the way out." "Strangerously" is yet another "found" portmanteau substituting metonymically *peligrotescamente* (*peligro* = danger; *grotescamente* = grotesquely); here "strange" stands synonymously for "grotesque." More important, sound is meaning: "Balanswaying," associated with the original meaning, re-creates the image of the elderly man trying to keep his balance on the bus and exhibits, besides, the text's balancing act between English and Spanish in a book that incessantly explores the spontaneous, yet almost prefigured, correspondences between languages.

Again, the most (in)famous model of moving puns from one language to another is probably James Joyce's Italian re-creation of "Anna Livia Plurabelle." This translation, "a complete rewriting, a later elaboration of the original," came out of the text's, and the author's, metamorphosis in another language; Jacqueline Risset, in her essay "Joyce Translates Joyce," writes that "the creative principle, the text's dynamic, is carried *inside* the language of the translation." (10) Joyce's puns were Italianized, names became more satirical, more explicit, enriched in multiple puns. Joyce responded to what he experienced in exile as the new language's flexibility, from the Trieste dialect he and his family had learned to speak, to the high literary language of Dante. He felt liberated by the spoken within the literary, a new way of *speaking,* of expressing feeling.

Puns and exile go hand in hand and not only because puns often involve translingual play. The exile acquires an objective, "binary" view of his adopted language and culture, the second language making her aware of the mechanisms of language, both one's own and the other.

For Joyce, Italian was "liberating" because, in his ear, it was a hedonistic escape from English and all its censorial apparatus. For Julien Green, the Franco-American writer, French was more abstract, English more concrete, and therefore he would say/write things too bluntly in English precisely because his non-native ear was insufficiently sensitive to the connotative weight of words. For Cabrera Infante, English, the language of the movies as well as of his favorite books, became a toy, a plaything.

If puns point to language's imperfections, to words' opacity, names – particularly names that "signify" – dramatize the impossibility yet necessity of translation. Names in fiction, particularly in satirical, self-commentative fiction, serve symbolic functions: A common noun is often hidden in a proper name. To translate the name destroys its unicity, yet if we don't translate it we don't understand it.

Cabrera Infante's title *La habana para un infante difunto* – which became *Infante's Inferno* in English – reveals not only an allusion to Ravel's *Pavane pour une infante défunte* but also to the writer's preferred name, the name the unnamed narrator earns at the end of the book when he is (re)born as a writer. *Infante* both misleads (he is no longer a speechless infant) and leads to a secret truth. The ear hears the name in the original title; in the translation it becomes even more explicit. An "abusive" substitution like *Infante's Inferno* draws attention to how Cabrera Infante's novel subverts the "normal" usage of his name, and by bringing attention to this key, sustains the subversive principle that produced the original term. In *Three Trapped Tigers,* wordsmith Bustrófedon and his friends perpetually play upon their own names and others': One proper name is never enough; each new name is another clue to an ever-evasive identity.

Titles, like names, "precede, float above and follow their bodies," as Lucille Kerr writes. "Titles help us to read, but are also read through, their texts." A title should open the reader to possibilities, Eco advises, not "regiment" his ideas. Names, like titles, are in a way enigmas that impel the reader to undertake the voyage of the text. In translating puns, names, and titles one needs to communicate "key words" without closing the door to associations. But the writer must avoid vagaries that would evoke irrelevant or fuzzy associations – especially in English, the language of merchants and mathematicians ever since the seventeenth-century "purification" performed by the Royal Society of London and lauded by the Bishop Sprat. The translation of key terms dramatizes the delicate balance between openness and closure that all translation, all writing must sustain.

The technical name for puns is *paronomasia,* "naming alongside," which is what all writing does. Writing is not the reality it describes but the words used to name that reality. Describing the process of translating prose could be an infinite task: Looking back to see how puns and names were translated can serve therefore as an emblematic way not only of understanding translating but original writing itself.

TTT: A Universal Code

In "This Condition We Call Exile," Joseph Brodsky observed that writers often acquire a significance and style as exiles that they didn't have as natives in their own land. Like Vladimir Nabokov, Cabrera Infante found a liberating literary medium, a creative impetus in linguistic exile in English. Defying prejudices against the "lowest form of wit," both writers have enriched contemporary English by restoring the pun's place in prose. But Cabrera Infante is not only an external exile; this Cuban's Spanish feels "thick" in his mouth, just as French did to Flaubert: hence the need to write, to stretch language to its limits. This thickness becomes even more pronounced in translation, where the referent becomes even more remote, where the feast of words moves on. For the sake of a joke in the English version of his works, Cabrera Infante often undermines a more serious moment in the Spanish version. Behind such a subversive act Cabrera Infante admits a critical motive: "Translating such a moment to English forced me to make fun of it." Through humor, we express sadness even more poignantly – as he has often said, puns hide pain.

The original *Tres tristes tigres* was, as Cabrera Infante put it, "an excursion into language," but it could also be considered refuge in his mother tongue, Cuban. Language is the baggage the displaced writer takes into exile, and with *TTT* Cabrera Infante aspired to transform spoken and written Cuban into a literary language. Inspired by Petronius's *Satyricon* – the original of which Cabrera Infante considers *TTT* to be a "failed translation" – he re-created the speech practices of various social classes of a particular region in and around Havana, and a particular era, the late Fifties.[1] Like the early satirist, Cabrera Infante attacks the roots of social hypocrisy by exposing the seamier side, focusing on the sexual via vulgar, conversational language.

American culture, north and south, is translational; we all speak imported languages. Cuba dramatizes this condition, as a crossroads of Africa, Europe, North America, and even China. *TTT*'s Havananites speak many tongues; a polyglot bible straight out of Babel, *TTT* tells that no single language is pure. And *TTT*'s absent tiger Bustrófedon, named after *boustrophedon* – the ancient Greek and then Hebrew method of writing from left to right and right to left like a plow – is a kind of macaronic godhead of language, out of whom all wordplays and multilingual witticisms spring.

In his urgency to lighten ponderous Spanish rhetoric, Cabrera Infante has continued along the path forged by two Latin American masters: Borges and Lezama Lima. Their poetic projects, which included the revival of the baroque splendors of Góngora and Quevedo, also involved a turning toward other languages and traditions. An anglophile like Borges, Cabrera Infante took as his models Lewis Carroll and Joyce in turning words inside out, in discovering neologisms, while Hemingway, Mark Twain, Raymond Chandler, and S.J. Perelman served as his Virgils in translating spoken speech into written language.

Faithful poetic translation could be called an exercise of parallel reveries in two languages. My collaboration with this Cuban and now naturalized British writer as his faithfully unfaithful translator began as an exercise in parallel repartees, reparteasing each other in English and Spanish, in a two-faced monologue of compulsive punsters.

By the time I arrived in London in 1969, an English poet, Donald Gardner, had worked with Cabrera Infante on several sections of *TTT,* particularly the chapter called "Brainteaser" (*"Rompecabeza"* – literally, "head-buster"; figuratively, "puzzle"), based on Lewis Carroll's word and poem games, and together they had produced a first draft of the translation. Of that first draft, only a parody of Poe's *The Raven* remains intact. (217–218) Gardner had to work with the French

---

1. *The Satyricon* was the adolescent Cabrera Infante's first erotic literature.

translation since his knowledge of Spanish was rudimentary; and since Cockney was not the best equivalent for spoken Cuban, he was planning a trip to New York to brush up on American vernacular.[2] Our Havanan in London thought it dubious that two weeks in another town would change a man's linguistic habits, so he was relieved when I appeared, equipped with Spanish vocabulary and doubtful double entendres signifying everything.

Cabrera Infante told interviewer Rita Guibert that I brought to *TTT*

> that sense of humor characteristic of New York Jews, which is based on play upon words and confronts reality with strict verbal logic. Nothing was closer to my purpose in *TTT* than the philosophy of life expressed by the Marx brothers, and in Jill Levine my three Marxistigers had met their Margaret Dumont! While by day Jill Levine-Dumont was busy destroying with alice aforethought the remains of the stiff-upper-and-underlips, the sometimes metaphrastic construction of the English version of *TTT*, by night I went on building my constructions of a phrase, of a word, of a phoneme – and even went so far as to treat proper names as subjects of linguistic experiments, as I did in Spanish. (414)

We had Marx in common, Groucho of course: Our shared language was the citywise humor of the American movies, as well as Lewis Carroll's universe of nonsense. (S)wordplay was our communal, if not sacred, ground.

Memory betrays: In order to illustrate the way we worked together on *TTT*, I'll rely on yet another text, our correspondence. A particularly abstruse section of "Brainteaser," for example, which in Spanish was titled *"Los Pro-y-Contra Nombres,"* became "Pro and Con Names." The play on "pronouns" – *pro-nombres* – in the original was displaced in English by "con names." Registers of fame were reduced here to lists of *calembours* based on the phonetic relations (or confusions) in and between several languages. For example, *"Philosuffers:* Aristocrates, Empiricles, Antipaster, Presocrates, Ludwig Offerbach, Luftwaffe Feuer-Bang, Marxcuse, Ortega and Gasset, Julius Marx, Giordano Brulé, Des Carter, S. Boyassian-Mamassian... " (288)

---

2. A journey to be financed by the American publisher Harper & Row, unbeknownst to the American editor Cass Canfield, Jr.

The original lists of wordplays combined streetwise humor with sophisticated multilingual allusions to Cuban and world culture, to pop and to the highbrow. These were reproduced in the English version with only minor changes: Original and translation would both be multilingual, both requiring the reader's participation as translator. But we needed a series of wordplays that rang a local bell for the American reader, just as many of the (particularly obscene) wordplays rang a local, untranslatable bell for Cuban ears only, such as S. Boyassian-Mamassian, alluding to oral sex. From the bottom of the barrel I dug up and sent Guillermo (in May 1970) a list of second-grade jokes, for which I added another category titled "Famous Books and Authors." This list included *Off the Cliff* by Hugo Furst, *Yellow River* by I. P. Daley, *Twenty Years in the Saddle* by Major Assburn...

My regressive humor set the wheels in motion. Several days later I got a letter saying: "About your list—here's my counteratachment [*sic*]." He had ingeniously changed the (sub)title into *Famous In Books* (or *In Famous Books*). His list included slight variations, as in Ugo Furst, but ended more promisingly with *Under the Lowry* (which he quickly revised into *Lorry*) by Malcolm Volcano. Since *TTT* attempts to recapture the Havana of the Fifties or *Remembrance of Things Past Translation* (408), our author suggested adding *Memoirs of an Amnesiac*, but the final list has nothing substantively to do with the original. And *Memoirs of an Amnesiac* got lost in the shuffle since piano-player-cum-actor Oscar Levant had already appropriated this found title, from that inveterate title inventor Erik Satie, for his loser's autobiography. The final English version includes such gems as *Crime and Puns* by Bustrofedor Dostowhiskey, *Comfort of the Season* by Gore Vidal Sassoon, and *In Caldo Brodo* by Truman Capone.

Cabrera Infante decided to add this new list *"In Famous Books,"* of *purely literary nature,* a more universal code than *choteo,* the local language of sexual humor. This supplement characterizes the principal subversion in *Three Trapped Tigers* and, indeed, in the English versions of most of Guillermo Cabrera Infante's works: They are consistently more *literary* than the original. The incommunicable in-jokes of Havanan popular culture and the associations provoked by the spoken play of sounds have been displaced by conceptual, graphic, *readerly* in-jokes. One common code (Cuban *choteo*) was replaced by a universal code, Literature, shared by readers despite language barriers, and *gracias a* translation.

By underscoring literariness, the translation functions here as parody, repeating forms but with a critical difference. "A more advanced stage," Borges once said of translation vis-à-vis the original. But then again, the original *Tres tristes tigres* itself already parodies the "narrative interruptus" technique of Laurence Sterne's *Tristram Shandy,* of Joyce's stream of consciousness and wordplays in *Ulysses* – particularly the "Nighttown" Dublin-by-night section – and, above all, of Petronius's *Satyricon,* the first urbane night-voyage-of-discovery novel. And beneath Joyce's twenty-four-hour urban odyssey *Ulysses* already floats Homer's *Odyssey,* whose main motif, lost wanderers in a labyrinthine world, inspired Petronius's *Satyricon.* Preceding *TTT* as an anthology of literary parodies, *The Satyricon* mimics the Greek novel form as it satirizes Roman *mores;* the book's mixture of humor and philosophy derives from the satirical form invented by Menippus of Gadara. One parody descends from another, producing a vertiginous effect, placing in question the mythic original whose translation *must* be read as parody, since parody exists only in the eye of the beholder. The reader of the translation-parody of *TTT* should be on similar footing as the original reader who shares the author's language and cultural tradition. Writing and translating take an equal status in their function as acts of communication, requiring the reader's reception and participation.

Just as the jokes in the original had a familiar association for the Spanish reader, so did a mutual bond, a familiarity, need to be forged through the translation. Since many multilingual allusions remained a puzzle to the Spanish reader, so was it appropriate for the translation to retain a similar multilingual hermeticism.

Writing is rewriting, or as Cabrera Infante tells Rita Guibert, "something added to the original text." (412) The translation process mirrored the process of writing the original, Cabrera Infante adding a parody here, a pun there up to the very last minute. A year later (June 2, 1971), when Guillermo was still adding (and I subtracting) words to a manuscript that the publisher Cass Canfield, Jr. thought was safely finished and in house, I received a letter advising me to substitute all the "of courses" in the book with variations – e.g., of coarse, off course, off courts, of courts, of corpse, of corset, off cords, of cores, of corps, off corpus, of Corpus, of Corse, of Corsican (Of course he can!), etc., etc. – "taking good care that it makes nonsense when you make the substitution." I responded two weeks later with the following: "FAIT ACCOMPLI, MISSION CARRIED OUT. . . . Here are a few samples of these mutated *of courses* in cross-stitch: Canada Dry (of corks), Laura Díaz, a widow (of Corpus), Livia's best pics (off curves), something about the Czar (of courcze), something about the isle of Cuba declining (off Kursk)." I went on to say, "but Harper is in an uprow, NO MORE CHANGES."

Fulfilling a Potential

Bilingual readers of the translation have observed, correctly, that author–cum–translators elaborated on the original, adding more allusions, mostly to American and English culture. *Three Trapped Tigers* is thirty pages longer than *Tres tristes tigres*. The surplus pages consist mainly of jokes, elaborations, "fulfillments" of words in the original, adding a subversive cargo to the book in its odyssey from Cuba (via Belgium, where Cabrera Infante's life as an exile began) to English.

The original's seriocomic devices serve a dramatic as well as festive function, accented particularly in the last long chapter, *"Bachata."* Here Silvestre and Cué, two secretly sad tigers, enact a duel of wits far into the night. As they cruise around Havana by night for more than a hundred pages, they make jokes and pick up girls – or vice versa – in order to avoid subjects of conversation too painful to confront. Behind the festivities of a now legendary nightlife, Cabrera Infante reveals the dramas of poverty, of wasted lives under exploitation, of wasted love in the politics of machismo, of talent squandered by sordid commercialism.

By elaborating on the wordplays, the translation tips the balance in favor of the festive, but again, Freud would remind us, there's nothing more dead serious than a joke; many puns (in *TTT* and in general) are not funny. The book's satirical, critical intent is not buried under but rather heightened by the additional jokes, burdening the reader of the translation more than the original's reader since puns – perhaps because of the pain impelling them – become oppressive.

The additional literary jokes compensate – deliberately or not – for the loss of the original spoken Havanan. *Un naúfrago* ("a shipwrecked sailor,") becomes "Badsin the sailor"; *la noche de sabado* ("Saturday night") becomes "Saturday night and Sunday mourning." Why? Because words, phrases in the original already abuse their conventional function, are already *charged* with suggestions. *Un naúfrago* refers to reality but also to myth: The discovery of America (Cuba, that is) was fraught with tales of shipwrecks turned into classics of English literature such as Shakespeare's *The Tempest* and Defoe's *Robinson Crusoe*. *The Arabian Nights* became a more important book in English, German, and French than in its original form, as Borges paradoxically demonstrates in his essay "The Translators of *The 1001 Nights*." Like these other "classics," it became the material of popular Hollywood movies, the found paradise or promised land for *TTT*'s nostalgic characters. Saturday night, a big night for casual sexual (mis)adventures, often ends in mournful Sunday mornings for *TTT*'s night owls; the allusion to the John Osborne play made into a 1958 movie is historically appropriate, his "angry young men" reincarnated in the disenchanted tigers. The suggestiveness of words is *TTT*'s message here, so that *meaning* surfaces even if it has slipped – in another cultural context – into another meaning.

The English version is more forced, more artificial, more literary, the Spanish more natural: Inevitably the original's effortlessness, its natural tie to a language, can never be replaced; the round vowels of Spanish cede to the angular consonants of English. The translation is not entirely a more literary version, however. As some bilingual English readers have noticed, the English translation is spiced with stronger, more blasphemous language than the Spanish version. For native speakers of English, of curse, English swear words would be stronger than Spanish insults. This works both ways: Since English was less charged with intimate connotations for the Cuban writer, he felt freer to use stronger words. But the relative freedom of speech in the United States vis-à-vis Spanish censorship then was a decisive factor.[3]

The creative translator fulfills "latent truths" lying fallow, "unrealized" in the original.[4] Borges's Pierre Menard reflects such a view in pretending to rewrite *Don Quixote,* an act that constitutes a loving violation of the original, as if this "re-writer" knew the *Quixote* better than Cervantes; as a reader, he does know it better. One could say this was the faithfully unfaithful approach taken in *TTT,* except that the author was one of the translators.

The original's potentialities are fulfilled in translation both by seeking the original's source and by representing the original's passage through time. *TTT*'s sources include American mass culture and English literature; the historical moment of the translation is the early Seventies, when New Yorkese and Black American speech function as the closest cultural equivalents to the slurred, slick speech of the mostly mulatto or black characters in *TTT*'s Havana. Like all rhetorical acts, translation is limited to a historical moment and intends to produce an effect upon a given audience: *Three Trapped Tigers* was written in 1971 for North American readers.

A Timely Example: The Title

The way we reached the title of the book in translation crystallizes our efforts to restage the original's play between sound and sense.

Cabrera Infante stressed the title's ambivalent referentiality by calling it instead a name, that is, an arbitrary linguistic convention. He undermines the sacred unicity of names and the semantic role of titles, here in conversation with Guibert:

> What's in a name? Merely the three first words of a tongue-twister I believed Cuban but actually belongs to Spanish-American folklore. I used it because I wanted the book to have the fewest possible literary – which are

3. Joseph Brodsky views with some cynicism the newfound freedom of writers released from repressive societies to delve into eroticism and foul language, as following the fashion "of one's free-market colleagues." (18)
4. Thus spoke Hölderlin, poet-translator of Pindar and Sophocles.

always the most *extra*-literary – connotations. Starting with the cover, I wanted the book to suggest practically nothing about its content, and this was the nearest thing to an abstract title, since the number "tres," the adjective "triste," and the common noun "tigres" are united by nothing but the difficulty of pronouncing them, and because it is a made-up phrase. Namely, a phrase that has lost its meaning by senseless repetition like jingles or swear words. . . . I was also pleased by the doubtless poetic justice of a once formal tongue-twister ending as a mere meaningless game, and also by the inevitable metaphysical connotations – after Blake – of this wild beast among wild beasts (an animal which. . . inhabits other tropics, other jungles) and that diffuse feeling of uneasiness called sadness (the most "literary" of metaphysical ills and the most "human" of animal feelings) expressed by a Latin word. Besides, I have all my life felt perturbed by the frightful imagery of the three, glowing obscurely in the jungle of the mind. (413)

The "frightful imagery of the three" suggests Christian and Oedipal concerns – the awesome threesome of the "family romance" – but our concern as translators was language's manipulation of its speakers and listeners. If one were to favor sound at the complete expense of meaning, the English equivalent of the popular tongue twister *"tres tristes tigres en un trigal"* (three sad tigers in a wheat field) would be "Peter Piper picked a peck of pickled peppers." But even though the original title's nonreferentiality forms part of its message, it also invokes associations and meanings Cabrera Infante intentionally seeks.

Titles are often the last to fall into place in the process of composing a book. When the book is finished – or when the writer has completed his reading – is perhaps when it can finally be represented by its title. *Tres tristes tigres,* though an early idea, became the final title when its author wrote the last chapter upon his last return from Cuba to Europe, definitively convinced that his Havana had disappeared. Cabrera Infante evokes that last visit most directly in *"Bachata,"* where Arsenio Cué and Silvestre celebrate, mainly with words, their vanishing Havana by night. As Cabrera Infante remarked in the interview with Torres Fierro: "Back in Madrid in 1965 I composed the grand fugue that is "Bachata" – and *TTT* was not only completed but it also recovered one of its first titles." (91)

The three tigers turned out to be fundamental to the book's structure. The phrase "three sad tigers" alludes to Cabrera Infante's paper

tigers who prowl by night, *TTT*'s main male characters. There are really five – actor Arsenio Cué, writer Silvestre, photographer Códac,
bongo player Eribó, wordsmith Bustrófedon – but at least three main
characters appear in every episode either as subjects of the action or at
least as "subjects" of conversation. The careful reader of *"Bachata"* will
observe, for example, that either Arsenio and Silvestre are discussing
another tiger, such as Eribó, or one of them is thinking or soliloquizing
about another two others, as when Silvestre, the narrator of *"Bachata,"*
thinks about a name-calling contest between Códac and Bustrófedon.
The three tigers had to remain in the title of this book about a group of
paper tiger friends who are one nostalgic voice, all fragments of the author's consciousness, and especially about language's celebration of itself.

A list poured forth: "three tired tigers" (we feared readers would
yawn), "three flat tigers" (also dangerous), "three triped tigers" (too
forced), "three-tongued tigers" (had to be pronounced with an Oriental accent according to Severo Sarduy, cleverly underscoring Cuban
multilingualism – but Cabrera Infante's book does not highlight Havana's Chinatown as does Sarduy's *De donde son los cantantes*), "three
triggered tiggers" (only readers of *Winnie-the-Pooh* would remember
Tigger), until finally we agreed on "three trapped tigers," trapped in
memory, in the book, in English exile forever. Cabrera Infante said in
a letter (September 1970): "If the present title is no good I suggest,
simply, *Tres Tristes Tigres,* just like that. All the other alternatives I
don't like: Three Sad, Tongued, Triped, etc., Three Trapped is by far
the best. But it is always up to the publisher, who should know the
best," he remarked, not without irony.

Extrinsic conditions enter into the makings of books, and certainly
of titles: What will draw the reading public's eye? The publisher did
settle for this suggestive title. Trapped doesn't mean happy and could
be contiguous to sad, which already does and doesn't mean sad – it's
there for the tongue twister – for the tigers' melancholy is both cosmic
and comic. Festive and elegiac, the book is both joyous and sad. Sad
in the title is not monolithic: In the book's web of associations, sad
and trapped are metonymic complements – we're sad because we're
trapped in our mortality. The tigers are caught in language's empti-
ness, a "sound and fury signifying nothing." Nothing's sadder than a

tiger trapped in exile, a tiger whose territory is now an absence. He sounds ferocious but he feels sad.

In the battle between sound and sense, *Three Trapped Tigers* is a compromise: Its meaning relates only partially to the original title's, and obviously the oral tongue twister (produced by a failed alliteration: tr–tr–t) is replaced by a graphic rather than a phonetic alliteration. But this betrayal seems to have worked, as William Gass writes: "*Three Trapped Tigers,* from title to epilogue, with its final words, 'cant go no further,' is a book made of language. . . . " (52)

TTT demonstrates that language conceals more than it reveals. This abstraction becomes concrete in the many conversations and monologues throughout the novel that serve to hide the characters' feelings, or to omit or distort information because of the defense mechanism of repression, because of the inevitable limitations of point of view, because ideology in the broadest sense always shapes and sculpts our utterances. The author duplicates this unyielding alienation of language by his own necessarily treasonous (though successful) attempt to document the jargon of a lost Havana. Furthermore, his active involvement in the translation of his original "translation" produces the effect of emphasizing language's alienation. One becomes another in another language.[5]

The book that went to press in 1964 in Spain was *Vista del amanecer en el trópico* (the original title, a title that became another book) came out as *TTT* in 1965, rewritten by the Spanish censor's pen, or more precisely, passed under the Franco-censor's eraser. The original, as it often occurs, constituted several versions and stages leading up to *the* original as published but never really *finished,* a conviction the Cuban writer shares with Flaubert, a literary father and an infamous perfectionist. But then again Cabrera Infante perversely, or writerly, took a liking to some of the "revisions" imposed by the censor. As one who's always revising his texts, always preferring the next version to the last, Cabrera Infante pronounced to Guibert: "Perfection is not a state, but a goal." (417)

5. Julien Green remarks about his first book in English: "What I expected to read was a sort of unconscious translation from the French, or at least a very close equivalent, whereas what I saw might have been *written by another hand than mine.*" (228; my italics)

The Betrayal of
Rita Hayworth

Writing Against Authority

I_F A spoken tongue twister was sacrificed to a written alliteration in the title of *TTT*, it would appear that ambiguity yielded to clarity – as often occurs with translations under the pressures of commercial publishing – in the translation of Manuel Puig's title *La traición de Rita Hayworth.*

Movies, mainly popular American "women's" movies, had been the vehicle of escape for Manuel Puig as a sensitive young boy growing up in the Thirties and Forties in the oppressive atmosphere of a small town in the Argentine pampas. As an adolescent seeking his sexual identity, Puig experienced male and female models of behavior in his world as stultified and stultifying. To achieve success and happiness, men had to be aggressive, women submissive. Movies represented these values, but in glamorous, glorified terms, and the imaginative young Puig could identify safely with both men and women on the screen, live vicariously in this unreal world, which became for him the "only reality." The budding writer's first aspiration was to invest his creativity in the cinematic site of imaginary freedom, but as a film student at Cinecittá in Rome in 1959, he soon discovered that he felt incapable of assuming the authoritative role of director, that his pleasure lay not behind but in front of the screen, in spectatorship.

Throughout all his works the alienating as well as inspiring influence of models imposed by American mass culture would provide a pre-text as well as a pretext for writing. His first novel, *La traición de*

Rita Hayworth, began as a film script, but Puig realized that the auto-biographical "material was too complicated to be analyzed in film." He explained in an interview (*City* 5) that

> I needed more space and freedom. I wasn't sure about any of those characters. The kick was to find the truth about these [people] who had been with me during my childhood: my cousin, my mother, my father, my closest friends. (69–70)

Monologues, conversations, letters, diaries, and other forms of every-day narration would serve here to retrace his past, the relationships, the movie fantasies at the root of his identity and sexuality.

Why he couldn't "analyze" these characters with sufficient "freedom" in the cinematic genre becomes abundantly clear in the trajectory of his writing. *Kiss of the Spider Woman,* his fourth novel, realizes a direction begun in *Rita Hayworth,* where Toto, Puig's alter ego, "reconstructs" the plot of one of his favorite films in a school composition (chapter XII). Toto inserts his own interpretation of *The Great Waltz,* subtly changing and completing the plot and characters in ways that reveal or carry out his own fantasies. *Kiss* is structured almost entirely upon this device. The exploitational popular films that Molina, an imprisoned homosexual, verbally re-creates for his cellmate, a political prisoner, demonstrate how Puig unveils mass culture in order to analyze the values and ideologies that rule lives and mediate desires.

Rita Hayworth is structured by texts spoken and written solely by its characters, silencing at least on the surface the presumed narrator. The latter's function seems limited to putting these texts in chronological order, except for the last chapter, giving them descriptive titles (such as "Toto's Monologue, 1941,") and titling the book that contains them. Puig passes no authorial judgment upon his characters; as Lucille Kerr observes, complementary, even contradictory readings are possible. Puig questions the authority of the father, and of cultural models, by allowing the characters to speak for themselves. Such rebellion against authority could never be simple: As Puig himself confided to Cuban photographer Germán Puig (no relation), if he couldn't be a great director, he would become a great writer. Puig comments in the *City* interview: "Authority frightens me. I hate it. I don't accept it, but at the same time I find great difficulty in rebelling against it, in facing it directly." (71)

The Title, Indeed the Name

The title literally represents the ambiguities of the characters and of the novel's discourse, suspended grammatically between two opposed meanings. Again, titles guide us but are also interpreted through the reading of their texts. The "Betrayal of Rita Hayworth" refers us to Toto's outing with both parents to the movies, to see *Blood and Sand,* starring Tyrone Power and Rita Hayworth. This episode and its aftermath constitute the "key" or primal scene, so to speak (in chapter V, narrated by the nine-year-old Toto), which sets up Toto's sexual ambivalence and unresolved identity.

But the reader's first association is extratextual: "Why Rita Hayworth?" A Marxist reader would view this reference as a symbol of the false, alienating values imposed on a marginal culture by a dominant imperialist culture. True enough. And if we dig further, we discover that this proper name is a pseudonym, that Ms. Hayworth was really Margarita Cansino, the daughter of a Spanish dancer who to survive, but even more to succeed, "betrayed" her Hispanic origins by adopting a name and values of this dominant culture.

The title, indeed the name pulls us "in several directions at once," writes Lucille Kerr, referring at once to the real world and the world of fantasy. (27–28) But Rita Hayworth's signification is ambiguous especially because, even though she explicitly betrays Tyrone Power in the movie *Blood and Sand,* what she *means* to Toto is implicitly betrayed.[1]

This particular movie outing is special because it is the first and only occasion father accompanies his wife and son to the movies. It is Toto's conscious hope that his father will like the movie and want to go again, and his unconscious hope that his identity will not be polarized against the male model, that he will be able to be a man because not only

---

1. Jonathan Tittler points out that "the plight of the viewer is simple in comparison to that of the star herself, who sees or imagines her own image on the screen and may be tempted to try to act out that idealized role off screen as well. The inevitable confrontation with the insuperable distance between Rita's selves leads to a second betrayal, which is lost in translating the title figuratively. The title in Spanish... (the Betrayal of Rita Hayworth) allows Hayworth to be the object as well as agent of infidelity." ("Betrayed by Rita Hayworth: The Androgynous Text," *Narrative Irony in the Contemporary Spanish American Novel* [Cornell UP, 1984], 80, fn. 5.)

women but men, too, like movies. This hope is crushed: Berto imitates (indeed appropriates) Toto's desire by going to and liking the movie, but he likes most the pretty, "wicked" actress. Disturbed by her wickedness (her power to castrate), Toto is in turn motivated to imitate his father's attraction to the woman who betrays the man who desires her. And after Toto is "seduced" in his desire to imitate his father into liking her, he (like Tyrone Power) is abandoned by his father, who finally rejects the movies because going to movies won't pay the bills, won't solve life's problems. Toto's version ends up confusing the two subjects, Rita Hayworth and his father: Berto is both identified with the subject to whom he's attracted and rejects her and the world of fantasy that she represents. Toto at first identifies with his father, to whom he is attracted, and finally rejects him and all that he represents, patriarchal oppression.

The novel ends with a never-sent letter by Berto to his brother that reveals the final irony. The betrayer is betrayed: Berto's insecurities – and consequent oppressiveness – originate in the powerless position he occupied in his "family plot" vis-à-vis an older brother whom he originally loved. Toto's victimization merely repeats that of his victimized victimizer. The letter restates what Toto's monologue began to demonstrate, as Kerr writes, "to be or to see oneself as the victim of betrayal by those to whom one is also deeply attached is to become the subject of an irresolvable ambivalence toward those same figures." (34) Toto as betrayer, manipulator of words (if not realities), is "born" here.

The polyvalence of the original title reflects, therefore, multiple betrayers and betrayals. Rita Hayworth (woman), Berto (man), or heterosexuality betrays – and is ultimately disavowed by the betrayed principal who becomes principal betrayer, Toto.

The English translation still betrays, of course: "Rita Hayworth" – the name – serves a different function in a foreign text than it does in American English. It signals the imposition of American popular culture in Argentina, whereas in English it signals merely the imposition of pop culture upon a literary domain. Nevertheless, the American English reader knows that he is reading an Argentine novel, in translation.

Translation betrays because, like criticism, it makes choices. Even though one can read two meanings into *La traición de Rita Hayworth,* this title *sounds,* strikes the Spanish reader's ear as a raw, forceful, even blasphemous statement. *Traición* is stronger than betrayal since it also means treason. "Betray," the verb, strikes the English reader as stronger than the noun "betrayal," and grammatical changes (noun to verb, for example) often serve a translated phrase better than lexical ones. *Betrayed by Rita Hayworth* sounded stronger, more emphatic in English, a language that privileges "clear senses." Colloquial immediacy should also be privileged in a novel that, like *TTT,* has been called a "gallery of voices," in which the characters speak for themselves in a living Argentine idiom. Ambiguity – or, rather, vagary – would weaken more than enrich the reading of the title in English. *The Betrayal of Rita Hayworth* sounds literary, *Betrayed by Rita Hayworth* sounds more spoken: This phrase should sound as if it were uttered by Toto, just as the original Spanish does.

The lesson Toto (Manuel Puig) learns in his coming of age, as several critics have observed, is to become a betraying subject. Nothing is ever resolved at the level of plot or discourse in Puig's novels. He betrays the reader, as he does the role of author, by not communicating a clear-cut message. Like Toto, he is an ambiguous manipulator. It is impossible to decide if his writings merely stylize, reproduce the voices of others without a judgmental function, as Kerr writes, or if he critically reevaluates the "subliterary genres, themes and languages, as well as the non-literary forms of popular culture, with which his writing is so dramatically engaged." (13–14)

Opio into Coca (Cobra)

THE TRANSLATION of titles gives us an emblematic view of critical and creative strategies involved in translating the text as a whole. Another "way in" is to isolate the translation of repeated devices or motifs that shape or provide an underlying unity. The "of course" variations in *TTT* were an instance of *added* wordplays to compensate for the loss of spoken Cuban and to underscore the (word)playfulness of the novel. Severo Sarduy's third novel, *Cobra,* provides us with a provocative network of allusive, reiterated terms, through which Sarduy weaves a rigorous, obsessive structure.

Cobra was the second Sarduy work I translated. One of my first projects was to translate for *Review* magazine "Eat Flowers," an excerpt from this novel-to-be, which first appeared in 1969 in *Imagen,* a Venezuelan literary journal. "Eat Flowers" became "The Initiation" in the final version of *Cobra,* an initiation that begins in "Le Drugstore" on the Boulevard St. Germain, the then chic new Parisian emporium whose interior is adorned with bronze sculptures of the lips and hands of famous people. The "Initiation" scene, culminating in a religious and sexual rite, involves a gang of motorcycle punks who metamorphose into Tibetan monks, one of whom shoplifts a scarf from "Le Drugstore." I still have a photo of Severo posing piquantly at the entrance, in front of a sculpted hand cupping a lamp, for his translator's "documentation."

The playful presence of North American pop culture and pop art of the Sixties in this perverse hallucinatory narrative, the fusion of the foreign and the familiar, attracted me as an aspiring translator. Sarduy's Cuban parodic wit was at first difficult to grasp because of the dense imagery and syntax, a verbal agility that obliges the reader – even the Hispanic reader – to become an active interpreter. A newcomer in a foreign country finds him/herself in a similar situation, motivated to learn the language in order to catch the jokes.

Cobra could be described as a Frankensteinian tapestry, composed of many languages, of the "leftovers" of texts, from Góngora to the *Michelin Guide,* from Cuban slang to French post-structuralist jargon. His "characters" (not characters in the realist sense) undergo continuous metamorphoses, reflected in the verbal disfigurements and alterations that Sarduy perpetrates. *Cobra* and his fourth novel, *Maitreya,* both satirize quests, from West to East (or vice versa), in which the Orient functions as a projection of the West's own (mis)interpretation. Columbus's initial "mistake," discovering the West Indies when he thought he had found the East, and the Europeans' consistent misunderstandings of the Native American languages and cultures throughout the discovery, conquest, and colonization of America, provide the historical backdrop for Sarduy's "traducements."

Part I of *Cobra* commences in Western Europe, in Paris, capital of exile and civilization, where Cobra is a transvestite actress/prostitute starring in the "Lyrical Theater of Dolls." The plot works its way "East" to Morocco, where Cobra, accompanied by sidekick Pup the dwarf, seeks a "conversion," a sex change. Part II begins with "The Initiation," which occurs simultaneously in profane Western and sacred Eastern settings. The book ends in India with an "Indian Journal" citing an excerpt from Columbus's diary, in which the explorer describes what he considers to be the East Indies, but which is really Cuba.

Sarduy's writing denies mimesis and exposes the artifice of all representation. His characters are ever-changing puppets in appearance and role, always projected as mutable, double configurations, drawn from pictorial imagery such as Velázquez's dwarfs and the surrealist Wifredo Lam's elongated Afro-Cuban figures. The English translation continues this denial of mimesis: The play on Pup and puppet in English, not possible in Spanish, carries further the original's French play on Pup and *poupée* (doll). English makes explicit the implied meaning of Pup(pet), a character without the realist trappings of a will and personality.

The subject Cobra, that is, the character and the subject matter, is an absence. *Cobra* – the title – is a polyvalent term, not all of whose meanings survive in the eponymous English translation: 1) the snake, of course, an Eastern religious symbol, and particularly the African Mandingo Whidah (a god worshipped by Caribbean African slaves). The pagan cobra snake invokes (phallic) erotic associations as well as a circular representation of time, the snake biting its tail; 2) the innovative CoBrA group of abstract painters (e.g., Appel, Alechinsky, Jorn) from Copenhagen, Brussels, and Amsterdam. Their expressionist gestural painting directly influenced Wifredo Lam, Cuba's most famous painter, and through him, Sarduy's approach to the written word as opaque, materialized, pictorial (Sarduy confirmed this lineage in conversation); 3) in Spanish the third-person singular of the verb *cobrar,* to receive wages; 4) the name of a transvestite who died in a plane over Mount Fuji. *Cobra,* as transitive verb, becomes intransitive, an icon of language as gesture, as materiality, becoming the convergence of a web of signifiers including Cuba, *obra* (work) *opio/apio* (opium/celery), and *barroco.* To translate the novel *Cobra* meant translating a 250-page pun, almost as untransposable as Octavio Paz's anagrammatical wordgame poem *"La Boca Habla"* (the mouth speaks) written for Sarduy and quoted in *Cobra.*[1]

The project of *Cobra* and of *Maitreya* (1978) converged with Sarduy's meditations on the (neo)baroque as a fundamental tendency in all art, particularly relevant to Ibero-America, direct heir to the Spanish baroque. He also postulates a connection between the baroque esthetic and non-Western theosophies, specifically Buddhism, and speaks of how baroque ornamentalism and the Buddhist void converge in representing the expulsion of the subject, the loss or absence of a center. In an essay, *"El barroco y el neobarroco,"* he offers a poetics of his own writing, and defines baroque methods or procedures:

> Another mechanism of Baroque artifice consists in obliterating the signifier of a given signified but not by replacing it with another, as distant as

1. *La Boca Habla:* La cobra/fabla de la obra/en la boca del abra/recobra el habla: El Vocablo. . . *The Mouth Speaks:* The cobra/speaks of the labor (or work)/in the mouth of the break (or opening)/recovers/speech: The Vocable. (152)

the second is from the first, but with a chain of signifiers which progresses metonymically and which ends up circumscribing the absent signifier, tracing an orbit around it, an orbit from whose reading – which we could call radial reading – we can infer it. (170)

From the "plot" of his novels – in which characters, settings, actions multiply and metamorphose to the point that the reader cannot determine psychology or causality – to the syntax of a sentence, Sarduy's writing demands a "radial reading." The reader must follow metonymic displacements from image to image, character to character, translating the text not into an explanation, a message, but into yet another fragmented, open-ended image of itself.

In *La Pensée Sauvage* Claude Lévi-Strauss defines *bricolage*, "tinkering," as the "method" of his anthropological research and as the discourse he uses to write about his research. He describes the *bricoleur*, or "tinkerer," as a prototypal figure who uses the "means at hand," who played a function in primitive societies and who can still be found, in his "prior" form, in the modern societies of today. Sarduy exemplifies such an artisan/artist, often referring to his writing as weaving, asking us to relate to the text as if it were a dense texture. *Cobra* speaks of *bricolage* in its repertoire of images of the "junk" in everyday Indian life that also constitutes the very material with which Indians construct their religious icons. The tinkerer's tools are "already there," heterogeneous and haphazard, and translate in *Cobra*, for example, into images of ready-to-wears, or surrealist wrought or found objects. In "White Dwarf" such nonreferential items are "snow" and the copper cones the Magician uses to produce changes in Pup; in "The Conversion," to perform sex-change surgery on Cobra, Doctor Ktazob (an Arabic-rooted name that could have been translated as "Cut-Cock") makes use of an unlikely instrument, rhetoric.

A principal strategy through which Sarduy reveals the improvised rigor of his text (and which he perceives subterraneously or consciously in all writing) is what visibly appears as an ebb and flow of repetitions and changes. Through a fragment, the repeated play between *opio* (opium) and *apio* (celery), I would like to retrace at least a simulation of the process of re-creating the anagrammatic effect of *Cobra*, its web of resonances, repetitions, and variations.

Sarduy mentioned the "untranslatable" play between *opio* and *apio* in a letter (April 18, 1973):

> This is quite difficult. . . . The point here is to hide a serious misdemeanor or error ["falta"] under a slight one... in which both words are pronounced almost identically. That is, here [Eustachio] traffics in *opio* but pretends to traffic in *apio;* only one letter changes the formula. Couldn't you find a solution with the word "horse," which I believe designates heroin in English, or something with "snow".

This note refers to *apio*'s first appearance (19): *"Encubría bajo un delito benigno – traficante de apio –, su verdadera infracción,"* which literally translates as "He concealed under a benign misdemeanor – smuggling celery – his real infraction." Sarduy's associative thinking certainly encouraged lassitude, the *freedom* to deliberate, without which creative translation is not possible.

Sarduy is always walking the tight*trope* between trope and meaning, supplanting signifiers with "floating" signifiers referring us back to wordplay, privileging the graphic materiality of vocables, which at the same time speak to us of language's continual slipping, both away from and toward meaning. Writer and translator here are drawn to delve into the unconscious of their own languages. The following reconstructs how *Cobra* (in English) follows the instability of *Cobra,* vacillating (*vacilón* in Cuban slang suggests "jiving"), jiving, zigzagging between trope and meaning.

To translate *apio* literally as "celery" would eliminate any possibility of recovering the "repercussions" that the *apio/opio* play produces in Spanish. The next step was to find a word similar in sound to *opium,* or that would graphically suggest opium, and would be at the same time an "innocent" word, signifying an object with no connection to drugs. But since celery is known in popular culture (in both Spanish and English) as a household aphrodisiac, the substitute would have to be ambiguous, both innocent and suggestive, creating not only a phonetic but a (euphemistic) semantic bridge with the prohibited term.

"Poppy" – "opium" constituted one possibility: The poppy is both a common flower, and the source of opium.[2] But phonetically the words are dissimilar (the *op* in both does not immediately strike the

---

2. The poppy is traditionally worn by war veterans on Veterans (formerly Armistice) Day.

reader's eye or listener's ear) and the referential connection is not ambiguous since the poppy is known as the natural source of opium. "Hop" came to mind: It's slang for opium, the *op* is more visible, and it suggests the innocent verb *to hop*. Too innocent though. Fitting a verb in the place of a noun here would have been awkward, and phonetically it is still too dissimilar from *opium*. How to find two heterogeneous yet intertwining words like *apio* and *opio* that differed by only one critical letter?

The first step out of this checkmate was to find another hard drug that was similar to opium, in effect (to create euphoria) and in source (imported from Asia or from the Third World, for consumption in the West) – yet keeping in mind the anagrammatic connection with *cobra*. Cocaine. And the slang expression "coke," also short for Coca-Cola, came to mind. Reconsidering this "solution" now produces a vertiginous sense of historical hindsight: Cocaine's notorious role in recent North and South American relations makes its presence in a Latin American novel translated into English even more relevant than it had been in the 1970s. As for Coca-Cola, it is both an innocent and noxious product. An emblem of North American economic imperialism, the carbonated drink is trafficked, like opium or cocaine, throughout the world, East and West, North and South.

Like celery, Coca-Cola had the popular reputation for being a not-so-benign transgression. The first formula for producing Coca-Cola contained cocaine; like the drug, the drink came from the coca leaf. By 1906, however, all traces of the drug had been removed from the leaves used to produce the drink.[3] This indelible fact did not erase from the books, however, the old wives' tale that Coca-Cola contained cocaine, a myth perpetuated by the knowledge that Coca-Cola contains another more "benign" drug, caffeine. American slang is the foremost perpetrator of Coke's black legend, since "coke" is also called "dope." Cotton mill workers in the early twentieth century called the trucks that dispensed Coca-Cola to them "dope wagons" (probably because of Coke's "pick-up" effect):

3. See E.J. Kahn. Jr., *The Big Drink: The Story of Coca-Cola* (New York: Random House, 1960), 99. This data was brought to my attention in 1974 by Paula Speck, a student at Yale University, on the occasion of a symposium on the New Cuban Novel, where I first presented some of the examples and observations in this chapter.

Just how "dope" came to be associated with Coca-Cola is uncertain. However, from "Coca-Cola" to "cocaine" to "dope" would seem to be a reasonable derivative chain. H. L. Mencken said in *The American Language* that "dope appears in virtually all American craft argots as a designation for a liquid of unknown composition," and Coca-Cola handsomely meets the specifications of this definition, for its precise contents have never been disclosed. (103)

Since the writing of *The Big Drink,* another "twist" has been added: The "original" Coke (not the original cocaine-distilled brew) is now called the "Classic" formula, to distinguish it from yet another simulation, a new and different "Coke."

The ambiguities of the "original" Coca-Cola make its insertion into *Cobra*'s web of elusive and allusive references a logical consequence: The ruins and remnants out of which Sarduy weaves his texts include the invasive repercussions of North American commerce and popular culture. Coca-Cola, an emblem of the American way of life as propagated in popular advertising, is a benign and not-so-benign transgression already implicit in the original *Cobra,* in which garish posters of American movie idols stand alongside retouched Rembrandt masterworks.

Not only was *coke* a pun – one word that had two meanings – and similar in sound and spelling to cocaine, but it could even more explicitly serve – like *apio* – as a partial anagram of *cobra*. I translated *traficante de apio* (celery smuggler) as "bottling coke without a license," both expressions suggesting in different ways the contradictory "benign transgression."

The next appearance of *apio* as a mask for *opio* occurs in a playfully pseudoscientific context describing only one factual property of opium, its sleep-producing effect:

> Si – añadió el Facultativo –, los curanderos legendarios que fundaron el Sikkim, para combatir el albarazo o blanca morfea, un herpes corrosivo, o más bien una lepra que atacaba al ganado, inyectaban a las reses un alcaloide del apio disuelto en agua fría. En las montañas los pastores usaban nieve. Poco a poco estos últimos fueron descubriendo que los animales, después de los enemas, al mismo tiempo que entraban en un sopor sin límites, crecían milagrosamente. (73)

Which came out in the final translation as

"Yes" – added the Physician –, "the legendary witch doctors who

founded the Sikkim, to combat the white leprosy or *alba Morphea,* a corrosive tetter, or rather a leprosy which attacked cattle, injected the cattle with
an alkaloid of coke dissolved in cold water. In the mountains the shepherds
used snow. Little by little these shepherds discovered that the animals, after
the enema, and at the same time they entered a boundless sopor, grew mi-
raculously. (52)

The *Encyclopaedia Britannica* helped justify the free play of substituting cocaine for opium. Opium is a juice, extracted from the poppy,
that is white at first but which turns black in contact with the air. The
chief active principle of opium is the alkaloid morphine. The uses of
opium can be medicinal; in the form of morphine it can be used as a
painkiller. But it can also be smoked, eaten, drunk, and injected as an
illicit drug, and can be used for the manufacture of heroin. It is, therefore, an extremely metamorphic substance. As with all his tropes, Sarduy takes *opio* and extends its metamorphic possibilities to what he
calls "hypertelic" extremes. Such semantic liberties permit his translator to abuse one drug by transforming it into another related substance. The poppy grows in many different places, though it is identified mostly with China. Illicitly used, opium produces drowsiness,
sleep, and finally comatose effects.

Cocaine does not have as many forms and uses as opium, but it does
share certain qualities and societal associations, and thus serves many
of the functions of *opio* in the text. Cocaine is also white, and remains
white; it is a crystalline alkaloid extracted from a leaf that grows mainly
in Peru and Bolivia but also in Indonesia. Latin America enters into the
field of connotations, which doesn't occur with opium – though in
Sarduy's world, again, the Far East presents an inverse, implicit mirror
of the West (Indies). Called "snow," it appears in powder form and is
usually sniffed. Opium appears in either liquid or coagulated lump
form. Cocaine can be used medicinally as a local anesthetic; as an illegal
drug, its effect is almost the opposite of opium's – it causes sleepless-
ness, loss of appetite, nausea, emaciation, and convulsions. The ency-
clopedia concludes soberly that the addict ends up pitifully irritable,
reduced.

Opium reigns over this paragraph of *Cobra* (73) in the form of the
white dwarf and white leprosy, with it Morphean effect and its association with the Far East – where Cobra encounters another concept of

time, sexuality, and identity. "Coke" erases the Morphean chain of paronomastic allusions extending explicitly to "morphological" (on the same page) and metamorphosis. But on the other hand, besides making more explicit the metamorphic play with the vocable *Cobra,* and naming a narcotic referent, it creates the metonymic association with whiteness. "Snow" in English most commonly signifies cocaine, and to a lesser degree heroin. Like opium, cocaine is cultivated in the Far East, specifically in Indonesia–though it's not associated with China as opium is–so that it does not completely displace the Oriental atmosphere fundamental to the text. The most significant (or better, signifying) supplementary aspect of this subversive substitution is that cocaine reinscribes a South American context.

Opio next appears in unmasked form, as a painkiller during Cobra's surgery: *"O en la operación, sientes que se inclina la mesa. Oyes un chorro caer en una vasija de aluminio. Te dan opio para que resistas."* (104): "Or in the operation you feel that the table slopes. You hear a stream falling into an aluminum container. They give you cocaine so that you can stand it." (78) Note here in the Spanish the predominance of *Cobra's* O, meaning "zero" and "or." The *o* in *O, operación, opio, Oyes, chorro* becomes less emphatic in the English "Or," "operation," "slopes," "cocaine," "so," where perhaps other sound plays, in an alliterative move from vowels to consonants, compensate: "contain," "cocaine," "can."

The final example I'll cite here–to display the substitution of one network of vocables by another–alludes to the Chinese torture of the one hundred slices. This horror was described more "painstakingly" in Cortázar's *Rayuela* (*Hopscotch,* 1964), and elaborated (or belabored) further by the Mexican novelist Salvador Elizondo in his novel *Farabeuf.* (The description, in all three texts, is based on a faded newspaper photograph.) This most horrible mode of execution, brought in as an analogue of Cobra's "conversion," is the most vivid, literal form of "metonymic dismemberment" in which subject is transformed into object:

> *Sea un hombrecillo que sonríe, atado a un madero. Atracarlo de opio. Uno a uno, sin sangre–en los tendones de las articulaciones breves tajos–, separarlo en pedazos, uno a uno, hasta cien.* (114)

Which became:

> Take a little man who smiles, tied to a beam. Cram him with cocaine. One by one, bloodlessly – brief cuts in the tendons of his joints –, separate him into pieces, one by one, up to one hundred. (87)

Cocaine is clearly a semantic transgression here; opium is the drug the Chinese torturers would have used to liberate the consciousness of their victim, whose engraved smile must be a grimace of pain. Thus, Sarduy's already hallucinatory abuse of the written word in general and of the metamorphic substance of opium in particular is extended by the impulse to follow a labyrinthine path of resonating, self-reflecting signifiers where the fringes of words change in each new setting. The kindred translator must transgress, extend herself, reach out in order to reconstruct *Cobra*'s elusive code, a code in which literary sound often makes literal sense.

Love Conquered by

All-iteration

Thou art translated.
Shakespeare[1]

In the Poetics, Aristotle says (in the words of his translator), "a good metaphor implies an intuitive perception of the similarity in dissimilars." If *Three Trapped Tigers* turned out to be a "good metaphor" of *Tres tristes tigres,* it is partly because a shared bilingualism between author and collaborator transcended manmade language barriers, and even the battle of the sexes that raged in Cabrera Infante's imagination.[2] He and I once considered writing a book together, partly because he thought I had too much of an ego to be a mere translator, and yet I have feared to tread where he dares. His ambivalence about intellectual women led to a possible title: *Horror Valkyrie.* He wrote a letter on this imaginary project that turned into a treatise on titles (Feb. 2, 1980):

> Let's do something together other than writing each other letters, translating while having a lot of pun and talking over the phone as if Don Ameche had just invented it. Let's be bald and make it a threesome together with the bald soprano. Horror Valkyrie is a good title, though I don't feel frightened

---

1. Bottom's metamorphosis in *A Midsummer Night's Dream* into an ass, quoted from Mel Gussow's review of Jan Kott's *The Bottom Translation* in the *New York Times Book Review* (June 14, 1987), 27. Kott interprets Shakespeare's use of the term *translation* as "the sudden discovery of desire."
2. According to Anny Amberni, French translator of *La habana,* GCI confessed to her his fear of the woman to whom he dedicates "The Amazon," the longest chapter in the book. This episode doubled in length in GCI's rewriting, obliging us (the publisher was alarmed by the book's girth) to suppress a chapter about the now married narrator's casual yet sought sexual trysts with women encountered on the street or in buses. I had converted the oxymoronic title *"Casuales encuentros forzados"* into "Casually Enforced Encounters," adding alliteration to insult in the original "Casually Forced Encounters."

46

or threatened by tall-tale blondes. . . . Now seriously I think it's a good idea to do this book together. We can call it Follies à Deux (which I seriously think is a good title but I don't believe it's commercial enough) or Three for Two. But never mind the title. There are many titled people in England who are unable to make a Night's Errand.

Our correspondence (literally and figuratively) held true as we progressed through a third major translation that began in 1979, the year of *La habana para un infante difunto*'s publication in Spain, and culminated in 1984, the prophetic year in which "Havana for a Dead Infant" finally became *Infante's Inferno*.

Why Infante and why Inferno (apart from its alliterative coupling with Infante)? We should keep in mind always the provisional nature of titles – and of texts. One of the early titles of *La habana* had been *"Las confesiones de agosto." Confessions of August* would have been a double entendre playing upon the confessions of St. Augustine; Cabrera Infante's narrator not only reveals – like the saint – but revels (or ravels) in past sins as well as his passage through life into the world of writing. Also August is hurricane season, the month of apocalyptical natural events in the Caribbean. So let us again journey to the source(s) to observe how the title surfaced, as with *Three Trapped Tigers,* when the book was nearly in the publisher's hands.

Cabrera Infante had now changed his tune about leaving titular decisions in the publisher's hands. Cass Canfield, Jr. had censured a portmanteau Cabrera Infante attempted to implant on the title page of *Three Trapped Tigers:* "Translated by Donald Gardner and Suzanne Jill Levine *in closelaboration* with the author" was reduced to "in collaboration." This cass-tration of his neologism was a bone of contention, even though, when it comes to title pages, the publisher has the right to exercise *manu militari*. In a letter (June 22, 1981) discussing possible titles for *La habana*, Cabrera Infante asserted his superiority over editors:

> What I am sure of is that we shouldn't leave this in the hands of Cass nor show signs of vacillation. Be as sure-footed as we were with the other two books. It's my experience that editors always want to contribute and always think of themselves as connoisseurs.

The "other" of the two books is *View of Dawn in the Tropics* (1978). An "editor" may be one's fellow combatant, but, unless the author is a canonized commodity, war waged between author and publisher will often dethrone the author; Cabrera Infante acceded later in this same letter: "The title, finally, will be determined by the publisher, as it happened last time. . . . " Editor and publisher are the same person here, but in the author's unconscious these *personae* are antagonists.

Cabrera Infante first mentioned to me in 1970 the book that was to follow *TTT*, which he then called *Cuerpos Divinos*. "Celestial" or "Heavenly Bodies" could be wonderful double entendres here but Cabrera Infante warned then in a letter (May 27, 1970) that this was "a title not to be translated": There exists a book titled *Heavenly Bodies*, and "Divine Bodies" says nothing. *Cuerpos Divinos* became *La habana*, pivoting first upon the Mallarméan but then impressionist motif *"L'après-midi d'un faune" (d'infant)* – the poem translated into music by Ravel. Cabrera Infante's explanation (May 10, 1975) for this metamorphosis recalls Ravel's view of the creative decision-making process:

> I continue writing my *Cuerpos Divinos*, although I have had to discard an important part and all that's left is the prologue which Emir published [in *Mundo Nuevo*, July 1968] and Julián Ríos reproduced. I've decided that this was the wrong path and that now the book is both simpler and more complex. The prologue is simply a phrase from Mallarmé, which fits perfectly, since I've turned the book into the memories of a Faun in his afternoon or après-midi.

(He continues to write *Cuerpos Divinos*, now one of his *next* big books.) And the title of this book, as already mentioned, turned into a parody of yet another Ravelian impressionist title, *Pavane pour une infante défunte*. But I'll take a few steps back (or forward).

When Cabrera Infante officially introduced me to the book as its prospective translator (February 1, 1979) he quipped about alliteration as the chief "difficulty" in the stylistic canon of English prose:

> I think you'll like it. There are many puns, some in English, others in French. . . . But the rest (a problem for you) is filled with alliterations, a device which the books of rhetoric declare dangerous for prose. You'll have to translate it into verse, then. Many of the alliterations are imperceptible, but others are very visible, forced. It occurred to me that alliteration is an erotic construction, because of the intimacy between one word and the

next, at times becoming triollism. . . . In any case you'll soon see. . . 606 pages of difficulties.

He also raised the problematic issue of the title:

> Cass already has a photocopy of my book, which is called (first time I divulge the title outside of the family, but as you will be one of the authors) LA HABANA PARA UN INFANTE DIFUNTO. I'd like the title in English to be, if possible, Havana for an Infant Difunct. I already know that there's a violation of order here, but it's the best title I can think of, since you don't seem too keen on Dry Dreams. I haven't mentioned anything about this to Cass yet. In any case the title in Spanish is not *Tres tristes tigres,* but on the other hand (a masturbatory idiom) my memorable novel is something else, full of sex and cinema.

La habana followed *TTT* almost as a sequel, confirming Joseph Brodsky's description of the exiled writer as one who "even having gained the freedom to travel. . . will stick in his writing to the familiar material of the past, producing, as it were, sequels to his work." (18) *La habana* continues to pay homage to Havana lost but this time as the city of an adolescent's discovery of love or (more to the point) sex. Written by the narrator in the afternoon of his life, it is not a night in the life but the memoirs of memories of two decades, the Forties and Fifties, the adolescent's morning and early manhood's high noon when this Cuban Casanova and obsessive voyeur chased after every girl or woman in sight.

"I decided on the title almost upon finishing writing the book, but for me the first writing means little. . . . Almost all the wordplays, puns and alliterations are done in the rewriting," Cabrera Infante states in an interview with Julián Ríos. He continues:

> Curiously, the title influenced the beginning of the book – even though it was already written, there's no doubt that a phrase that I incorporated afterwards was given by the title. [The phrase is, in translation: "I had stepped from childhood into adolescence on a staircase."] That is, the fact that the *infante,* the child, had "died" upon arriving in Havana and the adolescent was born. Then the book becomes the adolescent's long struggle to become a man, a battle which he doesn't win. He tries to achieve this through women, but only becomes more and more infantile with women.
>
> At the end it seems that he's finally become a man [through a relatively more mature though extramarital relationship] but in the epilogue he is lit-

erally devoured by a woman as if he were no longer an *infante* but a baby. (156)

This autobiographical book centers upon man's fate as eternal infant in mother's arms but also uncovers its author's identity when (as Emir Rodríguez Monegal writes) the speechless infant finally becomes defunct, metaphorically represented at the book's end, where an enormous vagina spews forth the Infante, born again as a writer. Infante had to be in the title.

La habana is a book both nostalgic and satirical, like the semiclassical music of the impressionist composers. Ravel and Debussy, the narrator explains in the chapter titled, after Debussy's waltz, *"La Plus Que Lente,"* influenced the campy composers of certain popular Cuban sounds serving as background music to the narrator's conversations and romances with women. Among these impressionist pieces Ravel's *Bolero,* a French parody of a Spanish form appropriated by Cuba, has evolved into an erotic cliché, even a pornographic chestnut on at least three continents; Sarduy labels it, in *From Cuba with a Song,* "the trademark of every striptease." Cabrera Infante expresses nostalgia for a mythical past, as did Ravel and Debussy, but also parodies past forms and performances in order to create not only art out of life but life out of death.

Pavane pour une infante défunte, Ravel's original, was already a *boutade,* a modernist piece playing upon the form of a sixteenth-century court dance. Cabrera Infante comments to critic Ardis Nelson: "Ravel was more than an impressionist, much more than an imitator: he was a parodist, a poet of pastiche and panache. . . . In other words, a man after the author's own heart." (91) Furthermore, Ravel himself admitted – a musician after all – that he chose the title not in homage to a dead Spanish *infanta* but for its lilting alliteration, imitating his mock *pavana*'s nostalgic sway.[3]

3. The *pavane* serves as a structural device in *La habana*, Ardis Nelson asserts [91]: "The pavane is a slow, processional dance of the late Renaissance, which winds slowly forward, although steps may be taken backward. A similar pattern is seen in the temporal progression in the novel, which, while mostly linear, occasionally reverts to the focal point of the first chapter, 'La casa de las transfiguraciones.' In a variation of the dignified dance, the procession divides with partners separating, circling the room and then rejoining. This recurring motif of seeking one's other half culminates in the phantasmagorical adventure at the end of the book, when an alluring woman... entering a movie theater invites the narrator with suggestive body language 'to the dance of life.' "

Cabrera Infante "bets," in an interview with himself titled "Horror Kirie," that Ravel, like himself, thought of the title as a "[late] Romantic afterthought." (9) Like Ravel's title, *La habana para un infante difunto* is not to be taken literally. The Infanta perhaps never existed in the dream of life, just as what remains of Havana is an image, a phrase of music, a string of words. Plays on words and alliteration were incorporated, Cabrera Infante has insisted, in the rewriting, that is, the writing. The pleasure of the text here (for writer and translator) lay in shaping the sentence, in letting words produce words.[4]

If the title *Tres tristes tigres* was a spoken tongue twister, a failed alliteration (complemented in English as a visual, *written* alliteration, the phonic translated into the graphic) in which the first two words begin the same, and the third *almost* the same, *La habana para un infante difunto* is an achieved alliteration, announcing verbal language's most musical device.

The memory of music as well as of the spoken voice is all that remains of Infante's Havana, his Paradise Lost. Music, "the essentially untranslatable," Susanne Langer has said, is the unspoken, universal language that writing aspires to, or so the anonymous, eponymous narrator (mis)quotes Walter Pater. Alliteration expresses, frees the impulsive, rhythmic nature of language. Language *is* music to the child and to the poet, just as words become magical objects to the child, to the poet, and to the exile who discovers a new language. Music pours out in spoken language in *TTT,* particularly in the rhythmic monologues featuring Music's maximum Muse, La Estrella, a black bolero singer, and Eribó, the mulatto bongo player, and of course throughout the book's incessant songs, jingles, and oral wordplay.

But *La habana,* its author has emphatically distinguished, is a *written* book. Where *TTT* was a gallery of voices, the narrator of *La habana* is a supremely solitary figure, like the *pavo real,* the peacock from which the *pavane,* an often solo dance, originates. Like his paper tigers, he is

---

4. "I would like to produce books which would entail only the writing of sentences," Flaubert wrote to Louise Colet, June 25, 1853, *The Letters of Gustave Flaubert 1830–1857,* ed. tr. Francis Steegmuller (Harvard UP, 1980), 189. "The exciting part for him was working on the style, on word-choice, resolving the problems of naming, of modifiers, of euphony and rhythm," writes Mario Vargas Llosa in his intelligent study *La orgia perpetua: Flaubert & Madame Bovary* (Barcelona: Seix Barral, 1975), 52; my translation. See *The Perpetual Orgy,* tr. Helen Lane (New York: Farrar, Straus & Giroux, 1986).

enclosed in the book, in his hall of mirrors like Haiti's King Christophe. Despite all the women reflected, he experiences the greatest moment of love, or rather orgasm, through masturbation. *La habana* traces the narrator's supreme efforts to conquer loneliness, a loneliness experienced perhaps more keenly by the author in exile, in memory.

The pun plays an important role but alliteration takes over, perhaps because *La habana* is a much more sexually explicit, less censured book than *TTT*. An early structural principle in poetry, alliteration evolved into a comic device, as in Shakespeare's comedy *Love's Labour's Lost,* alluded to in *La habana* in the phrase "a labor of literary love" (70), when the adolescent narrator is trying to seduce a girl by reading erotica to her. Alliteration has always been a mnemonic aid (dancing daughters, founding fathers), often exploited by commercial advertising to fix a product in the consumer's malleable mind. Since *Infante's Inferno* opens a Pundora's Box of memory, mostly erotic memories, the sensual device of alliteration best harmonizes with the book's sexual content, and comes closest to music, the conduit of memories. In the spirit of Dr. Johnson, who speaks of the "unexpected copulation of ideas" in verbal wit, one could say that alliterating words literally copulate.

"Infante's Inferno" provides an appropriate alliterative play on the author's name, but what does *La habana* have to do with Dante? Our guide through this "inferno" of Havana lost tells us we'll find more than one "vigilant Virgil for every damn Dante." (108) Cabrera Infante's real-life Virgil, the homosexual writer Virgilio Piñera, referred in a misogynist vein to the vagina as Hell. Havana is a sexual Hades for the adolescent Infante, but already in *TTT* Havana looms like an infernal Nighttown. Photographer Códac describes Havana's night world as a modern "musical circle of hell" (289); nostalgic for the missing muse La Estrella (a grotesque Beatrice), he descends into one of Havana's many subterranean clubs only to encounter Cuba Venegas, a siren of the night. Eribó, the nickname for S. S. Ribot, another dweller of this underworld, means "hell" in Afro–Cuban dialect.[5] Tourist Mr.

---

5. There existed (unknown to GCI) a French linguist named Ribot who believed in the "instinctual" origins of language. Théodule Ribot, a nineteenth-century French experimental psychologist, studied the origin of speech and the evolution of abstraction. He contended that "the completely developed languages... bear throughout the print of the unconscious

Campbell refers to Havana oxymoronically as "Dante's *Invierno*" (190), the winter of discontented northern visitors who come to exploit the atmospheric and sexual heat of the tropics. And in *La habana*, in the initial and initiating chapter *"La casa de las transfiguraciones,"* the adolescent discovers "the tenement as hell" with its different light and infinite sexual transfigurations going on in every room. We transfigured this chapter title in English as "The House of Changes," giving it an appropriate Chinese *I Ching* ring, not only because English prefers simple words over the multisyllabic but because the *I Ching* focuses on the dual nature of (wo)man, the obsessive subject of the book, the dynamics of yin/yang. Other resonances are more autobiographical and more Cuban: The Chinese dragon lady was Cabrera Infante's first literary crush. Also, prophetic like the *I Ching,* the tenement building introduces the young narrator to the mysteries of sex and Havana, and among the many women a Chinese beauty, hence prefiguring his destiny.

But the "Ching" ring brings first to the bilingual mind *chingar,* Cuban slang for sexual intercourse. Alliteration is language's poetic mimicry of Eros; the pun is a weapon on the battle of the sexes, in which apparent hostility often cloaks underlying love. Such a verbal battle of the sexes is staged between Olga Andreu and Roberto Branly in *"La Plus Que Lente":*

I remember the day Branly became notably noticed by Olga Andreu. He came to see her bowl of brand new goldfish, and asked with almost scientific curiosity: "Are they adults?" But Olga (christened Volgar by Branly) made Branly's game into a set from her settee, a repartee à la Satie:
"Adulterers" said Olga. "They're fiendish fish."
"What are their names?" asked double Branly: "Daphne and Chloe?"
"No" said Olga, "Debussy and Ravel."
"Oh, I get it," said Branly, approaching the golden bowl but not bowled over. "Debussy must be that one with the flaxen scales."
"Algae."
"Olgae?"
"Vegetal filaments that float, vaguely."

---

labor that has fashioned them for centuries: they are petrified psychology." (James Stam, *Inquiries into the Origin of Language* [New York: Harper & Row, 1976], 250.)

"Are they from the impressionist school of fish?" asked Branly.

"Yes, Debussy even composed *La mer,* an impression."

"Quite impressive." Branly said. "Though I doubt he did it. Nobody at sea composes La mer and a goldfish wouldn't compose *The Fishbowl* either, I hasten to add."

Olga wanted to scare Branly: "The other one, Ravel, a composer of waltzes and boleros, wrote the *Pavane for a Dead Punster.*"

Branly pretended not to feel the hook and had the last word–fish: "I suppose that one afternoon Debussy will write *L'après-midi d'un poisson d'or.*

Catia, almost overcome, turned to ask me: "Is he crazy?"

"Merely enthusiastic."

Cabrera Infante first mentions this "musical" chapter in the same introductory letter (February, 1 1979): "This episode has changed a lot since you last read it and it is one of the pieces de La Resistance (music for the underground) in my novel."

A brief chapter synopsis: At Olga Andreu's intellectual gatherings or *tertulias,* the adolescent meets and falls in love, unrequitedly, with Catia; Debussy's nostalgic little "waltz" accompanies this episode about an adolescent crush that ends in inevitable disillusionment. The group gathers to listen to classical or rather impressionistic music, a music movement in which – Cabrera Infante writes in the same letter – "Olga involved Ravel, whom Satie nicknamed Ravol, adding insult to injury by claiming that Ravel firmly believed that in music, theft is mere rubato. Here not only a wordplay falsely attributed to Satie is added – "Ravol" – but Ravel's role as a parodical creator is under-*scored* in the claim that imitation is not theft but a part of creation – in this case comically a musical frill, rubato playing on robbery."

Hence Satie intrudes upon the witty repartee in the English version, in which a Ravelian joke, "Pavane for a Dead Buffoon," becomes more alliterative as "Pavane for a Dead Punster." *"La Plus Que Lente"* (chapter IV) was the first episode translated – as a kind of warming up exorcism. It was the first to appear in print (in the Mexican journal *Vuelta*), and we thought it could be serialized in English as a set(tee) piece. Cabrera Infante not only insisted upon the importance of the Sati(e)ric maestro, but recommended that I listen to music by the *impressionists while* translating. He explains in English in a letter dated December 27, 1979:

54

The reference to Satie is very pertinent because Satie – very sarcastic, very anti-Debussy – is also one of my favorite personnages in the history of music. Satie is besides cited to satiety throughout the book, like the end where the Narrator enters the vagina and declares that it's a "pieza" [both "piece" and "room" in Spanish] in the shape of a pear. Do you remember Satie and his "Trois pieces en forme de poire"? It would be good if while doing this part of the book and in "The Most Beautiful Girl in the World" – where the narrator finally consummates the love act, in this case with a girl who wants to make love to the sound of Debussy's "Sea" – that you listen to – or sightread, picaroon of a piano player, you – a lot of Debussy, chunks of Ravel and all of Satie's piano works.

Already a habituée of that languid, nostalgic music, I took his advice literally and listened incessantly to Ravel and Debussy, fatiguing my turntable as I translated to the hypnotic melodies and rhythms of Debussy's *Sea* and Ravel's *Valse*. Borges and Bioy Casares apparently abused Brahms in like manner while composing their *Bustos Domecq* stories in collaboration, turning his romantic symphonies into innocuous wallpaper.

The following comments in the same (long, single-spaced) letter stress the "transelaborations" perpetuated in this passage, as well as Cabrera Infante's subversive participation in the process:

Have we lost somewhere the golden bowl bit? Don't you think that we could say "Branly approaching the golden bowl"? I like poking fun into old James's ashes.

Set and later settee, all right? Fiendish fish better than devilish. Flaxen scales gives the reader's Debussy's La fille aux cheveux de line, your own translation of it plus musical scales. And the plural of alga should be algae. Then we have Olgae as an absurd plural. *It works even better than in Spanish.* The impressionist school of fish I think it's good, don't you?

Nobody at sea, though not exactly the equivalent I think that it conveys the idea of being at sea and lost. "I hasten to add" I think it is rather funny for Branly to say. Now scare is related to scale, thus we have a fish to fright. Punster is better than Buffoon, though I believe that the Ravel title is kept in Spanish elsewhere. Feel the hook continues with the marine metaphores [*sic*] and hook is also a punishing blow. I put word-fish to play with sword and word and fish. . . . The last lines are straight from King Kong and it is an exchange between Bruce Cabot (who asks this question about Carl Denham) and the captain of the ship who literarily says: "Merely enthusiastic." I only left out the word skipper in Cabot's question. But the merely here is perfect, conveying the sparseness of captain Conrad, the Debussyan mer and the usual adverb. It is a very terse line.

The quotation from *King Kong* would remind only the most knowledgeable film buffs of the King Kong quotation serving as terse epigraph to this verbose book: "Blondes are pretty scarce around here." We shouldn't forget that *King Kong* is essentially a romance, about the impossible love of an ape for a woman. The obsexed narrator of *La habana* finds his truest analogy, perhaps, in this king.

Names Proper, Improper, and Just Plain Common

Name: the word seems to be a compressed sentence, signify-
ing being for which there is a search.

PLATO, *Cratylus*

THE PARADOX of proper names with evident
meanings is that they must become common (they must be translated)
and yet remain proper. Such names serve a semiotic function, like
common nouns in everyday usage, but in satirical literary art they *represent,* suggest connotations to the reader; their conventional usage is
"abused." By retracing the translation of names, we come to see how
these vocables imply meanings that become explicit in translation or
suggest meanings that are displaced in translation by contiguous
meanings. Names involve relationships within and between languages
and texts, between word and referent which become reshuffled in another context, and the translation of names signals the ways in which
the original and the translation decipher each other.

When Guillermo Cabrera Infante first described *La habana para un
infante difunto,* he listed among its difficulties "a playing with proper
names considered as common names." (February 1, 1979) He went on
to cite an example: "One of the heroines is named Margarita and there
are allusions to the phrase Margarita para los cerdos. Pearls before
swine is fine but then all the other allusions to Margarita are lost. . . . "
Margarita means Daisy, which in English descends from Day's Eye.
Day's Eye would have been an apt nickname for this formidable female
character who turns out to have one breast, but then there's the allusion
to her favorite drink, margarita. How necessary and how difficult to

57

translate names, beginning with Infante itself, which does not quite mean infant. When *La habana para un infante difunto* became *Infante's Inferno,* Infante as a proper name remained, but its common meaning (as in French) had to be "read" through the text. Not only did the implied proper noun become explicit, but the explicit common noun became implied. "Infante" remained the same but became something different in translation.

The following are a few among many transmutated names that lost connotations and gained others, and whose satirical effect had to strike the reader's eye and/or ear. "Some puns die in translation, while other puns are born," dixit Cabrera Infante. Nicknames, with concrete meanings, are more commonly used in the Romance languages than in English – and the English translator must often be more resourceful than the Romance writer.

Dulce Espina (literally, "Sweet Thorn"), the pseudonym Cabrera Infante chose for one of the women seduced by the narrator, defines a character whose sugary sweetness hides an underlying thorniness, as interpreted by the misogynistic narrator. It's a corny name, suggesting a leading lady in a soap opera or even a soft porn queen, with a common meaning. My fellow translator came up with a brilliant stand-in: "Honey Hawthorne" maintains the sugary and thorny connotations and suggests another, relevant one: whore(Haw)ishness.

"Hawthorne" brings inadvertently to bloom other buds: the book's rich allusions to the universe of literature. Cabrera Infante's *Inferno* comments ironically on the romance tradition, within which Hawthorne's Puritan fable on the wages of Love (or sex) is inscribed. There's Hawthorne, the pathetic British agent in *Our Man in Havana* (inversion of our Havanan in London perhaps?). And the thorny motif of (in English translation) the "hawthorne lane" in *À la recherche du temps perdu,* the *locus amenus* where Marcel first sees Gilberte, which then becomes a nostalgic refrain throughout the volumes. Cabrera Infante shares with Proust not only remembering but also a (male view of the) whore thorns of love. Down Mammary Lane.

Dulce into Honey inspired my next translation, Sarduy's *Maitreya:* El Dulce, a desirable young man, and one of the many reincarnations of the future Buddha, became "Honey Boy." In the translation of names with concrete meanings one should, again, select the living part. Spanish grammar creates substantives by prefacing an adjective with an article; the literal translation into English would be "The Sweet One," but "one" is such a weak, neuter pronoun, and "Honey Boy" is anything but neuter.

The names of double (and chubby) divas in *Maitreya*, La Divina and La Tremenda, provide similar food for thought. Divine, the transvestite in John Waters's films, seemed a shoe-in. The particular problem here was the feminine address *La*, used commonly in Spanish to designate a female personage as in *La Pasionaria*, the muse of the Republican forces in the Spanish Civil War. *"Divina"* and *"Tremenda"* are also common epithets, particularly in gay South American jargon. *Tremenda*, an oft-used Cuban hyperbole, has lost its original bombastic force; the same occurred with the tired adjective "nice" in English, or *linda* in Argentine. The necessary note here was affectation, exaggeration. Why not take advantage of the lofty and yet satirical address "Lady," used with irony, but also in homage to Billie Holiday, in the lingo of black jazz musicians. Hence Lady Divine and Lady Tremendous. The local flavor of *tremenda* vanished, but translation (like all writing) attempts somehow to communicate: *Tremenda* refers not only to her tremendous artistic qualities as a diva, but, even more so, literally to her size.

The first Sarduyian doubles I tackled, in *De donde son los cantantes*, were two acolytes or "helpers": Auxilio and Socorro. These two words mean "help," normally used to yell for help, but they also doubled as comically archaic proper names, particularly Socorro. Auxilio and Socorro (avatars of Kafka's bungling assistants?) provide a common thread throughout this three-part disjunctive novella, thus helping the plot along, first as chorus girls and lastly as devotees of Christ. I chose, in faithfulness, Help and Mercy, Mercy more discernibly a possible real name like Socorro. The hilarity is produced by their juxtaposition, as if each time the names are mentioned, one were calling for Help! Mercy!

In *La habana* as in *TTT*, name-inventing becomes yet another category of name-translating. Again, the Olga/Branly repartee:

Eran los días en que Roberto, nacido Napoleon, Branly, que entró a formar parte del grupo como especialista en humor vítreo, decía tener un amigo apodado Bombillo y otro apellidado Chinchilla y no sabíamos cual era el apellido y cual el apodo, dudando que la piel de Chinchilla fuera genuina y preguntando cuantas bujías encendía Bombillo. . . . Pero Olga (a quien Branly bautizó Olgasana). . . (238)

Which became in English:

Those were the days when Roberto, born Napoleon, Branly, who joined the group as a specialist in vitreous humor, was said to have a friend named Leo Tiparillo, and another called Chinchilla, and we couldn't tell the surnames from the nicknames, doubting that Chinchilla's hide was genuine and wondering how many matches it would take to light Tiparillo. . . . But Olga (christened Volgar by Branly). . . (112)

Cabrera Infante remarked (December 27, 1979): "The Leo Tiparillo bit works very well. . . named after Leo Carrillo and your own tiparillo. . . and also Volgar."

Here he jumbles in Borgesian mode reality and fiction by juxtaposing the names of real-life people (Roberto Branly, Olga Andreu) with invented names such as *Bombillo,* meaning "Light Bulb," and *Chinchilla.* He also plays Joycean phonetic games with real names such as "Napoleon Branly" (or Brandy) or "Olgasana," that is, *Holgazana,* meaning "lazy," and here insinuating lazy Olga but also healthy Olga (Olga sana).

The image of a lit bulb, and particularly the verb *encender*—meaning "turn (the light) on" but suggesting also "light (a fire)"—brought to mind "tiparillo," in my effort to find rhymes with *illo.* Tiparillo suggested the character actor Carrillo to movie buff "Caín" and so he added "Leo": Leo Carrillo, like Rita Hayworth, was of Spanish descent and usually played friendly, chatty fellows in broken English. The vulgarized Russian song about rowing a boat down the Volga river was not irrelevant to Olga, the Russian-Jewish girl. Though vulgar does not mean lazy or healthy, lazy, healthy, hence earthy Olga evokes the contiguous image of a vulgar Olga. It's important to note here the shared references to North American popular culture and to the popularizations of foreign cultures.

Boquitas pintadas (1968), Manuel Puig's second novel, parodies the serial romance and like *Rita Hayworth* chronicles provincial life in the small town of Colonel Vallejos with an almost hyperrealist effect. Many names of people and places in this satirical work "mean" something: regionalist nicknames as of the maidservant La Raba, or proper names that have a symbolic value while remaining "proper," as with the lecherous Doctor Aschero and the general store *La Criolla,* or even emblematic names like Juan Carlos. Juan Carlos, the embittered young man who seduces all the women in this novel, recalls the figure of Don Juan. His initials also suggest, in irony or not, Jesus Christ. Juan Carlos dies significantly during Holy Week, as a "martyr" to TB, love, or *ambos,* "resurrected" by the wishful fantasies of Nené, a former girlfriend, and by the text, to a life of eternity.[1] Since the Don Juan myth has transcended its Hispanic origins, all readers can recognize – if not as readily – the Don Juan in Juan Carlos. Just as we come to recognize the infant in Infante.

Some Names Are Born

Antonia, alias Rabadilla, alias Raba: Rabadilla (*Raba* for short) "the tail of a chicken," alludes to the maid's prominent rear, which stands out as a synecdoche for her body, her "biological" destiny, ultimately her social role. *La Raba* metonymically links cause and effect, her anatomy with her downfall perpetrated by seducer Pancho. "Goose Ass," "Bunny Tail" came futilely to mind, but suddenly a brainstorm: I remembered Fanny, the name of a large, warm-hearted woman who had been like a grandmother to me. Fanny/*Rabadilla* turned out to be a magical correspondence, acceptable women's names in two different languages that could serve the same "end." *Rabadilla,* rural, concrete, relates more directly to its referent; "Fanny" is associated through simile (fanlike) to its form. Fanny is a slang word for the buttocks, but since it functions as a real name, it is also more indirect. Fanny is less local than *Raba,* further removed from a literal etymology, hence more literary.

  Dr. Aschero: Aschero functions as both a proper name of Italian origin – identifying his immigrant origins, suggesting *nouveau* vulgarity, as opposed to native-born gentility – and as a "sign" associating him with *asco,* disgust. He is a vile villain who takes advantage of his posi-

---

1. Lucille Kerr comments that this "replay" both debases and glorifies the Don Juan figure in an insecure, insincere, yet romantically inspiring avatar. (98–100)

tion of power to seduce young women in his employ, among them Nené.

Again, when Joyce translated the "pun-names" in "Anna Livia Plurabelle" into Italian, he "Italianized" them, multiplying the significations of the names, creating double, triple puns. In like fashion Aschero had to evolve into a different name that would crystallize the character.

Aschero subsumes a multilingual Argentina where Italian has mingled with Spanish; *Lunfardo,* an urban slang spoken in the *barrio sur* of Buenos Aires is heavily Italianate. But does the relationship between Italian and Spanish find its equivalent in the United States? In the United States, Italian immigrants recall associations with the Mafia, as opposed to the social superiority of *"Mayflower"* Americans. The Argentine equivalent of the *Mayflower* type is the *criollo,* the native whose ancestry goes back to the first Spaniards to set foot on American soil. But there are more social and linguistic connections between the sons of Spaniards and Italians, Latins all, than between American English and Italian. *Aschero* is a Spanish pun, and Italian's Lunfardesque contribution to Argentine Spanish is unique.

A solution: I dug into the telephone directory and came up with "Nasti." Not as physically suggestive as Aschero (*asco* is synonymous with "nausea"), Nasti nonetheless describes this scoundrel. Nasty and disgusting are synonymous in effect: The reader misses out on the stomach-turning connotation but can draw the logical conclusion that the original *implies:* If he's disgusting he is also nasty. Puig thought Nasti was too transparent and decided to tone it down to Nastini, a ridiculous Italianate name producing a comic *effect* for the American reader, just as Aschero makes the Spanish reader chuckle. Nasti/Nastini is perhaps another of those magical correspondences in which "the creative principle" is carried forth "*inside* the language of the translation." In its non-Latin origins nasty meant "foul, dirty, nauseous." If one were to dig – perhaps too deeply – into linguistic mysticism, nasty/*aschero* share the syllable *as.*

La Criolla: the *almacen,* or "store-tavern," what in the United States we would call a general store, where Juan Carlos often goes slumming with Pancho the bricklayer. The cognate in English "Creole" originates in the same Latin root, *creare* (*criar,* Sp.), "to breed," with a similar meaning: descendant of settlers in the New World. But *criollo* and *creole* take on different regional, racial, and social connotations. Creoles are descendants of European or Negro settlers "bred" in the West Indies; creole smacks of soul food and New Orleans's Latin Quarter. *Criollo* means native-born Argentinian: The upper-middle-class usage, represented in Borges's or Bioy Casares's works, connotes pride in being *criollo*. But in Puig's context of lower-class rural people it suggests "half-breed," *negro* (not African but rather of Indian origins). Both *criollo* and *negro(a)* are denigrating terms used by Puig's middle-class characters when they speak of Pancho and Raba. For the tavern's name "The Creole Girl" (the place where J. C. and Pancho pick up *criollas* like Raba) we finally came up with "The Gaucho Inn," the place where Pancho and J. C. drink and whore like rough-and-ready gauchos. *Criolla* and *gaucho* are linked by association, and *gaucho,* though exotic to the American reader, evokes a recognizable, relevant image. Remote but intelligible.[2]

2. Donald Keene has observed that when translating obscure or culture-bound allusions, the translator should try to produce an effect that is "remote" but "intelligible." See "The Translation of Japanese Culture," in *Landscapes & Portraits: Appreciations of Japanese Culture* (Tokyo & Palo Alto: Kodansha International Ltd., 1971), 322–329.

Part II:

Spoken into Written

Writing here is only an attempt to capture the fleeting human voice.

G. Cabrera Infante

TTT: Writing the Spoken (in Which the Spoken Becomes Written)

GCI WROTE two caveats to *TTT* that we didn't include in the English version. One of these *advertencias,* which addresses his intention to reproduce spoken Cuban, can be translated as follows:

> This book is written in Cuban. That is, written in the different dialects of Spanish spoken in Cuba. Writing here is only an attempt to capture the fleeting human voice. . . . The different forms of Cuban become (or I think they become) a literary language. Nevertheless, a particular Havanan accent predominates as does an even more particular nocturnal slang which, as in all big cities, tends to be a secret tongue. The reconstruction was not easy and some pages should be heard rather than read – it wouldn't be a bad idea to read them out loud. Lastly, I would like to borrow the following words of advice from Mark Twain: "I offer these explanations for the simple reason that without them, many readers might think that the characters are trying to speak alike without succeeding."

Why was this preface omitted? The particularly Cuban speech and Havanan accents in *TTT* inevitably vanish in its English version. And the English reader would find a statement innovative in the American idiom a century ago now unnecessary.

Should the translator supplant one local dialect with another? Or somehow suggest the vividness of the original "Cuban" through a composite of spoken accents from American English? Every translator has a personal version of what a particular slang sounds like, and of which slang is a more appropriate substitution. In the Penguin preface to *TTT*'s Menippean model, the British translator of *The Satyricon* argues for a less localized slang in order to give an impression of what might have been spoken in a given milieu. Sullivan didn't want to impose a particular period or place in England upon Petronius's Rome, and yet he heard the less lively but more "compact" British English as nearer to the Latin colloquial speech than American slang. The American translator Arrowsmith argues, on the other hand, that *The Satyricon* required the "context and vigor of a particular language, at once vividly colloquial and vigorously literary. . . . American English has that full ripeness." (23–24)

For the "sound" effects in *TTT* we produced a simulacrum of the particular accents and vocabulary of southern Black Americans, the closest culturally and ethnically to *TTT*'s many mulatto and black characters. We had to mark believable distinctions between different characters' speech, identifying differences of race and class between writer Silvestre and bongo player Eribó, for example, or between actor Arsenio Cué and kept woman Magalena Cruz. To bring the tone down to earth, we Americanized Gardner's earlier Cockney version: *bloody* to *damn, filthy* to *dirty, weeping* to *crying*.[1]

When I first met Cabrera Infante in London he was struggling over the beginning section of the book, *"Los debutantes"* ("The Beginners"), which, following the emcee's introduction, set the lively spoken tone of the book. "Beginners" is a double entendre: The first speakers are children, literally beginners in life, but the other beginners introduced in the early sections of the book are mostly young men and women from the sticks trying to begin to "make it" in the big city. These inaugural tableaux include

1) feisty *Cuba Venegas* (whose real name is Gloria): Her sexy good looks lead her to become a model who hangs out with photographer Códac. Her rise to infamy is reported in a letter by the puritanical Delia Doce, a Havana friend of Gloria's mother, Estelvina, who had placed her daughter under Delia's protection. The letter reports that as soon as Gloria reached Havana she flew Delia's coop. Delia Doce's slightly illiterate, old-fashioned prose expresses disapproval of Estelvina's

---

1. British English would have its playful heyday in *Infante's Inferno*, reflecting not only Cabrera Infante's years in Britain but also the baroque flourish of this written book narrated by a single literary voice.

daughter Gloria (now Cuba) who instead of being a good girl and working in an office and studying to better herself at night school, has gone into show business, or rather, into living a loose life.

Guillermo added a comment in the translation to emphasize Gloria's disdainful view of book learning (quoted by Delia to Estelvina) and her preference for the glamour of "real" life: *"ella no pensaba estudiar ni cosa que se le pareciera . . . "* (28) became "she had no intention of studying anymore . . . and furthermore she added that if she had any studying to do she'll be doing it from now on at the academy of life, her very words." (ms., 20) We changed "academy of life," which didn't sound simple-minded enough, to the "School of Hard Knox." I misspelled knocks to go along with the uneducated Estelvina's spelling, graphically transcribing the phonetic: In Spanish, *v* and *b, s* and *c,* and other consonants can be easily confused. (17) Similar spelling confusions in everyday letter-writing, based on pronunciation, come up again in Puig's *Boquitas pintadas.* Since English is often not spelled the way it sounds, I had an even broader range of possible misspellings to play with.[2]

By capitalizing the School of Hard Knox so that it can be taken literally (as if such a school existed) as well as metaphorically, the translation underscores what is already clearly implied in the original: Delia is a good-hearted, naive person, and it would seem that she's taking Gloria at her word, just as indeed she had accepted Gloria into her house in good faith. The School of Hard Knocks, a lower-middle-class expression (which my mother used often, also without irony) exemplifies how we re-created the reader's relationship with the text. The expression is everyday vulgate, suggestive of the "class struggle" underlying Delia's letter and Gloria's avid ambitions for Glory, which she begins to achieve by changing her name to Cuba Venegas. The School of Hard Knocks is very locally American but paradoxically brings to life the spoken immediacy of the original text; it abusively supplants the original but sustains its effect.

2) *Beba Longoria's* telephone conversation: *"Livia? Beba, Beba Longoria. La misma. Como andas miamiga?"* (43) "That you, Livia? It's me, Beba. Beba who? Beba *Longoria* that's who." (34) Beba reports to

2. See *TTT,* 16–23, and *Heartbreak Tango,* 90–102.

her friend Livia her triumph as the girlfriend of a colonel in Batista's army. Here we lose the comic Caribbean slurring of words together *(mi amiga = miamiga)*, comic because the written evokes the spoken, which can only be replaced less effectively by other speech idiosyncrasies, as in the repetition of the same word(s) for emphasis: "who?. . . that's who."

3 *Magalena Cruz*'s foulmouthed argument with her grandmother, as she leaves home definitively to become another kept woman of another corrupt politician: *"La dejé habla así na ma que pa dale coldel y cuando se cansó de metel su descalga yo le dije no que va vieja, tu etás muy equivocada."* (34) "I let her go on and on and on just so she could get to an end and when she got tired of shooting off her big mouth and kinda breathless, I told her but dahling you got it all wrong." (24) To suggest this even more slurred speech, we thought of repeating kindred sounds, as in "on and on. . . an end."

By reading out loud together, by throwing words and phrases around in person but also in correspondence, we sought solutions that *sounded* the best, as with the title of the alternate *"Ella cantaba boleros"* ("She Sang Boleros," literally) episodes. Here Códac recounts the story of the obese black singer La Estrella in a Babelic nightlife babble that incorporates multiple voices, from Alexis Bayer's lisping gay cant to La Estrella's slurring drawls. "Bolero" in the Cuban canon, not Ravel's apocryphal Spain, is a slow crooner's ballad of which there is no exact equivalent in English. The ballads of the Forties and Fifties sung by Frank Sinatra perhaps approach the nostalgic, even poetic mood of these songs and of Códac's narration with musical accompaniment, but do not match the exaggerated sentiment of the boleros.

La Estrella is a fictional avatar of a black singer famous in Havana named Fredy, whose death in 1961 – a voice vanished vorever – motivated Cabrera Infante to begin writing the book that would become *TTT*. The music of Cuba, once embodied, was not entombed. On the melancholy Belgian night he heard about her death he began writing the first segment of the *"Ella cantaba boleros" suite*. As he recalls in the interview with Torres Fierro:

> Suddenly it all came together: Fredy's death, the rebirth of the song [Agustín Lara's "Noche de Ronda"] which she signified and the word bolero (this is important: that word, so Spanish and yet so Havanan), when I

thought of rendering an homage to Fredy, but at the same time attempting to do *P.M.* through other means: in that moment I saw clearly – an inspiration without a doubt – how the words and the music and the vision which appeared in the little movie about habaneros having fun – and thus "She Sang Boleros" was born. (89)

Fredy's death coincided with Castro's censorship of *P.M.*, a documentary film about Havanan nightlife. Translating haunting voices into writing, a frozen simulacrum of the fluid originary voice, into a book – space trying to capture time, the space that music plays in – Cabrera Infante tried to imagine what "the flame looked like." This visual metaphor for aural memory from Lewis Carroll's *Alice in Wonderland*, "And she tried to fancy what the flame of a candle looks like after the candle is blown out," remained as the only original epigraph to appear in the English version, despite Cabrera Infante's love for multiple epigraphs.

The single most important fact about *TTT* is that he wrote it in exile, remembering Havana in the basement of the Cuban embassy in Belgium, where he had been banished gracefully as cultural attaché. Cabrera Infante explains to Torres Fierro the initial writing of the book was an "ecological mania to preserve the night fauna so well portrayed in *P.M.* and destined to disappear" and then "a nostalgic attack over the habitat of that fauna, the *genius loci* of the book – Havana, and concretely Havana at night, because the book collects many nights which want to become a single long night." (90–91)

The book was also published in exile, in Spain. But the book's exile from a strictly Cuban common ground precedes its author's. Its models ignore national boundaries: Raymond Queneau's crazy Parisian *roman comique, Zazie dans le Métro,* fuses with Joyce's Dublinesque *Ulysses.* The first title of the book that Cabrera Infante later qualified as "horrendous," *The Night Is an Endless Hole,* inspired in Fredy's story, darkly invokes Céline. But *TTT,* a long day's journey into the orgiastic fleshpots and verbal fireworks of Havana nightlife, sings more to the tune of the joyous Joyce or comical Queneau, saluted in *TTT* as Arsenio Cuéneau!

Music already translates what cannot be said in words, but even the word *bolero* loses its common Cuban meaning in translation, a word, as Cabrera Infante says above, "so Spanish and so Havanan." Guillermo and Gardner had come up with "The Dark Lady of Song," a clever parody of Shakespeare since here the lady was literally dark, Cha-Cha-Chakespeare being a fundamental thread in the web of English literary references in *TTT*, and an allusion appropriate to the poetic theme of the late-lamented Lady. *"Ella cantaba boleros" is* lyrical but *not* in the manner of a sixteenth-century sonnet. This title *sounds* like a nostalgic line from a popular song of the Fifties or early Sixties. I suggested "I Heard Her Sing" because the story is told in first person by the photographer Códac (appropriately named), remembering the magic moment when he first heard her sing, *and* because it sounds like a phrase from a song *in the same way* the original title does. The Beatles' "I Saw Her Standing There" came to my Sixties American mind, in magical conjunction with Cabrera Infante's transplantation to swinging London, reverberating from the musical revolution that exploded in Liverpool.

The following transformation of a tune, taken from the "Beginners" section, in which the writer Silvestre describes his boyhood trips to the movies with his brother to see American Westerns, portrays the spirit of the changes that occurred between the first and the final draft of *TTT*. Silvestre quotes "The Santa Fe Trail":

(*TTT*, 38):   *Voy cogiendo el camino*
                 de Santa Fe
                 Voy cogiendo
                 corriendo
                 el camino de Santa Fe

(First draft):

                 I'm taking
                 I'm running
                 on the trail to Santa Fe

                 I'm taking I'm taking I'm taking I'm
                 taking the trail to Santa Fe

(*TTT*, 29):   I'm on my way
                 Yes on my way
                 on the trail to Santa Fe

I'm on my on my on my way
on the trail to Santa Fe.

Like Silvestre and his brother, translator and author also hit the Santa
Fe trail, seeking a silver mine of lyrical clichés, the rhymes and
rhythms of American English.

"The Ides of March":
Post-TTT Exercises

Literature is all that is read as such...
G. CABRERA INFANTE, *Exorcismos de esti(l)o*

TTT WAS WRITTEN to be read aloud, and the American English translation followed suit, but doesn't the written page in translation inevitably make the textual texture of the spoken more *pronounced?* To remake a text that amuses or moves the reader by the sheer fact of being written in a very local, hence very "real" version of spoken language is surely a task worthy of Pierre Menard. After *TTT* I briefly experienced (to avoid "experiment," that scientific word Cabrera Infante detests) with Menardian fervor Cabrera Infante's *Exorcismos de esti(l)o* (1976), a collection of comic miscellany in evident homage to Queneau's *Exercices de style.* These set pieces really are exorcisms, excessive games with language and literary forms high and low, Cabrera Infante blowing off steam accumulated in *TTT,* especially in "Brainteasers," by continuing to abuse texts and to amuse himself. He explains in an interview in the *Paris Review:*

> *Exorcismos de esti(l)o...* means many things: the exorcising of style, exercises in summertime, even the lure of the pen – all in a send-up of *Exercices de style.* This is one of my favorites among my own books, and it closes the cycle begun in my collected movie reviews, *Un oficio del siglo XX* (1962). In *Exorcismos,* I expanded my experience (not experiment, a word I loathe when I see it applied to art instead of science) with Havanese, the idiom of *habaneros,* who might perhaps be called hablaneros or total talkers. (166)

I chose to do for *Review* (Fall 1974) an "exorcism" titled " 'Los Idus *de Marzo', según Plutarco . . . y según Shakespeare, y según Mankiewicz, y según el limpiabotas Chicho Charol."* (16) In this monologue, a shoeshine boy narrates to a silent client his innocent or at least biased version of the plot of Joseph L. Mankiewicz's movie version of Shakespeare's tragedy *Julius Caesar.* " 'The Ides of March,' According to Plutarch . . . According to Shakespeare, According to Mankiewicz, According to the Shoeshine Boy, Ol' Leatherlip," a delirious piece in vulgate, exposes a very literary subject: how culture is handed down through the metamorphoses of interpretation, that is, translation. Writers (Shakespeare) interpret history and/or writers (Plutarch); one genre translates another (in this case, theater reconstructs history and film pirates theater); and readers or spectators of another age, language, and class interpret history-as-popular-legend converted into high art to return inevitably to the *vox populi.*

The translation of this piece confirms once again that literary parodies of the spoken become, need to become, more *written,* more literary when transposed into another language. Unlike the original parody, the translation mimics a written text.

"Los Idus . . . " already challenges the reader, becomes a veritable obstacle course in interpreting, indeed in translating spoken Cuban. Chicho's speech is "recorded" phonetically and forces the reader to translate it into a more communicative code. *C* becomes *s (socio = sosio), s* disappears, making two words into one *(quete = que este),* and *r* becomes *l,* as in Hollywood's popular and racist representations of Chinese pronunciation. The problem of reading Chicho is multiplied by all sorts of wordplays and alliterations. These can be read as Chicho's "natural" invention, but we know the author is using Chicho as a mouthpiece for his own double entendres: The noble Brutus becomes *Bruto* in Spanish, which also means stupid.

"The Ides of March" is a grotesquerie, low humor straight from the gutter, the satirical representation of a racial cliché. This text descends from a popular tradition that harks back to the *Menippea* and certainly to the Renaissance farce and Spanish Golden Age *entremeses,* in which social satire often plays upon the innocence or ignorance of the underdog. The black man as the butt of humor is a theme of low farce in both Cuban and Anglo-American vaudeville, particularly his misperceptions of the rules of the game in white society and his mispronunciations.[1]

"Boy" in English figuratively, demeaningly denotes a black man of unspecified age who can be unmistakably identified in the Spanish by the Cuban reader. His language, his unabashed illiteracy, his low station in society, and even his name (*Chicho* suggests "burnt," thus by metonymy darkened; *Charol* means "patent leather") belie his racial and, in this milieu, social identity. Ol' Leatherlip attempts to duplicate the parodic effect of the original name by identifying the character with his trade, but also multiplies or makes more explicit the parodic thrust of the text by the addition of "lip": The text we read is indeed a product of Chicho's "lip service."

Chicho is linguistically, even psychologically plausible in Cabrera Infante's rendition. The humor here derives from the contrast between Chicho's low or comically incorrect language and the complex literary plot he tries to unravel, as well as the written play with spoken language that turns the piece into a graphic puzzle that the reader must unravel.

The translation attempts to reproduce both the tension between low language and high art and written and spoken, but the problem that remains is how to maintain Chicho's plausibility. For the sake of humor — the piece's *raison d'être* — verisimilitude is inevitably undermined when the text loses its raw material and passes into English. The humor derived from writing words the way they are slurred in Spanish, again, cannot be repeated to the same effect in English. "This guy" approximates the tone but is not as comically confusing as *quete (que este)*. The spoken can only be rendered into yet another version of the spoken, but also the original already demands, implicitly speaks of translating into "proper" writing when it is read in Spanish. Here's the first sentence of this ludic interlude in spoken "Cuban":

bueno sosio la cosa e quete tipo Sesal no quie sel rey pero si quiere o no quie pero si quiere la corona que no e pa tanto poque no ejuna corona deoro ni de plata ni con joya ni na ni na sino quee de yelba asi como de gajo emata y no se polque tanta boba — que sí se la pone que si se la quita quetan neneso como un siglo. (p. 35)

---

1. See chapter VI, "You Always Can Tell," of *Infante's Inferno,* prefaced by a reference to the figures of "Blackie and the Spaniard — traditional comic characters, from as far back as the gay nineties." (193)

For the non-Cuban readers' sake, here is the above *translated* to proper phonetics, if not grammar:

> *bueno socio la cosa es que este tipo Cesar no quiere ser rey pero si quiere o no quiere pero si quiere la corona que no es para tanto porque no es una corona de oro ni de plata ni con joyas ni nada ni nada sino que es de yerba así como de gajo de mata yo no se porque tanta bobada – que si la pone que se la quita que están en eso como un siglo.*

Now, in Slanglish:

> Well man the thing is that this guy Ceezer dont wanna be king but he really duz or duznt but he really wants the crown which dont mount to much cos it aint made of gold or silver or tin or nuttin but sum weeds or branches and I dont know what's the big deal about him puttin it on or takin it off which they fuss about for ages.

Cabrera Infante's comment on this translation (May 25, 1974):

> I really like it, especially since I know how damned difficult it was, so much so that I wonder how you could understand the whole thing, since I myself got confused at certain points of this exercise. I think you've transposed it very well into American.

In the original, the authenticity of the transcription of spoken Cuban is what brings home vividly the distortions but also hidden truths of interpretation, that is, translation.[2] I write "hidden truths" because behind Chicho's innocence and misunderstandings (of, for example, the symbolic importance of the crown, which he perceives literally as being a thing made of "weeds or branches") there is implicit criticism. The movie is a melodrama, and its referent, the high-minded, "high art" drama (and in turn its point of departure, ancient history) seem on the surface irrelevant to Chicho's daily existence, except in and/or through Chicho's interpretation.

Chicho can certainly identify hypocrisy, deceit, and betrayal in the followers surrounding Caesar, except that Chicho uses a word that translates as "asslickers" rather than the word "hypocrites." And he finds a political issue that strikes home: When the populace crowds around Caesar begging for favors, Chicho interprets their pleas for

---

2. "Natural" inconsistencies in the "transcription" include *porque,* pronounced once without the *r, poque,* and the next time, with the *r* slurred into *l, polque* – two possible pronunciations in lower-class Cuban.

"amnisty" for some relative. Maybe Chicho can understand this detail because, like the Everymen of Rome, he lives under the double shadow of a dictator's tyranny: Chicho speaks as a citizen of Batista's Cuba, but Cabrera Infante writes the text in the Seventies of Fidel Castro. Chicho doesn't consciously admit historical parallels, but they are implied in his unconsciously devious though direct discourse, as transcribed by his invisible scribe.

The translation can't possibly reproduce Cuban Black speech but vaguely simulates spoken Black American, the closest equivalent. What makes this speech humorous to the reader in Spanish, however, is that it already is written. Chicho's speech becomes literature, that is, Cabrera Infante subtly undermines Chicho's mentality by making jokes that *could* sprout from Chicho's streetwise know-how but which *are* the author's. Something needed to be added in the English, beyond the simulated Black American: What made Chicho's speech humorous is the way Cesar becomes Sesal, so I made Caesar into Ceezer, writing it as it could be heard. Again, I could invent graphic distortions in English precisely because, unlike Spanish, it often doesn't (duznt) sound as it is written, but failure always lurks: An invented distortion is certainly not as funny as a "natural" one.

I had to go further, and, following the author's lead as in the Brutus/ Bruto play, play with words. When Chicho says Caesar's smart but perhaps too smart for his own good, repeating the word *vivo* (wise guy), which takes on an ironic twist since this *vivo* (live wire) ends up *muerto* (dead), I say "and Ceezer who's no geezer" with tongue in cheek since he will never reach old age. And I responded to Brutus and Bruto with "his pal Brutish comes along who aint so brutish." "The crown which dont mount to much" plays with the spoken, which slurringly leaves out syllables, and with a sexual suggestion, "mount": Chicho compares Caesar later on to a cuckolded husband who's the last to know – in this case, that he's in danger of being assassinated – so that a sexual innuendo fits well in Chicho's vulgarized version. These additional jokes compensate somehow for the loss of the local, and correspond to the text's underlying "thrusts."

The translation recognizes its status as translation by "spickin" instead of "speaking," self-consciously saluting the language of the original and participating in the two-tongued play between English and Spanish already in Cabrera Infante's original. Translation means substitution here, as in *TTT:* In both cases, the reader is led to respond to a humor based on language's distortions and language distorted.

Here is the rest of the translation. Some added or changed puns and alliteration are in italics:

> The thing is that this guy Cashius who's givin Ceezer the *hairy* eyeball wants the little ol' crown too altho it's only made of newspaper and he's eyein it from above on a balcon ey with one colum after anotha and he smiles kind of off the side of his mouth and that's when this other guy his pal Brutish comes along who aint so brutish but who's damn brutish at the end cos Ceezer is like he was his father in a manner of *spickin* and who really loves him and is goin to hand him down the kingdom someday with the crown and the branch and the whole *shebang.* But this here Brutish what he duz is start whispering in corners with Cashius and conspiring and all that and Ceezer who's no *geezer* makes like he dont know what's happening but he must know unless kings are like husbands who are always the last to know. Well, the thing is that Brutish knows it and Ceezer's friends suspect it and Ceezer's wife dreams it and the Sen'dors know it and everybody and his *aunt* knows it except Ceezer who keeps making speeches and walkin up and *down aroun Rome* wrapped in a white sheet the whole damn day until morning. Then comes this guy with a beard and a roll *of toilet paper* in his hand who the friend of some fortuneteller who already tol Ceezer what was goin to happin to him on the *Idas or Ideas of* March which seems to be a bad month, for crazy people and *hares and so on,* and Ceezer who jus dont want to unnerstand and when the bad guys come over to im it aint that way cos before he saw a fat man happily bouncing down the stairs and Ceezer has this thing with fat guys that he sez you shunt mistrust em but the skinny guys you should, poor Ceezer who dont know that fat dogs bite harder than skinny dogs cos theyre fat and grab you wid their strong jores and the party's over. But this Ceezer guy goes ahead as if nuttin happened and on and on til he gets to the Senit which is a cave of Ali babas and the fifty theeves and is chock full o' asslickers who are lying on the floor and crawlin over and kneelin before Ceezer askin to get on the *gravy train* and to get amnisty for some relative and with all that bunch of beggars Ceezer dont see the reel bad guys comin and with what intensions besides the knives which arent *sceesors* but *bonafido* knives theyre hidin under their sheets. Well the thing is they cover him with knife *wombs* cos in dose days they didn't have guns or revolvers and they sew his sheet with knives but before this guy

Ceezer who's as tough as *snails and tougher than the marbles, even the loose ones, in that statchue of his right next to im* turns halfway aroun like this and sort of from his profile he seez his son who aint his son but is Brutish come over but he sez his son and then Ceezer *spicks* to him in *sumfin* that sounds like Italian and his son who aint his son dont seem to know Italian cos he dont breathe a word but clams up and keeps a tight upper and lower lip and makes a tremendous slash in the bread basket and finishes him off and Ceezer dies like this wrapped up in his sheet which can also be used as a funeral shroud. And then comes Marlo Brando who dont have to be no *Marlowe* to finger out who killed Ceezer, and that they'll kill him too if he dont watch out and he picks up Ceezer who's lookin more and more like a salad and carries him out to the stairs and makes a tremendous fuss saying that he didn't come to berry Ceezer but to put him up *dere and down below* lissening to the speech there's a load of people who now that Ceezer died there's a bigger crowd than before and a tremendous meeting and sayin that thing about not comin to *berry confucion* and a mess cos it seems there's a war but there isn't a war and you dont see one fight and afterwoods, what happins afterwoods? Well, Brutish does and Brando comes to say he was brutish but also nobull and Cashius who's no clay pigeon like Brutish and even more brutish *besides being British* cos he kills himself when nobody not even enemies are around on his birfday cos it seems that's the way ancient peoples killed themselves to die on the same day they was born and that's the story, Joe. Hey, you want plain or black?

War and confusion are the outcome of Brando's speech, confusion reigning over the literal-minded spectator Chicho, who never sees war acted out in this movie pretending to be a play (or vice versa): hence, berry confucion. Brutish led to British in reaction to Chicho's reaction to this travesty of high-style British acting. *Alice in Wonderland*'s March hare enters on cue as our Marlowe Chicho gropes to interpret the words of the Shakespearean soothsayer who whispers or probably shouts into "Sesal's" ear about March being a bad month for *gente ida* (crazy people), *ida,* the past participle of the verb *ir,* literally, "gone." Associative thinking drives the groping interpreters Chicho and his translator from the mysterious Ides to the more accessible *ida* and *Ida* (the feminine name) and to *Ideas,* to berry the reader in confucion.

Yes, I'll admit I've taken liberties for humor's sake, making Ol' Leatherlip a mite more sophisticated and self-conscious than the relatively raw Chicho, but the seed of these liberties lies in the original itself. Cabrera Infante uses Chicho's speech as a vehicle of parody, imposing his subtle and critical differences upon "another's" discourse, a discourse (re)created by him out of the piquant potpourri of spoken Cuban.

The Way They Talk: The (Hyper)realism of Manuel Puig

How to find, as in *TTT,* a colloquial speech and slang that would bring to life *La traición de Rita Hayworth* and *Boquitas pintadas?* The geographic setting, a dreary small town in the endless pampas of Argentina, could remind the American English reader of Kansas. And yet the Spanish, Italian, even Russian-Jewish immigrants who inhabit this bleak new world have more in common with the melting-pot New York than with a comparatively more homogeneous Midwest town. Current slang in the early 1970s was out of the question since both Puig novels take us back to the Thirties and Forties.

I relied on my familiarity with old movies, the memories of older friends and relatives, and even *The Dictionary of American Slang,* which dates the origin and usage of terms. I attempted to infuse Puig's dialogues with homespun phrasing like "Mom, don't think I get that much advantage out of the house either" (8) to give the flavor of a social milieu recognizable to the reader without erasing completely the unique identity of the novel's language and culture. A balancing act, always.

From Toto's monologues in *Rita Hayworth,* culminating in his "rewriting" of "The Movie I Liked Best," to the borrowed language of everyday life, as in traveling saleswoman Choli's telephone conversation with Mita, the musicals and melodramas of Hollywood, as well as remembered voices from the past, are the sources of Puig's narrative world. Choli speaks of "interesting women" who are "hiding a past," leading exciting and adventurous lives, in an effort to represent or fantasize her own life as if she were an avatar of Joan Crawford, or of her idol Mecha Ortiz, an Argentine version of Crawford or Norma Shearer.

The dialogued chapters (1,2,4) in *Rita Hayworth* presented what initially seemed like insurmountable difficulties. In chapter 1 ("Mita's Parents' Place, La Plata, 1933") and chapter 2 ("At Berto's, Vallejos, 1933") conversations are transcribed without any descriptive or narrative context, and the names of the speakers are omitted. The reader gradually figures out who's who by the casual hints dropped by the speakers, speaking *from within* their world and *not to* the author or reader, who both play the role of eavesdropper. And we "hear" – in chapter 4 – only Choli's side of the conversation, from which we are forced to induce Mita's possible responses.

Puig provided me with the missing identities of characters and parts of dialogue without which I couldn't have understood completely the implications of remarks that were confusing precisely because they were so real. In "natural" conversation people convey meaning more through their facial expressions and intonations than through the actual words, and Puig's characters at Mita's parents' house and at Berto's play the roles of either uneducated people or Italian immigrants whose brand of Spanish is often awkward if not ungrammatical. The translation had to both communicate and obscure meaning by imitating conversational language in its "purest" form, had to border on the ungrammatical (for example, by comma splicing) and yet use a speech that was "natural," idiomatic.

Here is the first shockingly trivial sentence of *Rita Hayworth,* first in the original, then in the translation's first draft, and finally the final draft. Reading the phrases aloud (as with *TTT*), in some instances into a tape recorder, helped me find the most natural phrasing and intonation:

Original: "– *El punto cruz hecho con hilo marrón sobre la tela de lino color crudo, por eso te quedó tan lindo el mantel.*" (7)

First draft: "Brown thread cross-stitched over beige linen, that's why your tablecloth turned out so beautifully."

Final draft: "A brown cross-stitch over beige linen, that's why your table-cloth turned out so well." (5)

The first clause of my first version sounds too technical to be uttered in casual conversation between housewives; these women, after all, would take for granted that you do a cross-stitch with thread. Also, "well" sounds more common and colorless than "beautifully," and the point here was to reproduce banal language, amusing and striking in a literary context precisely because of its colorlessness.

Further down the page Mita's mother and sister Clara comment that they see her so seldom, now that she's married and has moved with her husband Berto to Vallejos, a town in the interior. The mother complains:

Original: "*Los días se pasan volando, el primer día parece que no, parece que rinde muchísimo, pero después los días se pasan sin darse cuenta.*" (8)

First draft: "The days fly by then, the first day it doesn't seem so, it seems like you're getting something done, but then they're gone before you know it."

Final draft: "Vacation days fly, the first day she's here doesn't seem so short, it seems like you're getting a lot done, but then the time is gone before you know it." (6)

The first draft is literally closer to the Spanish in the use of the impersonal "it" and nonspecific "days." But the statement in Spanish, supported by Clara's previous remark, "She ought to come twice a year to La Plata instead of only once," emphatically *implies* that Mita's mother is talking specifically about vacation time, regretting that it seems so brief because it's the only time she gets to see her daughter. The vague indirection in the original shows that she's being evasive, even euphemistic, which is common in everyday speech.

Boquitas pintadas continued to challenge me with what Puig called his "kitchen sink prose." The first episode of part I presents the condolence letter – and subsequent correspondence – written by Nené to the mother of Juan Carlos upon his death. Nené, a frustrated housewife in a repressive society, had denied herself the satisfaction of having an affair with the man she desired. Her language is fraught with euphemistic clichés whose exaggerated images produce both a comic and pathetic effect.

Nené asks, in one of her first letters to Doña Leonor, how the widow and now mother in mourning is faring, and then remarks *"Yo sigo todavía muy caída"* (13), literally, "I continue to be very fallen" – that is, down in the dumps. Puig encouraged me to make Nené's clichés sound as corny as possible.[1] By metonymic association *caída* (fallen) suggested in English "down"; "fallen" would have been incorrect and misleading, however, since one might think she was claiming to be a "fallen woman." I wanted to find an even more dated and absurdly concrete expression than "down in the dumps" that would strike the reader as silly and definitively old-fashioned, hence *Roget's Thesaurus* rewarded me with "I'm still so *down in the mouth*" (12), a very appropriate image for Nené, who indiscreetly spouts out of her mouth, via the pen, all her discontent with her marriage.

Nené's indiscreet correspondence continues into episode II. Nené has still not received an answer from Doña Leonor, which frustrates her even further. This silence becomes one more painful aspect of her life she has to deal with, or can't control:

Original: "*Si me pasa algo malo no sé como voy a aguantar. ¿Por qué es que no me escribe?*"

And further down, her husband has obviously noticed her bad humor:

(mi marido) . . . "*Dice que ando con cara agria.*"

English: "If something else goes wrong with me I don't know how I'll have the strength for it. Why is it you don't write to me?". . . .
    "He says I have a sour puss all the time." (21)

Literal: "If something bad happens to me I don't know how I'm going to stand it. Why is it you don't you write to me?. . .

"He says I have a sour face."

There is a kind of crescendo in this first paragraph of episode II that tries to hide yet reveals anxiety, culminating in the almost childish plea (to deaf ears): "Why is it you don't write to me?" Where "I don't know how I'm going to stand it" sounds like transliteralese, "I don't know how I'll have the strength for it" resonates with memories of my own

---

1. The "corn" uttered by Puig's characters translated more effectively into English than in French; see further discussion in part III.

mother's tone and use of the word "strength" in connection with the emotional trials of family life sapping her "strength." *Andar* in the last phrase *"dice que ando con cara agria,"* literally means "walking" or "walking around" but really connotes a continuous action, or mood, hence the emphatic "all the time." Immersing myself in the homey language that the mimetic genius of Manuel Puig reproduced so vividly, I found myself "sounding" the depths of my childhood, among adults, for kindred feelings of frustration and desire – and for the words that both hid and expressed those feelings – in an attempt to bridge, once more, the foreign and the familiar.

Part III:

The Source of the Source

Even when the translator seems attracted only by the novel and strange, by the foreign and the exotic, by the innovations of experimentations of an alien avant-garde of which he wants to become the honorary representative, the translator is always a humanist, a worshipper of tradition, a believer in the eternal values of arts and letters.

RENATO POGGIOLI

Itself a Translation: TTT

MEMORY, a treasonous translator, is the motivating *motif* in both *TTT* and *La habana,* as Arsenio Cué sarcastically intones in *"Bachata":* "The Remembrance of Things Past Translation." In the imaginary interview of himself in *Liminar,* Cabrera Infante wrote (I translate):

> — But this latest book is like a memoir.
> — Like a memory, like a memory. That great translator [in the feminine] who is memory has translated my memories. But there never was a falser book. You already know that *to traduce* in English means not to translate but to betray. My memory betrays me. Memoirs are the most deceitful books around. Autobiographies are acts of bad faith. (p. 8)

One of many explicit examples in *TTT* of memory's "bad faith" is the presumed transcription of the dreams a female character narrates to a psychiatrist; we are led to suspect she is Laura Díaz, the love object of both Silvestre and Arsenio. Laura is one of several female translators *and* traitors in the male's eye (I) view in Cabrera Infante's narrative world. We (and probably she) never know if she's lying or telling the "truth"; Laura's transcribed dreams recall Freud's theory of dreaming and of dream reporting and analysis as translation processes. Memory and language are fellow traitors, translating what they intend to capture.

TTT is constructed not only upon the memory of voices but also of written texts, we must remember. When Cabrera Infante reduces *TTT* to the status of a "failed translation" of *The Satyricon,* the first

erotic book he got his hands on as the narrator of *Infante's Inferno* con-
fesses, he is presenting only the tip of the iceberg. *The Satyricon* is already a palimpsest, a parchment we have inherited in fragments in
whose "substratum" we can glimpse other texts, such as Lucan's *Pharsalia,* an epic parody that Ezra Pound "rehandled" in his *Cantos,* notably in his *Homage to Sextus Propertius.* Sullivan, the translator of *The
Satyricon,* speaks of going to the source of the source by studying Lucan and other models that inspired Petronius. But what particularly
served as a model was Pound's re-creation of the *Pharsalia.*

Sullivan needed to travel back to the source of the source, and to the
modern parody of that primal source, which brings to life its effect to
the modern reader, in order for his translation to repeat the original's
use and abuse of source material, that is, to (re)produce the original's
effect on its reader.[1]

Translation becomes an explicit poetics in *TTT,* synonymous for
memory and for the act of writing, which transcribes memories. One
has only to think of the emcee's bilingual speech at the opening of
TTT, "Showtime! Señoras y señores. Ladies and gentlemen... ,"
where the novel's first character is a simultaneous interpreter. Then
there is the polyglot Bustrófedon, who endlessly transmutes names
and refrains, and parodies Cuban writers, "translating" their styles as
he imagines what and how they might have written about the assassination of Trotsky. In "The Death of Trotsky as described by various
Cuban writers, several years after the event – or before," a Pierre
Menardian chapter on history as (mis)interpretation, parody serves
the cathartic function of exorcising – and exercising – influence as well
as critical mockery.

The most explicit presence of translation is doubtlessly the section
titled *"Los visitantes"* ("Vae Visitors"), in which the invisible author
parodies translators and translations by presenting versions of an anecdote about two North American tourists in Havana. Silvestre's "cor-

1. When Matthew Arnold observed that the best translation of Homer was perhaps the King
James version of the Bible, he meant that this text best reflected the effect of Homer. The *relationship* of Homer's reader to the *Iliad,* in which the book's effect was "odd and antique" but
also "familiar" – both "plain" and "difficult" – found its parallel in the English reader's reception of the Bible. See Gilbert Highet, *The Classical Tradition* (New York & London: Oxford University Press, 1949), 484.

rect" translation, followed by Rine Leal's awkward translation – both commissioned by an editor named "GCI" – reproduce a story written by a Mr. Campbell, about a supposedly stolen walking stick. There are four versions since the tale is twice-told: the conflicting versions of Mr. and Mrs. (who really isn't Mrs.) Campbell, and their corresponding "translations."

TTT closes with remarks on translation's treason: On the next to last page Silvestre, as he is falling asleep, has the last "word-fish" on *traditori*. He remembers or is already dreaming about Lino Novás Calvo's mistaking sea lions for lions in his translation of Hemingway's *The Old Man and the Sea*, the translated dream translating this error into another, turning on false cognates: *morsas* – sea lions – and "sea morsels." That the error, conspicuous in the last line of the novella, was made by one of the consecrated Cuban writers parodied in "The Death of Trotsky" makes it all the more grave – or not, since Hemingway chose Novás Calvo as his translator, and gave the translation his official approval. But then again, as Cabrera Infante has noted, Hemingway's knowledge of Spanish was far from perfect.

The "second" language in pre-Castro Cuba

Translation in *TTT* (in the emcee bilingual speech, in the trumped-up Campbell story) speaks to the United States' exploitative relationship with Cuba. English, for Latin America, particularly American English for Central America and the Caribbean under the shadow of the Northern Hemisphere, represents both the detested language of an imperial presence and the desired language of economic and cultural power. It is, as both Cabrera Infante and Puig have shown, the language of desire through the glamorized mediation of American cinema. English is a source to which we translators of *TTT* had to return, but the sociolinguistic value of the book's bilingualism is distorted unavoidably in the English version. English words and expressions in the Spanish reflect the pervasive presence of North American culture (via tourism and the movies) in Cuba; the Spanish that appears in the English text, to maintain the bilingual character of the book, may strike most English readers as mere "south of the border" local color.

Three Trapped Tigers performs a triple translation act precisely because of the author's and the original's duplicitous relationship to English, to a web of English-language texts (including movies), translated into the Cuban idiom. Returning to English, one of the sources of the source, signifies betraying the original's critique of the language of the exploiter, but also, finally, exploiting or cannibalizing the exploiter. As Cabrera Infante says to Torres Fierro, English is the language of his favorite literature, high and low:

> [In London] I go to the movies, as always, I see a lot of television and I read English literature which for a long time has seemed to me the best in the world, from Chaucer to Burgess: a long extension of literary creation. (103)

He was ready and willing to substitute, to eradicate untranslatable Cuban folkloric references, as when he turned the "Coffee Cantata" (a Cuban salute to Bach) into "Auld Lang Syne," replacing an auditory game with words with a visual gag. The *"Cantata del Café"* goes like this: *"Yo te daré, te daré niña hermosa, te daré una cosa, una cosa que yo solo sé, café!"* (Literal translation: "I'll give you something, pretty girl, something only I know: coffee!"). This nonsense song in the hands of adults takes on a double entendre with a single sexual sense, coffee euphemizing sex but also meaning itself, a common enough referent in Cuba, a coffee-drinking country. The *infantile* game, a tongue-twisting musical exercise composed by "Bustroffenbach" (one of the many pseudonyms for the pseudonym Bustrófedon), involves repeating these limericks five times, each time substituting all the vowels with one vowel of the alphabet. Thus Bustrófedon parodies popular oral traditions, turning them inexorably into literature: *"Yo to doró/ye te deré/yi ti dirí/etc."* (212–213) The song is obviously untranslatable, since the reader would have to recognize the original in order to recognize the parody; more important, the play of sounds is lost in any literal translation.

A recognizable original for the Anglo-American reader was chosen – the "New Year's Hymn": "Lest old acquaintance be forgot," became "Last aald acquantanca ba fargat/Lest eeld acqueentence be ferget . . . ," etc. Obviously it works only visually: Writing again takes precedence over speech through translation's metamorphic process here. But Cabrera Infante insisted upon making this "sacrifice" in or-

der to preserve an intention: to parody, to resuscitate popular traditions, turning folklore into literature, and at the same time returning to
a source language, English.

Parody

Cabrera Infante was adamant, however, about *faithfully* translating his
sometimes faithless, and even ruthless, literary parodies. "The Death
of Trotsky" is, within the fiction of *TTT,* the tape-recorded transcription left by Bustrófedon to the "tigers" of his (or rather his creator's)
caricatures of the stylistic idiosyncrasies of Cuban writers. But if parody requires a collective remembering in which texts or a body of texts
are brought to mind by what the reader is reading, how, I thought as
cotranslator, would the American/English reader recognize the models of these parodies? If parody functions only *if read* as parody, the
non-Hispanic, nay, the non-Cuban reader would be utterly lost.

He responded to my suggestion that he either suppress the parodies
or replace those parodied with American writers like Poe, James,
Faulkner, and Hemingway who had served as exorcisable influences
upon Hispanic writers, in the following letter (London, May 15,
1970):

> Re: The Parodies. Carlos Fff [Fuentes] has been given [*sic*] me the works to
> change it as you suggest. He even suggested they might be written by him,
> John Callman [*sic*] and, lost but not less, Cort-azar! (I could suggest your
> name, first but not foist, off kurst.) But I think you are all wrong and that
> what the book is is what the parodies are: cona and underdevelopmentary
> my dear What's'on. Nobody ever worried about not getting who the hell
> was Joyce parroting at Nausicaam in You Lissez. The shame goes for Max
> Boredom and all of them. If the par O Dies are bad in Spanish its [*sic*] all my
> fault. If they are no good in English its our collective fault. What I mean is
> that you dont need (and by you I mean you English-speaking you) one
> more parodist after all the people ohfool Do I-t Mack Donald was able to
> make a book with – fifty something authors and parodists. Who needs an-
> other parody of Hemingway after E. B. White or Wolcott Gibbs? Who
> needs another Super-faulkner after the Peter De Vries piece? Et Cacaetera.
> Mailer could be an interesting subject were he not subconsciously parody-
> ing Hemingway et all. As to Donald Barthelme it would be against the
> grain of the book which was written, after all, many years before I discov-

ered him – this was when Snow White was published in England in 1968. In other words, no and two thousand times no!

We can now read this missal as an eloquent manifesto even though some of the arguments boomerang. John Updike panned our punful *TTT,* labeling the book "derivative" in contrast with *One Hundred Years of Solitude,* an "original" Latin American book: "one might. . . conclude that the novel was derivative, that its excitement derived from the translation of the methods of *Ulysses* into Cuban idiom, and that, restored to Joyce's mother tongue, it shows up as a tired copy." (91) Updike's complaint (who needs another Joyce?) masks an ideological prejudice. How dare this Cuban author appropriate words, language, and avant-garde narrative structures, when he should be chronicling oppression and revolution? Updike seems to forget that "magical realism" was a term invented by a German art critic, Franz Roh, to describe expressionist European art of the Twenties, and that the magical realist style evolved out of European surrealism. Says Updike, "we blearily realize that, whatever happened in Havana in 1958, this book isn't going to tell us." (92)

"Derivative" is what all literature is: All our rhetoric – call it innovative or traditional – derives from the vast repertory of Greece and Rome. Updike's review exhibits not only blindness to the book's intentions but a canonical caveat handed down to those marginals who "cross over."

Cabrera Infante's argument – paradoxically identical to Updike's – speaks, nevertheless, on behalf of the liberties a marginal work should be allowed to take. As subversive collaborator I still sought a compromise, as the following epistle (May 20) shows:

> The Parroties (Part II): The bump on top of my head has become a flashing lightbulb or How to Lose Friends and Influence People: Why not compromise by making parodies of Famous Latin American writers, i.e. Borges, Cortázar, Fuentes, Vargas Llosa, García Márquez – Fans here would get a kick, You would give a kick or two to your pet Mafiosi, and we could keep the Carpentier and Martí since they too are infamous. . . .

To which a final counterattack (GCI, May 27):

> – Parodies LatAm Writers In Store for Cuerpos – . . .
> Samples of *Cuerpos Divinos* (title not to be translated) would emit:

Chapter Cortazarino
"Encontraria la Manga. . . ?" and then the rest.

Chapter Fontesinus

A Sonali das Gupta, en recuerdo de la
lluvia de rupias en Ay Bombay!

The famous phrase from Cortázar's *Hopscotch:* "Would he find la Maga?" becomes in caricature: Would he find his sleeve? – *Maga* and *Manga* being dangerously similar. Cabrera Infante mocks Fuentes's tendency to name drop, parodying Fuentes's dedication (in his novel *Birthday*) to "Shirley MacLaine, under the rain in Sheridan Square." I still argued: What's wrong with including – anachronously – Barthelme if "The Death of Trotsky" chapter defies Chronos by including a "version" by José Martí, dead decades before Trotsky? Apart from taking a swipe at Julio Cortázar and Carlos Fuentes, in this same letter Cabrera Infante brings boldly to the foreground critical issues:

1) Why can't a marginal text be both obscure and authentically itself. Or, why can't a translation be as idiosyncratic as an original?[2] *TTT is* a Cuban book; the issue here is "political" in more ways than one. Updike's dig and even my unintended censorship function as cultural politics, in part denying a marginal work the privileges of a mainstream book. More important, the original parodies of Trotsky's assassination in Mexico thinly disguise Cabrera Infante's political disillusionment over the regime's Stalinist betrayal of the Cuban revolution. The writers satirized must be Cuban, among them Martí, martyr of Cuban independence in the late nineteenth century.

2) In self-translation, translating and originary writing serve each other: Cabrera Infante considers here a future work in which he will parody Latin American writers, which in turn will influence decisions

---

2. Seamus Heaney speaks of what is acceptable/unacceptable in translation in an entirely other vein. English and American English poets feel their language has been displaced from its mainstream position – established by Pound, Eliot, and the modernists – by Russian, Eastern European, Spanish, and Spanish-American poets, whose experience of a harsh reality is far more desperate. Poetry means more than language and tradition to these poets; poetry becomes a "necessary and redemptive mode of being human," i.e., survival. We (the English language) therefore accept the abstractions commonly used in foreign poetry, which would be forbidden in our native English, especially since the modernists established that poetry should speak to "particularity." (See "The Impact of Translation," *The Yale Review,* Autumn '86, 1–14.)

he makes about the translation. Manuel Puig did the same when, collaborating on the translation of *Boquitas pintadas* into *Heartbreak Tango,* he discovered materials he would later use in the original composition of *The Buenos Aires Affair* and *Kiss of the Spider Woman*.

3) The anxiety of influence surfaces here: Cabrera Infante speaks of the "inappropriateness" of supplanting Cuban referents with North American influences, except where such influence appears explicitly or implicitly in the original, as in the Campbell parable. Furthermore, he protests against "anachronistic" influences, e.g., parodying Donald Barthelme, whose "Snow White" came *after TTT*. Yet some of his parodies are by definition anachronistic. As mentioned earlier, Martí died decades before Trotsky; Virgilio Piñera and Lezama Lima, both alive at the time *TTT* was published, are described (prophetically) as deceased.[3] Influence is in the eye or ear of the reader, as Borges has taught us. "I would remark that Kafka's work casts a curious ulterior light on 'Bartleby'" but "the first pages of 'Bartleby' are not anticipations of Kafka but rather allude to or repeat Dickens... ," Borges comments in his essays "Melville" and "Kafka and His Precursors," on the paradoxical status of mentors and disciples.

Many of Cabrera Infante's decisions seem inconsistent, based on the (sometimes posthumous) "anxiety of influence," but inconsistency is often the stuff art is made of. We can see how his intuitions are based on what is and isn't "true" to the original's relationship to both itself and to its new life in translation: Barthelme would have been out of place in the parodies, even in translation. On the other hand, it was appropriate to translate the Martí poem into a parody of a poem by Edgar Allan Poe, who has had an extraordinary influence on Spanish-American writers via his recognition by the French postsymbolists. Poe's ornate, Latinate language and morbid sensibility provide a bridge between English and Romance poetic languages. In Puig's *Buenos Aires Affair,* we replaced the quotation of a poem by the sugary post-Romantic poet Gustavo Adolfo Bécquer with Poe's "The Sleeper." More than any literal translation, Poe's text was the closest equivalent in its morbid mood and rococo language as well as its deathly theme. (4–11)

3. An ironic postscript: A review of GCI's book *Holy Smoke* speaks of GCI's "blend of satire and whimsy" as "reminiscent of Donald Barthelme,... hilarious,... darkly nostalgic." (*New York Review of Books,* May 8, 1986, 35.)

Vae Visitors

"The critic who goes searching for the 'original' of this text is on a fool's errand," Lori Chamberlain says in *The Poetics of Translation in Postmodern Writing,* in a discussion of how *TTT*'s "concern with translation mirrors its concern with the doubling of writing," through her reading of "Vae Visitors." Chamberlain sums up the "plot" of this many times tall told tale as follows:

> [Mr. Campbell's] narration concerns his brief visit to La Habana with his wife, his purchase of a walking stick, apparent loss and subsequent retrieval of this walking stick, and the ultimate discovery that he has, in fact, ended up with two identical walking sticks. There is an archetypal quality about the story, with its quasi-magical stick, mistaken identities, and doubles. Appended to his story are corrections written by Mrs. Campbell, corrections which attempt to expose the "lies" of Mr. Campbell's version. (202)

Mr. Campbell, a buffoonish avatar of Hemingway, has supposedly published the story in *Beau Sabreur,* a fictive American magazine, and "GCI" has found it and wants to publish it in the Cuban magazine he works for, *Carteles.* The story is first literally translated by a real life friend of GCI, Rine Leal, whose last name ironically means "loyal." A letter from "GCI" to Silvestre (474) explains that the second "translation" of the Campbell story, titled *"El cuento de un bastón seguido de vaya que correcciones de la Sra. de Campbell,"* transelaborated – back? – into English in *Three Trapped Tigers* as "The Tale of a Walking Stick When Followed by Madame Campbell's Corrections in the Comic Style," is actually the first, Rine's awkward translation. Typically, this literal "translation" is a more elaborate version than Silvestre's, with more details, footnotes, and allusions. Its rhetoric is more mannered, and comically unidiomatic; it is indeed a *cuento,* a short story, as opposed to a *historia,* a narration of events.

The supposedly original English version will never be seen, however, since the translations are in reality parodies of what a prejudiced American tourist would write about La Habana and of what happens when English texts are translated into Spanish. These translations mock Lino Novás Calvo's translations, but Cabrera Infante parodies the strategies and mistakes of translations to show that all writing suffers from betrayal.

Mr. Campbell presents himself as a reasonable man, dragged into uncomfortable situations in a foreign, underdeveloped country by Mrs. Campbell's typical bourgeois enthusiasm for "enchanting" exoticism. Mrs. Campbell's corrections serve to expose Mr. Campbell's prejudices, sexual and otherwise, and to expose his self-inflationary strategies as a writer, "calling into question the truth value of writing in general." (LC, 206) Each denies the other's version: They come off as hysterical, sexually repressed, or complicated Americans; he, a racist and a misogynist, and she, a castrating bitch. As Cabrera Infante reminded me in one of his notes to the next-to-last draft of the translation, "she hates films," which means that not only Mr. Campbell but our author wages a battle of the sexes against her.

"GCI" continues to undermine "truth value" when in his note to Silvestre he explains that Mr. Campbell is a confirmed bachelor, not yet forty, insinuating that the Missus is a mistress, as in the case of so many Misters and Missuses who check into hotels. Or she's the invention of Mr. Campbell, just as Mr. Campbell is doubly invented by Cabrera Infante, first as an old writer with a walking stick, then as a younger man who obviously doesn't need a walking stick. (The walking stick plays the pop-Freud role of an absent phallic signifier here.) This apparently heterosexual story is undermined not only by jokes about *maricones* in the story but by its true origins: The "original couple" was not a man and his paramour (pretending for decency's sake to be married) but two male friends, Cuban tourists in Barcelona! And the story – not the stick – was given to the real Cabrera Infante by cinematographer Nestor Almendros, whose painstaking revisions of Cabrera Infante's version became the basis of Mrs. Campbell's "corrections."[4]

In Silvestre's improved version of *"Historia de un bastón y algunos reparos de Mrs. Campbell,"* ("The Story of a Stick, with Some Additional Comments by Mrs. Campbell"), his principal "revision" places "the adjectives that were in front of the nouns after them," (475) since Rine, following English syntax, had put the adjectives in front, whereas in Spanish they commonly follow the noun. But, even in Silvestre's sup-

---

4. Mr. Almendros, as well as Mr. and Mrs. Cabrera Infante, were kind enough to provide me with this "background material."

posed good translation, subtle stylistic irregularities smack of translation. Rine's literal translation precedes in a supposed "real" time, but in the book follows, elaborates on, and parodies Silvestre's version, by making a mockery of translation and of storytelling.

The translator/critic of the two translations should make Silvestre's seem like a correct revision of its own parody, so that the reader will accept the fiction of comparing them, even though, finally, that critical comparison is problematic because there is no original. Examining the same sentence from both (Mr. Campbell's) versions, first in the earlier draft of the translation, then in the final draft, helps show how we tried to set off these two "translations." The fictive setting of this remark by Mrs. Campbell is that Mr. Campbell has a bad leg, which attracts him to the *compensatory* walking stick in the first place, and Mrs. Campbell is saying that he couldn't have brought his own car to Cuba, which is what he had wanted to do:

> *Early draft:* "Honey with your leg in this state you wouldn't have been able to drive."

> *TTT, (178):* "Honey, with your leg in this state you simply cannot drive."

The phrase in the early draft is translated literally. However, since this is Silvestre's good, unliteral translation, I chose to put the phrase in the present tense, to make it direct and conversational, which is how it sounds in Spanish: The conditional tense is more spoken in Spanish than in English. The present tense provides the needed emphasis in Mrs. Campbell's words to reveal her as a bitchy, domineering American woman, the image that Mr. Campbell (or Cabrera Infante) wishes to portray. Here's the same phrase in Leal's outrageous translation:

> *Early draft:* "Miel, she said, "with your leg in that (pointing to it) condition, you couldn't possibly have driven a car."

> *TTT, (191):* "Little dear," she said, "with your leg in that (pointing to it) condition, you couldn't possibly have driven a car."

To create the illusion of a literal translation into English as Cabrera Infante did into Spanish, it was necessary to think of a word-for-word transposition of Mr. Campbell's original account as if it had been written originally in Spanish. *"Miel"* is Leal's "loyal" translation into

Spanish of the English endearment "Honey," but the fact that *miel* in Spanish has no other meaning than the literal is lost on the English reader. Rather than keep *miel* in the English translation, I changed it into a cumbersome diminutive: Diminutives, frequently used in Spanish as a sign of affection, are usually clumsy when translated literally into English. "Little dear" in English reproduces the effect of the barbarism *miel* in Spanish, and, besides, the diminutive makes explicit Mrs. Campbell's supposedly castrating, be*littling* attitude toward Mr. Campbell. Faulty communication between North American tourists and Cuban "natives," between translation(s) and presumed original(s) is the main thrust of "Vae Visitors." This thrust is inevitably diverted in the language of the exploiter, but humorous devices did in part bring home translation's exhibition of writing's failure.

Vista(s) of Dawn in the (Tristes) Tropics: History/ Fiction/Translation

> *There is no cultural document that is not at the same time a record of barbarism.*
>
> WALTER BENJAMIN

History Is a Story

*V*ista del amanecer en el trópico was one of the original titles of the book that became *Tres tristes tigres,* a book that was going to counterpoint Cabrera Infante's *carnevale* to the satyrs and nymphs of Havana nightlife with sombre documentary vignettes of history in the making–the revolution against Batista that ended with the victory of Fidel Castro. "Both a chronicle and a utopic vision of that moment, the original novel was to view in the tropical dawn of Cuba, the dawn of a new historical age," Emir Rodríguez Monegal wrote of the book that finally became *Vista del amanecer en el trópico* in 1974.

But in 1965 the self-exiled Cabrera Infante, convinced that the revolutionary government was turning into a repressive regime, particularly after the censorship of the film *P.M.* and other restrictive measures, disengaged from his work in progress the politically engaged vignettes. The twenty-minute documentary *P.M.,* filmed by his brother Sabá Cabrera and Orlando Jimenez, was a vivid testimony in black and white to nightlife in old Havana, except that most of the characters captured on the film *in actu* were black or mulatto, dancing to hypnotic cha-chas, rumbas, mambos, and boleros, drinking and occasionally getting into a brawl. It was not a vision of the "reformed" Cuba that the regime wished to publicize. And it was the first time, Cabrera Infante told Torres Fierro, that an artistic work was censored in Cuba "not for expressing counterrevolutionary ideas, but because of its form as well as content." (87) What his brother was not allowed to show in film, he would therefore tell in literature.

Literary preferences even more than Cuban politics motivated the transformation of *Vista* into *TTT,* however. The original project followed the formula of his first work of fiction, a collection of "lyrical" stories and "epic" vignettes titled *Así en la paz como en la guerra* (1958, *In Peace As in War*). In a similar fashion fiction and history conjoined to form another total Sartrean fiction, proposing a view of history and fiction as a continuum. But the text that turned into *TTT* recognized no other counterpoint than its own verbal music, making history and politics into a *basso continuo.*

Several years later Cabrera Infante collected the vignettes – which now began with the earliest chronicles of Cuba and ended in the early 1970s, since he had continued to compose new vignettes – and by means of the cinematic technique of montage, he created out of them a book. Or rather, in making a readerly discovery, he was finally able to write the book, as he explains in the interview with Torres Fierro:

> One day, upon reading the new vignettes, which had been published in places as diverse as Mexico and Czechoslovakia, I realized that they had a common denominator: violence. Cuba's history seemed wrought out of violence which contradicted its peaceful tropical geography. Using these vignettes and others which I wrote on Cuba's most remote and most recent history, plus actual testimonies (for example, in the last part of the book), another *View of Dawn in the Tropics* arose, this time turning the exemplary title into an ironic one: History now viewed as a simple story, historical life transformed into mere writing, into versions of reality – or rather "reality". (86)

Completed during sombre years of political persecution in exile, *Vista* was a less joy(ce)ful book than *TTT*. The vignettes are concise Hemingwayesque glimpses of a moment, an incident, a place, a character, or a text, as William Kennedy observed, "in the tradition of the vignettes of *In Our Time*." (136) Many of them describe photographs or engravings – literally moments captured in time in which the still, the visual image becomes dramatized for an instant, petrifying History in a graphic referent. Some are spoken testimonies, transcripts of conversations that actually took place. Inscriptions on photographs, fragments of recorded speeches, national hymns, legends, hearsay, quotations, transcripts – these are the ruins, the textual remains of History that constitute history-as-told in *Vista*.

The counterpoint between the lyricism of Cuba's nature and geography and the epic of history had become a subtle fugue. But Cabrera Infante, a fanatic subverter of academic or journalistic clichés, even his own, hated the term "vignettes." As with most writers who try to break new ground with each new book, he didn't want to repeat literary strategies, having used vignettes in his collection of stories. But there was another reason suggested, in a letter to me (October 4, 1975) as we were working on the translation:

> I promised Prometheus [allusion to a Havanan theater group in the 50s] not to use that word any more with *View of Dawn in the Tropics,* but I don't know what to call these fragments: perhaps viewgnettes? And there's a critic in Spain who insists that the book is a novel, with all the generals and the comandantes becoming one captain. What do you think?

His main concern here was that "vignettes" spoiled the structural *view,* that is, the reading of the book as a whole and not as a series of brief narratives. This was a serious concern from a pragmatic as well as a literary perspective. After the Spanish publisher had mistakenly advertised it as *"una serie de relatos,"* Cass Canfield, Jr. hesitated to publish the book. He insisted, correctly so, that volumes of stories do not sell well, and that *View* should come out when the new novel was ready to roll too; he finally agreed to publish it only after his author went over the book carefully with him and showed him its undeniable unity. Cabrera Infante wrote in a letter (September 18, 1976): "Cass had the idea that they were a series of vignettes about Cuba under Batista and not what the book is: a history which denies history and an epic told in lyrical terms about the history imposed upon the geography of that long unhappy island." These last words "long unhappy island" allude to Hemingway's passing description of Cuba in a kind of elegy to the Gulf Stream, which appears in his book *Green Hills of Africa.* This elegy turned out to be a provocation: Cabrera Infante ended his panoramic *View of Dawn in the Tropics* with a subversive translation of the original quotation.

Hemingway's vision becomes a source of discussion and questioning in Cabrera Infante's view. Despite its author's preoccupation with what could be considered derivative, *View*'s originality lies in its critical dialogue with other historical and literary texts, in its violation of the boundaries between history and fiction, between original and translation.

From *Vista* to *View*

Though Cabrera Infante participated less in this translation than in either *TTT* or, later, in *Infante's Inferno,* he still co-elaborated significantly.[1] Excessive elaboration would have upset its delicate balance, the grave contrapuntal effect of its lyricism, understatement, and straightforward violence, but he did add some new vignettes that underscore an ironic, pathetic view of the "best intentions" of revolution. He carried on a correspondence with me over a period of four years (1974–1978), which dealt with all aspects of the translation, from the most practical issues, such as getting the book published or pondering its reception, to answering my many translation questions, discussing the concept of the book, offering numerous editorial suggestions. He has now added further vignettes about the Batista era in a recent edition published in England (Faber & Faber, 1988), and has revised the text for the British reader.

The book's subtle variations of style and language, its demands for documentary authenticity, provided a challenge, while its elegant concision made it both pleasurable and more manageable than Cabrera Infante's more voluminous undertakings. On its deceptive simplicity in comparison with *TTT,* he warned me in a letter (November 12, 1977, I translate literally):

> *View,* despite its apparent easiness, has a lot of tricks to it, of style but also language. In the first pages I use many archaic documents mixed into the

1. GCI was still recovering from a nervous breakdown; under medical advice he refrained from excessive wordplay because of the contagion between the disassociation of words from meaning, and schizophrenia.

narration; some of the pages which seem as if they were mine – like that extraordinary graffiti we've just discussed – are really historical documents.

Italo Calvino remarked that a real collaboration between author and
translator begins with the translator's questions, and that "a translator
with no doubts cannot be a good translator." (109) And the poet-
translator Alastair Reid once pointed out to me an experience with
which I immediately identified, that of looking up words one already
knew: That is, translators have doubts even when they have the answers.

Anyway my first questions (November 28, 1975) when I'd already
begun to translate *Vista* were,

> Dr. Livingstone, I presume that on pp. 13–14 of *Vista* the quotations from
> Columbus are from his first voyage, correcto? On p. 17, do you remember
> from what section of Padre de las Casas' writings comes the quotation?
> Since both those works are translated, I thought it worthwhile to try to
> quote from the translations, if possible. Also, if possible, could you give me
> a list of the other works you quote from. Most of them probably aren't
> translated, but, if so, I should check into the translations.

His response (December 13, 1975) was prompt, despite protesta-
tion to the contrary:

> Dear Jill, forgive my delay in answering your letter in turn, but yours had
> gotten mislaid in this universe filled with papers that is my mundo infame
> [infamous world], not to be confused please with mondo cane or with in-
> mundo infante [filthy Infante but a pun, hence a better translation would
> be: Infante's underworld – underwear, get it?] and I couldn't answer yours
> without having it in view [in sight]: Land! shouted Rodrigo de Triana from
> the crow's nest – and you're right the quotation is from Columbus' first
> voyage, but I don't know if it [Columbus's letter] was translated from the
> Italian or from hispaniolo antico. I can't tell you anything about Las Casas
> – called Bartolomeo By C. L. Sulzberger! – I got that quotation like many
> of the others [dealing with the Conquest and Colonial Cuba] from
> Portuondo's History of Cuba. All the quotations come from there and
> those that don't come from that History, I've forgotten whence they come
> since I wrote those vignettes years ago. For example, the one where the
> general's mother refuses to recognize him because he surrendered and only
> accepts him when she finds out that he tried to commit suicide first, and
> others like that vignette. I don't think there are references to other universal
> works other than the obvious, Borges and Hemingway, for example, both

of whom have written about history and about Cuba; remember the "odious rumba The Peanut Vendor"? [This last quotation, from Borges's *A Universal History of Infamy*, was translated into English by Di Giovanni and Borges as "the deplorable rumba"].

At first glance, question and answer seem tautological: That most of the historical quotations came out of Fernando Portuondo's book was already known. But Cabrera Infante confirms this in detail, a comfort to the ever-doubtful painstaking translator, and he also underscores the tentativeness of his originals, or rather his "translations'" origins, and not only because he has forgotten, unavoidably or conveniently, these origins. Columbus's letters were translated from the Italian or, that is, as Rodríguez Monegal has noted in *Noticias secretas y públicas de America*, "Columbus's prose is an imperfect mixture of Italian, Spanish and Portuguese," which, one imagines, the King and Queen of Spain, or their secretary, had some difficulty in deciphering. (32) History inevitably mistranslates, Cabrera Infante confirms as he cites Sulzberger's version of Las Casas's name, and, of course, the Portuondo *History of Cuba*, an official textbook read by children in grade school. Cabrera Infante also mentions in this letter literary sources: Borges and the pervasive influence of Hemingway, particularly the Hemingway quotation in the last vignette, which he brooded over in a previous letter (September 27, 1975):

> Do you think that the vignettes (or whatever they're called) are coming out too Hemingwayan in English? I'm worried about that with some of them, particularly the older ones (like those you're translating now, the one with the two generals), that were written around 1963 or even before. It worries me because of the possible American reader (and especially critic). I know that in others they'll find influences of Borges, though in reality they are homages to the Argentinian – or direct quotations, as you know. But Hemingway is really so dead to me that it would be like performing funeral rites to name him among the influences of the book – although I chose for the end a direct quotation from him, this time consciously, since he is one of the few writers who have written on Cuba, not with the immediacy of the revolution in mind but rather the permanence of the island, which is really the theme of *View*, as you well know.

There is more than perhaps meets the eye in this exchange. The real theme of *View* turns out to be, via Hemingway, a sub*vision* of the original intention of the heavily Hemingwayesque vignettes: In effect, four centuries of political violence are framed by the first and last vignettes, which speak of the island's geographical permanence. Though its causes, from conquest to revolution, seem so varied in ideology, the repeated incidence of violence also speaks of another permanence, the age–old adage still true: History repeats itself.

But another transgression comes into view here. In my letter I ask, Am I to respect the source of your original, and quote faithfully your inevitably unfaithful translation of that original text quoted, or am I, like you (the author), to rewrite the original, quoting freely, that is, writing? Quoting becomes rewriting here: For instance, the phrase "Before dying, did the last hostage think he was dreaming?" (*View*, 76), more than a quotation, is an allusion to "Did he... [resume his sleep]... so that the murderers would be a dream... ?"—two different sentences at the end of Borges's story "The Waiting," which I've condensed into one for the purpose of comparison. (168)

Cabrera Infante was doubtlessly directing me toward the writerly course, at the same time denying unconscious influence in favor of conscious homage to Borges and Hemingway, two literary Virgils he could not ignore. Apart from sharing a way of practicing humor, what Cabrera Infante shared with Borges (and both he and Borges with Hemingway) was the books he read. Cabrera Infante remarks in an interview with E. Rodríguez Monegal (*Mundo Nuevo,* Paris, July 1968): "I wondered if Borges had read a story by Ambrose Bierce, which Hemingway had read so attentively, and which I myself had read and copied the technique of, in my story titled "Resaca" (Ebb-tide)." (47) Apparently Borges's story "El South" reflected "a similar device."

As Cabrera Infante clarified to me recently, it wasn't so much that he wanted to write like Hemingway, but rather that he wanted to be another Hemingway (or Faulkner or Fitzgerald), to have his fame. He had in any case exorcised Hemingway's influence through the exorcising (and homaging) mode of parody in *TTT,* in the supposed story/ translation of Mr. Campbell, the Hemingwayesque hero now a kvetching, prejudiced tourist. But not completely exorcised: The "anxiety of influence" lingers on, now multiplied in the dimension of translation, and he is concerned about the reception of *View* in English, the native language of Hemingway.[2] How to avoid being read as secondary, perpetrating the odious relationship between a mainstream culture and marginal Cuba? He had already been unjustly burnt over this issue.

Cabrera Infante phrases his concern here, however, not as anxiety but as parricidal criticism of a now passé Hemingway – "because of the bad reputation Hemingway has now":

> The particularly vulnerable zones are those written in Brussels. Those written in London are more *mine* [my italics]. What was written in 1963 is too much under the egis of Borges (aside from the textual quotations) and the form of my vignettes in that period owe a lot to Hemingway. (August 27, 1977)

The distinctions between the "derivative," earlier vignettes and the more original later ones, particularly "the originality of paralyzing history in photographs, graphic referents," certainly concern the writer. Ironically, what he defines as his original, final conception of the book, that of "de-signifying history, converting History into stories," could also derive in this instance from Borges's "timid games" in *A Universal History of Infamy*. But perhaps more relevant to the reader is how history, and fiction, are transformed into a text whose *originality* lies in its critical dialogue with these texts.

A Subtext

It would be useful to look at the original's original, not the island of Cuba but Hemingway's now much-prefaced description of the island in the stream. For brevity's sake, I am transcribing the particular seg-

---

2. The influence of Hemingway's poetic prose – which says more by saying less – can be traced throughout *View* and even into *La habana*. And it is precisely the process of translating *back* into English that brings to the surface this influence. In *"Amor propio"* (a one-page chapter of *La habana* describing the joys of masturbation) the culminating moment *"desparecido el ser en el semen que iba a pegar en chorros espasmódicos . . . "* could have translated as "the self disappearing with the semen splashing spasmodically. . . " ("splashing" substituting "spurting" to provide not only alliteration but *ass*onant rhyming), but, consciously parodying *Gone with the Wind,* we changed it to "the self gone . . . ". Now, looking back at Hemingway's ". . . all gone as the high-piled scow of garbage . . . spills off its load . . . ," I can't help associating Hemingway's streaming syntax and *seminal* semantics with that of his reader, GCI. See also in *View* the description of Capa's famous photograph of a Spanish Republican soldier falling in battle. (115)

ments of Hemingway's elegy to the Gulf Stream in *The Green Hills of Africa,* "cited" in *Vista del amanecer en el trópico:*

> when, on the sea... you... know that this Gulf Stream you are living with... has moved, as it moves, since before man, and that it has gone by the shoreline of that long, beautiful, unhappy island since before Columbus sighted it and that... those that have always lived in it are permanent and of value because that stream will flow, as it has flowed, after the Indians, after the Spaniards, after the British, after the Americans and after all the Cubans and all the systems of governments, the richness, the poverty, the martyr-dom, the sacrifice and the venality and the cruelty are all gone as the high-piled scow of garbage... spills off its load into the blue water... with no significance against one single, lasting thing – the stream. (149–150)

Now here is Cabrera Infante's version:

> *Y ahí estará. Como dijo alguien, esa triste, infeliz y larga isla estará ahí después del último indio y después del último español y después del último africano y después del último americano y después del último de los cubanos, sobreviviendo a todos los naúfragios y eternamente bañada por la corriente del golfo: bella y verde, imperecedera, eterna.* (233)

The "changes" are interesting: 1) Hemingway's "long, beautiful, un-happy" island becomes emphatically more unhappy in GCI's "sad, un-happy, and long." 2) And the "after the Indians..." series is trans-lated faithfully, except that the narrator omits the British, who perhaps played a more minor role in his view of Cuba's history, and adds the Africans, a principal racial group in Cuba, oddly omitted here by Papa Hemingway in a book about Africa. The addition of *"último"* is needed to give the dramatic emphasis that Hemingway's rhetorical repetition makes vivid in English. 3) The Cuban version condenses all the evils into *naúfragios,* literally, "shipwrecks," metaphorically to be taken as disasters: All the shipwrecked explorers and refugees signifying, after all, both individual and historical disaster. "Eternally bathed by the Gulf Stream" condenses all that Hemingway is saying about the natu-ral beauty, power, and permanence of the stream, in opposition to humanity's waste. But more significantly, the narrator shifts the focus from the stream to the island, which epitomizes nature – beautiful, green, lasting, eternal – except that *imperecedera* is stronger, more ac-tive, more directly associated with the history of violence just told, than the tranquil adjective "lasting."

View both quotes and paraphrases Hemingway, paying homage, but also subtly switching emphasis, marking a difference by using, or abusing, Hemingway's words to sing not to the stream but to the island. Cabrera Infante is perhaps saying without saying it that he is not an outside observer, an American *aficionado* viewing the stream from his fisherman's yacht, but a beached now exiled Cuban who has really known this "unhappy" island. Hemingway's nostalgic "long, beautiful, unhappy" becomes more poignant in the words of one who lived it from within.

And here, finally, the English translation:

> And it will always be there. As someone once said, that long, sad, unfortunate island will be there after the last Indian and after the last African and after the last American and after the last of the Cubans, surviving all disasters, eternally washed over by the Gulf Stream: beautiful and green, undying, eternal. (141)

One can observe a process similar to the original (re)writing. As with *último,* "always" is added, or intuitively retraced to the original's original, for the necessary rhetorical emphasis on permanence that the strong formal future tense gives in Spanish, just as the first sentence is turned around so that *always be there* is stressed at the strongest point, the end of the sentence.

"Long, sad, unhappy" becomes "long, sad, unfortunate." The original "unhappy" is displaced not only because unhappy picks up other connotations in its passage through Spanish – *infeliz* by a contiguity of notions means "unfortunate" – but because there is no progression between the synonymous "sad" and "unhappy" in English, as there is between *triste* and *infeliz,* in either meaning or emotional intensity.

Those of us who translate know that *y* doesn't always translate automatically as "and" since *y* can gracefully disappear between two words while "and" can sometimes stick out like a sore thumb. But here *Y,* as Cabrera Infante (May 12, 1977) insisted, "should be 'and,' linking with the unfinished first vignette that is, as the 'end' of a long or interrupted sentence, giving the book, again, its 'undeniable unity.'"[3]

---

3. The unfinished last sentence of the first vignette reads: "There's the island, still coming out between the ocean and the gulf: there it is... " (1)

On the question of *shipwrecks* versus *disaster,* he expressed the same doubt as I did: "If we put disasters we lose the connection with the waters and if we put 'shipwrecks' it's too dramatic, metaphoric. Toss a coin, girl, toss a coin." I did, and came up with *disasters* but precisely because *naufragios* literally denotes "shipwrecks" but connotes, in common speech, disasters in general, shipwrecks being one of many possible disasters – and a very common one around Cuba, but not the only, as *View* vividly tells. Again, the general term *disasters* made more sense in this final "eternal" summing up, a summing up that subsumes Hemingway's list of disasters. The word marks a three-way dialogue between the American English translation, the original, and Hemingway's original – just as "after the last" in the American translation marks the (mis)quotation by incorporating the contaminating Spanish "translation."[4]

Cabrera Infante has taken from Hemingway's version both what effective writing in Spanish permits, and what he interprets, from his view, as the more insightful version. An act of translation, of criticism, of creation. The American translation of *Vista* incorporates, perhaps without meaning to, a double vision: Hemingway's original and Cabrera Infante's interpretation. The Cuban writer quotes Hemingway's elegant meditation on nature's truth and human folly but implicitly descants Papa's estheticized view: The island is not a backdrop but very much the foreground. The linguistic difference between the original and its source vanishes in translation, but the critical difference has made its mark. Hemingway believed he was telling it like it was. Cabrera Infante, critically subsuming Hemingway's view, recognizes

---

4. A similar example of "contamination" in reinscribing a text in the original's "source" language occurred in translating the title of José Donoso's novella *El lugar sin límites,* a quotation from a passage of Marlowe's *Dr. Faustus* in which – after some evasion – Mephistopheles tells Faustus that Hell is always with us, is where we are. The title does not quote but alludes to Mephistopheles's pronouncement "Hell Hath No Limits" (a spoken phrase in sixteenth-century English), conflating this response and Faustus's question, "Where is the *place* men call hell?" Donoso translates the passage – and quotes it as the epigraph to the novella (question: "Donde queda el lugar... ?"; evasive response: "El infierno no tiene límites. . . . ") – into colloquial modern Spanish. Since Donoso's tragicomic grotesque tale takes place in a rural, feudal, yet contemporary Chile, "Hell Hath No Limits" would have been an unnecessary archaism, an archaism that already disappears in the Spanish original. The American English translation – "Hell *Has* No Limits" – is "contaminated" not only by its source text but by the passage of time; a phrase from the past is mediated by the translator/writer and (re)interpreted in the present.

that all writing is secondary, which may mean that he is closer to telling it like it is. One way to see this view is to look back in laughter at *TTT*, where Hemingway's influence is exorcised in countless ways.

The foreword to *Green Hills* was the source of one of the satirical epigraphs to *TTT*. Hemingway, taking himself – and realism – quite seriously, wrote with humor:

> Unlike many novels, none of the characters or incidents in this book is imaginary. Any one not finding sufficient love interest is at liberty, while reading it, to insert whatever love interest he or she may have at the time. The writer has attempted to write an absolutely true book to see whether the shape of a country and the pattern of a month's action can, if truly presented, compete with a work of the imagination.

The "action" of which the "work of the imagination" falls short, by the way, includes the slaughter of African animals by the stoic Great White Hunter. Why the Cuban would wish to bury the North American patriarch under numerous parodies is not difficult to understand. Cabrera Infante writes in his *TTT* foreword:

> The characters, though based on real persons, appear as fictional beings. The proper names mentioned all through the book must be considered pseudonyms. The facts are, at times, taken from reality, but are finally resolved as imaginary. Any similarity between literature and history is accidental.

He is pulling everybody's leg seriously, including Hemingway's. The first sentence is pleonastic play, mocking the movie industry's fear of lawsuits. (This epigraph, like the Mark Twain preface, "got lost" in translation for similar reasons: As a tired parody in English of the cinematic caveat, it didn't carry over.) The second sentence is a half lie because some of the names, such as Rine Leal, René Jordan, and Jesse Fernández, are real. But it's a pithy half lie, since names – like all words – are linguistic conventions: Even when "real" (in fiction) do they *really* signify an identity? The third sentence plays with Hemingway's preference for the real over the imaginary, and the fourth loudly sneers at realism, particularly Marxist socialist realism. Cabrera Infante takes Hemingway's text, and cinematic and sociological clichés, and as in dream speeches repeats the words but gives them a different meaning, revealing language's elusiveness despite all intentions to the contrary.

TTT's sense, language's non-sense, carries over to *View of Dawn in the Tropics,* except this time the joke is dead serious.

Cabrera Infante's final remark on the translation as it was about to go to press was (November 12, 1977), "What is coming out very well is the tone, between ironic and factual and often dead-pan écriture – how do you like the polyglotism?"

Infante's Inferno

There are many puns, some in English, others in French.

G. CABRERA INFANTE

CABRERA INFANTE refused to call *La habana* a
novel even though all writing is fiction to him. *La habana* is a memoir,
on the edge of autobiography, signalled already in the title by
"Infante." Alliteration, the autobiographical *"Infante,"* and the subterranean inferno metaphor for Havana and the female sex in both *TTT*
and *La habana,* as already discussed, make *Infante's Inferno* a logical
title. But there are other reasons that do not immediately meet the ear.
What strikes the reader of the original title is not only its playful alliterative form, the explicit reference to "Havana" and in comic self-
deprecation to a "Dead Infante," but also the visible parody of Ravel's
Pavane pour une infante défunte.

I have discussed the dialogue between Spanish and English in *TTT,*
and how this dialogue is both represented and sabotaged in translation.
La habana introduces yet another interlingual conversation, between
French and Spanish, evident already in the title beneath the title. As
Cabrera Infante said in his introductory letter about *La habana,* "There
are many puns, some in English, others in French." (February 1, 1979)
How does the close relationship between the Romance languages
Spanish and French translate into English? And if the *pavane* motif is
essential to the book, as suggested, how does one justify its loss?

La habana is a Dantesque voyage, in search of not one but many Bea-
trices, in search of not divine but profane love: The erring narrator discovers that true love is ultimately sexual obsession, that communion is
an illusion. In this parodical inversion the dead Infante remains caught

in the circles of the hell and heaven of Havana, a memory, a book, an infinite Proustian discourse.[1]

The English title is fateful and faithful: *Dante ante Infante*. Dante *and* Virgil (*io*, or "I"). As Virgil is Dante's guide to the underworld of the dead in search of Homer, so does the narrator, guided by Dantes and Virgils (and Sapphos) seek memory but also the "I," his writerly identity. If *La habana* satirizes Dante's search for true, divine inspiration by suggesting that the lover, like the writer, is alone, imprisoned in his own discourse, it also exalts in biblical dimensions the illusion of creation, Literature. Between Infante and Dante, another essential and Cuban Virgil intercedes: José Lezama Lima. His *Paradiso* (1967), a direct homage to Dante, re-creates a young poet's birth as writer and as sexual being in the urban paradise of Havana, providing a discursive Joycean and Proustian as well as Dantesque space for *La habana* to come.

The following translated correspondence traces, from another perspective, the multistaged evolution of the title.

When the original was still in manuscript, and before I translated *"La Plus Que Lente,"* Cabrera Infante wrote (December 2, 1978), "What do you think, seriously, of the title *Dry Dreams* for our next book?" As early as September 6, 1979, he was naming titles, some of which prefigured his next book, *Holy Smoke*: "I'm thinking of *To Havana and Not Havana*.[2] Or *Havana is not a Cigar* or perhaps *Havana Si, Havana No*.[3] But all are too glib, slick and though parodic not grave enough for my *Difunto Infante*."

The title had to be parodic but not merely burlesque: *Gravity* was needed.

SJL to GCI, September 22, 1979: "*Dry Dreams* is good. Another: *Pavana for a Havana Lost* (playing with Paradise Lost). (Here are a few

1. "Memory ruled by the city does not show encounters and visits, but, rather, the scenes in which we encounter ourselves." (Peter Demetz, intro. to Walter Benjamin's *Reflections* [New York: Harcourt Brace Jovanovich, 1978], xvii.) Benjamin's (and Breton's) view of the city streets as the "only place of authentic experience" coincides with GCI's – all of them preceded by that *flâneur* par excellence, Baudelaire.
2. Inspired in Hemingway's Caribbean drama (glorified in film by a young Lauren Bacall and her man Bogart) *To Have and Have Not*, in turn inspired in a phrase from *Don Quixote* – the Haves and the Have Nots. The title of the final chapter, or epiphanic "epilog," came out of these Havana jokes: "Movies Must *Have an End*" (my italics).
3. Poking fun at Fidel's anti-yanqui slogans.

for your amusement but not for the title: Dry Dreams of a Wet Back, Afternoon of an Infante, Nocturnal Omissions)."

SJL to GCI, August 8, 1980: "A possible title: *In Old Havana*.[4] In the interview [with Julián Ríos, *Espiral* 51] you suggest that DIVINE BODIES would be a good title for HAVANA, do you take it back?"

Sometime later, Carlos Fuentes commented to me that he had come up with the title *Infante's Inferno:* I passed this comment on to Cabrera Infante (SJL, August 15, 1981):

> This title, Fuentes' sinister idea, is certainly funny but could lead to the book being taken Holly too lightly (you know what I mean, I can just hear a critic saying "I had a hard if not hot time getting through Infante's Inferno... "). Infante's Inferno could turn the book into Havana for a Dead Duck, but what the hell... let's dive right in, if nothing better emerges from the Calldron.

Cabrera Infante quickly corrected me, reluctant to assume anxiety over a false influence, Fuentes (September 28, 1981):

> Dearest Daughter, *Infante's Inferno* is not an invention of Fuentes or by Morel but my own onus. Don't you remember? Please check up on my scarlet letters. The whole concoction was mine. I simply told Fuentes about this possible title in Old San Juan, P.R. and he gave me this bit of information that there was a book by some war correspondent called Durante's Inferno.

Sure enough (GCI, June 22, 1981):

> I fear that we haven't found our title (viscount? marchioness?) yet. But remember tardy TTT. HAVANE I don't like. HAVANA FOR A DEAD INFANT is a compromise with the original. And infant, as you know, is too tender, a baby, a suckling babe. It's almost HAVANA FOR A DEAD FOETUS!... I modestly think that one of the alternatives is INFANTE'S INFERNO because it's alliterative, Dantesque and slightly comical. There is besides, a book by a war correspondent in WWII, famous then, called *Durante's Inferno*.

In the same letter, Cabrera Infante continues,

> The title, finally, will be determined by the publisher, as it happened last time. But I've thought of another which maintains Havana (which as you've seen, is essential to the book) and at the same time something of the original infante (though no Ravel) besides being a wordplay, holding its pun high in salute. This title would be *Havana for a Knight* and to make it

---

4. Cinematic allusion to *In Old Chicago*.

more obvious (there are always slow, lip-readers) we'd add another epi-
graph to the King Kong one saying:
"But you were in Havana for a night,
Just gettin' the feel of the land."
Mae West in "Havana for a Night".
These lines come from her best record of the same title, a parody of the bolero "Vereda tropical" with English lyrics by Oscar Hammerstein. . . . Mae
West fits in with the theme of blondes and false blondes in the other epigraph. . . and with the mythic women of cinema and of the century, Fay
Wray clutched by K.K., Mae West squeezing men in her hands. The fact
that the reference is a popular song and not a symphonic piece doesn't matter. Nor that the title seems cheaper than the original (which always happens in the translation): The American reader doesn't know the original,
nor Ravel's *Pavane* for that matter. . . . What's important is that there be a
humoristic, slightly anachronical, pop element. There are also anachro-
nisms in Infante's Inferno – and if Infante gets lost, it's always there in the
author's name above.

The essential "effects" of the title (though "cheaper") should be
"humoristic, anachronical, pop," that is, parodical.

Finally (October 1, 1982) he pronounced: "Our title is: *Infante's Inferno*," and in long-hand, "This will make Dante Difunto."[5] This last
joke has serious connotations. Within Cabrera Infante's poetics of
translation, the Old becomes the New; the past (Dante) is transformed, displaced, translated into the present (Infante). The Old is paradoxically defunct and reborn.[6]

5. The process/reasoning behind choosing the allusion-saturated "Inferno" for the title can
be illuminated by the following statement by Umberto Eco:
The idea of calling my book *The Name of the Rose* came to me virtually by chance, and I
like it because the rose is a symbolic figure so rich in meanings that by now it hardly has
any meaning left: Dante's mystic rose, and go lovely rose, the War of the Roses, rose thou
art sick, too many rings around Rosie, a rose by any other name, a rose is a rose is a rose,
the Rosicrucians. The title rightly disoriented the reader who was unable to choose just
one interpretation. . . . A title must muddle the reader's ideas, not regiment them."
Postscript to The Name of the Rose. (3)
6. Enrico Mario Santí speaks of writing as "spatial difference," exposing "the sign's inherent
lack and its need to be supplemented by an endless chain of other signs." (*Pablo Neruda: The
Poetics of Prophecy* [Cornell University Press, 1982], 162) He cites Neruda's Cantos in *The
Heights of Machu Picchu,* which salute Dante but which displace his wor(l)d in the New
World, (re)interpreting Mesoamerica in Western terms. The historical process of interpretation and creation is described here as a "process of translation by which the past is transformed, with all its attendant revisions, into the present. It is the act of translation. . . that
provides the culmination to the earlier revision of literary history by becoming the figure that
adopts Western signs as part of a new beginning." (161)

If Ravel and Havana disappeared explicitly from the title, they were emphatically regained in the book, Havana a protagonist to whom many pages and puns serve homage, as in an alliterative pun, *"La habana... La Vana"* (237), which became a rhyming alliteration, "Havana, the Vain, Then." (135) Then, again, there's the *habanera* motif that we maintained by leaving the word for Havana woman in Spanish, since the English reader could associate it with the musical form *habanera*. And Ravel became a musical leitmotif as we reveling Ravelrousers of the unraveling word elaborated on Ravelian jokes – for example, in *"La Plus Que Lente,"* where Ravel, Debussy, and even Satie now play a more principal role than in the original, especially Cabrera Infante's favorite, Satie, who didn't even appear in the original passage.

The following is yet another instance of "unraveled Ravel" (to quote John O'Hara's *From the Terrace*) regained – cited from the chapter titled *"Todo vence al amor,"* turning Virgil's *Amor vincit omnia* upside down, in a kind of verbal 69:

The original:

"Bueno, yo cultivo mis flores" dijo y abrió el libro y volvió a leer, como con furia ahora: verso versus verso. (270)

Literal Translation:

"Well, I cultivate my flowers" she said and opened the book and started reading again, as if with fury now: verse versus verse.

The "transelaboration" – "Love Conquered by All":

"Je vais m'occuper de mon jardin," she said and was kind enough to translate for me: "Time to go back to my flowerbed." Merde! Je vais cracher sur la tombe de Couperin, I should have said, but she had opened her book and was reading with a kind of fury now, verse versus verse. (160)

Virginia, the girl pursued on this occasion by our incessant Don Juan, is in a library. À la *Satyricon,* GCI satirizes throughout the book the Frenchified cultural pretensions of the Cuban bourgeoisie.[7] The contrast between people's pretensions and their more authentic vul-

---

7. The French are the first to satirize their own classics. In Renoir's film *Boudu Sauvé des Eaux* (1932), a gentleman approaches the bookstore where Boudu the bum has found a home, asking, "Do you have *Fleurs du Mal?*" To which Boudu responds, "This is a bookstore, Monsieur, not a flowershop." The avid reader goes off in a huff.

garity recurs as a constant dialectic throughout *La habana,* as it does in Puig's *Boquitas pintadas.* Virginia is reading Baudelaire's *Flowers of Evil* under false pretenses, or rather trying to outpun the narrator by turning Baudelaire cutely into Voltaire's gardener. The only jokes the narrator tolerates are his own, and they are his own, and so he replies with a "ready repartee," alliterating, *como con furia ahora,* to mock the (to his mind) mock-intensity of her reading: verse versus verse.

We not only substituted but elaborated on jokes, out of necessity, but equally compelling was the perverse "pleasure of the text." The Spanish parody of Voltaire's *"Je vais cultiver mon jardin,"* that is, *"Yo cultivo mis flores,"* is based on the proximity of French and Spanish, a similarity that, as with the original's title "Havana for a Dead Infant," dissipates when English supplants Spanish. The "transelaborated" English version appropriately introduces French and exposes the disturbing, comical presence of (mis)translation implied in the original, now explicit in the translation. My *trouvaille* was inspired by a recording of Ravel's *Le tombeau de Couperin: "Je vais cracher sur la tombe de Couperin,"* in which Boris Vian's *J'irai cracher sur vos tombes* overflows into Ravel's homage.[8] This translated passage becomes more allusive, more musico-literary than the original, and perhaps more sexual, *cracher* suggesting French slang for "orgasm," *cracher dehors.* Alliteration lurks too, invisibly, in the conjunction of "should... she."

The humor, born of the close union between languages, works here because of a Gallic cultural perspective shared by Anglo and Latin America. Postcolonial Latin America has looked to Europe and North America, compensating for a lack of critical dialogue by *translating* into its own terms the so-called mainstream culture.[9] The hypocrisy in Cuban society mocked by the narrator originates in the alienation be-

8. Vian was a (quitessentially French) jazz enthusiast who "doubled as a Dixieland trumpeter in Paris clubs." (See E.J. Hobsbawn, "The Jazz Comeback," *New York Review of Books,* Feb. 12, 1987, 11.)
9. F. Jameson, "Postmodernism and the Consumer Society," *The Anti-Aesthetic: Essays on Postmodern Culture"* (ed. Hal Foster [Port Townsend, Wa.: Bay Press, 1983], 112). Jameson claims that cultural movements define themselves by displacing a previous cultural period (postmodernism seeks to displace modernism). Here Jameson quotes Octavio Paz's essay on translation and metaphor (from *Hijos de Limp*), which describes Hispanic culture as enriching itself by "translating" other cultures into its own terms. This process is compared to translation in which the text doesn't completely become another but rather the emphases are switched: The marginal becomes central and vice versa. (123)

tween model – be it popular North American or highbrow French culture – and Cuban reality. This distance between model and copy is a universal experience, certainly a very American experience: The North and South American aspiration to appear European is part of what is both alienated and authentic about America. The French phrase in the English translation accents thus the correspondence existing po(e)tentially between *La habana* and *Infante's Inferno*.

Between Texts and Sex

With its myriad sexual episodes, *La habana* is a picaresque bible, or better, one thousand and one lustful Cuban Nights (and days). How to reproduce the clichés and folklore that constitute *choteo*, a local language of sex and jokes?

"*Amor propio,*" title of the chapter that describes briefly, ecstatically, the adolescent's discovery of masturbation, produced in my associations a biblical heading: "Love Thyself." *Amor propio,* properly speaking, means "self-love," "self-esteem," but here it is used more literally than figuratively to signify sexual self-love-making. "Self-Love," or even the Gallicism "*Amour-Propre*" could have been perfectly proper titles but just didn't seem as ironical as the original "*Amor propio,*" playing literal love against a metaphoric sense of pride or vanity. *Amor propio* is such a common expression in Spanish; the word *propio* seems so concretely attached to ownership, loudly stressing the narrator's inevitable attachment to his own instrument of love. "Love thyself," taken from the rhetoric of the Bible (which, as Cecil B. De Mille was not the first to discover, is a very erotic book) reproduces a playful tension, between literal and figurative, between "good" and "bad" self-love, or perhaps between love and sex.[10]

Cabrera Infante responded ingeniously (February 24, 1980): "About Love Thyself's title, what do you think of Love Thy Neighbour? One's own penis lives practically next door, as a crow flies – or is it as the fly crows? . . . Now jokingly, I found the title a trouvaille. (Please

---

10. Jean Jacques Rousseau distinguished good narcissism *(amour de soi)* from bad narcissism *(amour-propre),* healthy self-esteem from unhealthy vanity. The ironic "Love Thyself," like GCI's, plays with the tension between these two poles (no pun intended), adding a hidden, third connotation, onanism.

note the correspondence between found and trouvaille...) Velly goo." His humorously porno*graphic* suggestion "Love Thy Neighbor" gave me the solution for the title of the next chapter, *"Amor trompero."*

The narrator begins this episode with a popular Spanish refrain: *"Amor trompero, cuantas veo, tantas quiero"* ("False love: The more women I see, the more I want"), which corresponds semantically more or less to the English saying "The grass is always greener... ". "Love Thy Neighbor" struck me as the appropriate introduction to this episode, which recounts the narrator's repeatedly unsuccessful attempts to seduce girls and women in movie theaters. "Neighbor" is comically accurate since the narrator would sit strategically next to unknown females, who literally became his temporary neighbors. "False Love" would not bring to the English reader's mind a popular saying like the profanity of "Love thy neighbor." The biblical "Love thy neighbor" lives up to the book's many double intertextual entendres, if not literally to *"Amor trompero."* "The grass is always greener" was incorporated into the text, substituting the original refrain, and Cabrera Infante parodically elaborated on it with "Your neighbor's grass is where it's green."[11]

One final folkloric sampler: the metamorphosis of episode VI, titled *"Mi último fracaso"* ("my last failure," 315) into "You Always Can Tell." This episode explores the perennial penial theme of an adolescent's sexual initiation, the narrator's (miss)adventures in brothels, and his final quasi-successful encounter with a streetwalker. As he takes leave of her, at the chapter's end, she remarks that she didn't think she'd have any customers that night, to which he responds, "You see?", so that she can complete the phrase with the punch line from a song in Spanish. "You never know." Immediately he thinks of an answer to her answer but doesn't utter it aloud, another line from another bolero: "You will be my last failure." "My last failure" does not evoke a song or a singer, the campy Olga Guillot, and therefore cannot epito-

---

11. See p. 94. Also SJL to GCI (August 8, 1980): "About to start work on "Love Thy Neighbor" – seeking equivalents for the refrain 'Amor trompero...' I now have two possibilities (aside from the literal); 'Love thy neighbor as thyself. What is thy neighbor's covet not' or, more earthy, 'the grass is always greener.' How's that for horse sense?"

mize the chapter's popular theme, which the Cuban reader would immediately recognize.

My first thought was "Better Late Than Never," a popular saying that could celebrate the character's first participation in sexual intercourse after discoursing upon it for 300 pages. Then "You Never Can Tell" came to mind, working well as the girl's parting words (changing "You never know" to "You never can tell"). But, as the final phrase has to be the narrator's mental repartee, Cabrera Infante suggested "you always can tell," an ironic echo, the narrator a constant echo of his narcissistic obsessions. Perhaps Freud was our (unconscious) guide, particularly in his essay on "The Antithetical Sense of Primary Words," in which he shows that yes often means no and vice versa: Could not the same apply to always and never?

"You Always Can Tell" covers a multitude of "sins": 1) The narrator automatically approaches the cruising *fletera* not knowing but somehow knowing that she is one, thus "you always can tell"; 2) *"Mi último fracaso"* is an affirmation that suggests the negative yet affirmative "You Never Can Tell," and the uncertainties of sexual initiation; 3) *"Mi último fracaso"* recalls another text, a song, just as *La habana para un infante difunto* recalls Ravel, asserting the verbal, the literary over a reality described. You always can *tell,* a misquotation from the lexicon of clichés, very much emphasizes the *telling* of this tale of tails in which even when the narrator can't always do he can always tell.

Between Cultures:

Boquitas pintadas into

Heartbreak Tango

How did "Little Painted Lips" become Heartbreak
Tango?

Boquitas pintadas: Parody or Nostalgic Requiem?

In *Boquitas pintadas* Puig continued to reconstruct
the provincial world of his childhood, a task begun in *Betrayed by Rita
Hayworth*. But whereas the first book was openly autobiographical,
Boquitas examines the townspeople of Colonel Vallejos with a more
sociological eye. Presenting the intertwining lives of characters from
different social castes, Puig attempts to understand, to analyze empa-
thetically the demise of provincial bourgeois values in Argentina. *Boquitas* is a tragicomic elegy to this past, specifically the 1930s and 1940s,
as suggested by the frilly title, lyrics from an old song saying, "I want a
kiss from their little painted lips." ("Painted lips" has a precious connotation and does not suggest painted, tainted "women of the street"
as it would in English.) The book has often been characterized as a parody, imitating the form of the soap opera or serial romance, which
serves as an appropriate frame for the melodramatic plot involving
doomed love affairs and triangles. Puig's mimicry of his characters'
speech and his reproduction of what the reader experiences as outdated
cultural artifacts produce an ironic, satirical effect.

Puig describes his "intentions" as follows, in an interview published
in *Translation:*

> When I wrote this novel, I was very interested in working with the lan-
> guage of the characters, because the way they spoke tells more about them
> than anything the author could explain. Most of the characters in the book

are first generation Argentines, of Italian or Spanish parents, most of them peasants who hadn't been able to give their children any cultural heritage. Their traditions were peasants' or underdogs' traditions, but they wanted to suppress or forget them. Much the same happened with immigrants who came to the United States. This meant that the children of these people had no models of conduct at home, and, least of all, no models of speech. They therefore had to invent a language of their own, using the culture they had at hand. All they had were the popular songs of the era, the subtitles of films, and stories in women's magazines. These models were not the best, but they were the only ones available to the lower middle class in small pampas towns. Mainly they were unrealistic and romantic. The language was overblown and was meant to impress quickly. That's why the tango is so truculent: because it had to make an impression on an audience lacking any subtlety. The characters in my book, based on the people of that era, try to use the language of *passion,* and they even think they act passionately, too. (34)

Puig sets out to expose the gap between the language his characters use to communicate, to fantasize about their lives, and the harsh, calculating reality of their existence. To produce this effect Puig had to re-create their language accurately, and yet introduce a distance between language and "reality" that the reader would perceive.

But Puig quickly balks at the label "parody":

I think it is misleading. I'm often embarrassed when someone says to me: "You mock the way poor people speak." That isn't my intention, and I'm sorry if it comes out that way. The point is that the ordinary speech of these people is already a parody. All I do is record their imitation. (35)

He clarifies that he does not merely imitate in a burlesque manner. However, in a formal sense, *Boquitas is* a parody, an imitation of a conventional genre with the intention of imposing a critical difference, of producing a double message involving both elegiac praise and satirical criticism. *Boquitas* criticizes the false or exaggerated sentimentality of the tango, the glamorized images of Hollywood that reify his characters' behavior, as well as the clichés and alienated journalistic, bureaucratic forms of everyday communication.

But the praise is also there: Puig takes the refuse of popular culture – song lyrics, advertisements, sensationalist journalism – and recycles it, creating something new. He could be considered a *bricoleur,* like Lévi-Strauss's primitive tinkerer, but more precisely following Adorno's use of the term to qualify the composer Gustav Mahler, who scandalized bourgeois esthetics in his time by taking folkloric musical themes and using them in new ways that resisted "passive listening." (298) Puig's books are entertainments, but for active readers; apparent praise of lower-middle-class popular forms involves a criticism of upper-middle-class esthetics. Puig's writing seeks the poetry in "bad taste," provokes the reader to enjoy and not suppress it as "good taste" has done, thus questioning the category of "kitsch," which presupposes a judgmental distance.[1]

Again, this empathetic reappraisal is also parody – which often transcends mockery and becomes sympathy. As we read *Boquitas pintadas* we grow to empathize with the characters despite their corny clichés, or maybe even because of the way they speak. They are all Don Quixotes, aspiring to what they are not, to what they cannot have. The borrowed words they unconsciously parody are ultimately "authentic," or at least the only language to which they have access. As readers, we no longer laugh at their absurdity but rather cry with their predicament, which is, after all, our own.

The Tango: Authentically Argentinian or Mendacious Myth?

An awareness of a book's intended effect on its original reader is obviously necessary in order for us to understand the difficulties of repeating that effect. The author's intentions may or may not be verifiable or even relevant, but I as translator have to decide what interpretative function I need to fulfill. In *Boquitas,* how to re-create in English the parodical effect that spoken Argentine has upon its intended reader? Let's examine the main impasse, which includes the translation of the title: how to reproduce in translation the "flavor," the function of the tango lyrics in the original version.

Imported films, or domestic films modeled after Hollywood imports, continue as in *Betrayed by Rita Hayworth* to be an influential medium to the characters of *Boquitas:* At one point, for example, libidinous Mabel fantasizes that her greatest desire is for Robert Taylor to

---

1. Danubio Torres Fierro, "Manuel Puig," *Memoria Plural,* 208. Lezama Lima in *La expresión americana* quotes Baudelaire as saying, "What is exhilarating about bad taste is the aristocratic pleasure of displeasing." (38)

enter her bedroom. But in *Boquitas* the tango, an "authentic indigenous" form, and a dominant manifestation of popular Argentine culture during the 1930s and 1940s, appropriately takes the foreground.

"The artificiality of those films," Alicia Borinsky observed,

> the way in which they make the viewer participate in their conventions, is
> similar to the structure of the tangos by Alfred Le Pera, tangos that we can-
> not help but imagine being sung by Carlos Gardel, the legendary tango
> singer and star of musical pictures, who interpreted the tragic tango lyrics
> with a sarcastic and oblique voice. (106)

The tango stresses the dark side of love: seduction and abandonment,
betrayal, the death of a lover. Gardel's irony doubtlessly responds to
the sexual battle the tango engages between the male's erotic domina-
tion in the actual dance and the content of the lyrics, which often speak
of betrayal perpetrated (when sung by a man) by the woman.

In the original *Boquitas,* quotations of tango lyrics appear as
epigraphs at the head of every episode, a phrase or a few words immediately touching the Argentine reader by invoking a well-known mel-
ody, and hence a mood or theme. Here is a list of the first four
epigraphs, accompanied by their "translations," or substitutions:

Boquitas pintadas

I. *Era... para mi la vida entera...*
("She was my whole life... ")
     – Alfred Le Pera

Heartbreak Tango

The shadows on the dance floor,
this tango brings sad memories
     to mind,
let us dance and think no more
   while my satin dress
   like a tear shines
– H. Manzi's tango "His voice"

II. *Charlemos, la tarde es triste...*
("Let's talk, it's a sad afternoon... ")

As long as you can smile,
success can be yours.
– radio commercial for toothpaste,
     Buenos Aires, 1947

III. *Deliciosas criaturas perfumadas,*
quiero el beso de sus boquitas
pintadas... ("Delicious perfumed
creatures, I want a kiss from your
painted lips... ")
     – Alfred Le Pera

She fought with the fury of
a tigress for her man!
He treated her rough – and
she loved it!
– ad for Red Dust, *starring*
    Jean Harlow and Clark Cable

126

IV. *". . . sus ojos azules muy grandes*
se abrieron. . . "
("... her eyes blue did open
wide...")
                        — Alfred Le Pera

My obsession, heartbreak tango,
plunged my soul to deepest sin as the
music of that tango set my poor heart
all a-spin.
— Roldan's "Blame That Tango"

These English "equivalents" are on the surface total departures. The original familiar quotations prefigure the characters, plot, and/or narrative form of each chapter. The Spanish-speaking but particularly the Argentine reader, whose feelings have been awakened by a musical memory, immediately captures the intonation of these words, what is implied between the said and the unsaid. Their exaggerated "bad taste" and the popular singer Gardel's sarcastic interpretations add a self-reflexive dimension, a distancing effect heightened by the novel's historicity. Their function as both nostalgic and ironic counterpoint is "heard" by the Argentine reader, but for the American reader, for example, a literal translation of poetic clichés like "She was my whole life" rings hollow. It could be a line from a popular song, but the specific tone, the contact between speaker and listener, is lost.

The tango "means" something else anyway outside of the "River Plate" (as the British nicknamed the region). For Europeans and North Americans, Latin American dance music has always had a stylized *Latin* connotation, whereas in Argentina the tango is as homespun as blues and jazz are in the United States. But it would have been absurd to substitute Billie Holiday's singing for Libertad Lamarque's, or Cole Porter's lyrics for Alfred Le Pera's. The original cultural referent would have been completely erased by such a drastic transposition. And American popular music, according to Puig's portrayal of Argentina in the 1930s and 1940s, did not invade the popular media and consciousness as significantly as the Hollywood cinema and consumer-oriented advertising.

Puig's vast knowledge of North American mass culture was invaluable to our creative collaboration. The solution we finally came up with was to translate some tango lyrics that were *essential* to the plot (I'll soon explain), but to replace at least half of the epigraph quotations with either tag lines from Hollywood films or Argentine radio commercials, originally borrowed from Madison Avenue inventions (see epigraph II). That is, artifacts relevant to the original context but that rang a funny, familiar, exaggerated bell for American readers. Puig comments in our interview:

> Because we couldn't use one-line epigraphs, as in the original, we found ourselves with too many complete songs, most of them unknown. They are sometimes picturesque, but without music they are not much as poetry. We thought of using other materials, such as taglines from American films. These are often quite funny and many of them ring a bell for Americans who went to movies in the 30s and 40s. (37)

The *Red Dust* tag line glamorizes sexism, machismo, and feminine submissiveness and is thus an appropriate epigraph to episode III, which introduces main male lead Juan Carlos, with whom women are always falling fatally in love. In "real life" we discover he's an insecure Don Juan, and his favorite girlfriend, Mabel, also introduced in this episode, accepts an archetypal submissive role in appearance but is really a tough and calculating woman.

These substitutions added a new dimension of interpretation, or more precisely, they emphasized certain elements in the text that had been more implied than explicit. The highlighted advertisements, as in the epigraph to episode II, underscore Puig's implied comment on the commercialization of culture as well as his intent, in writing the books he writes, to show how popular media have dissipated traditional distinctions between consumerism and art.

The *Red Dust* quotation is one of several movie epigraphs. By placing Hollywood movies on an equal plane with Argentine tangos it would appear that the translation suggests perhaps an equivalence between the cultural role of Hollywood productions, produced, Judith Weiss writes, in an "atmosphere of un-reality for a passive audience . . . [and] the role of Argentine music rooted in a popular past and enjoying popular participation in the present." (139) Making this equation could be dangerous, and subversive.

That is, if Puig's works question the alienating effects of North American cultural imperialism, doesn't the translation mitigate this criticism by stressing that culture at the expense of indigenous Latin American cultural phenomena?

Yes and no. Yes, the target culture does to a certain extent censor the ideology of the source text; an ideological subversion occurs by the mere fact of rewriting – appropriating – an Argentine novel in American English. Translation is a form of conquest, Ezra Pound, in Nietzschean spirit, has shown us. Like his model Edward FitzGerald, "transcreator" of the Persian *Rubaiyat,* Pound reversed the gender roles of author and translator, making the translator a virile violator of the original, now a feminine treasure trove. But the other side of the coin is, if the reader cannot recognize *Boquitas*'s parodical effect, its ideology is suppressed even more radically.

Besides, Puig's criticism has to be viewed in the broadest terms: He is not merely demythicizing but remythicizing, he is not merely calling attention to false or alienating models but paying homage to those movie stars who stimulated his imaginary life, giving a second life to sounds and images he finds worthy of salvation. To bolster Hollywood iconography in Puig's work in English is to pay homage to his homage.

The translation has followed the original, which already juxtaposes the sentimental tango and glamorous Hollywood movies within a critical narrative structure. We have to understand, as the Argentine reader does, what the book says about the tango and its supposed "authenticity," or more specifically, the middle class's relationship to a popular form that arose out of the "lower depths." Like jazz, the tango was accepted by the middle class only after it had been canonized in Paris, cultural capital of the world in the twentieth century. But in the process of passing from the *barrio Sur* and the brothels, the tango had undergone a "translation." What had been originally considered obscene (couples bumping and grinding in a tight embrace) had become melancholy, languid, and nostalgic.

While Puig's characters articulate their values in authentic Argentine terms, by juxtaposing what a character says and does/or thinks, the novel shows the reader how these original terms are false ones, translations, particularly for the "upwardly mobile" middle class. As Puig says, "The characters in my book . . . try to use the language of passion, and they even think they act passionately, too."

Only the working-class characters – in his view – wholeheartedly adhere to the tango's melodrama. It was precisely the tangos echoing in the thoughts of the main working-class female character, the maidservant Fanny, that somehow we had to translate "faithfully." In episode XI, Fanny listens to tangos on the radio as she scrubs the floors in the house of middle-class Mabel; as four tangos dance through her consciousness, she reflects on the stages of her love affair with Pancho that the different tangos evoke: illusions – seduction – abandonment – revenge.

But within the world of Puig's insecure bourgeoisie, the artificiality of the supposedly authentic gives us a clue to the motivation behind the apparently lighthearted title *Boquitas pintadas:* These words are not tango lyrics but are taken, treasonously, from a fox trot titled "Blondes of New York." *"Rubias de New York"* was a very popular song in the 1930s, sung, of course, by the legendary Gardel in an Argentine movie called *Tango on Broadway* – a movie that, for Argentines, glamorized the tango and their star in a Hollywood context. One could almost say that the fox trot lyrics *"Boquitas pintadas"* emblematize the tango's displacement, the uprooted roots of Argentine culture.

The Mexican Carlos Fuentes quoted the following *boutade* in an essay on the new Spanish American novel (1969): "The Mexicans descended from the Aztecs, the Peruvians from the Incas, and the Argentinians from the boat." A burlesque reduction, of course, but such indeed was the cradle of the quintessential Gardel, the illegitimate son of a Frenchwoman from Toulouse. Gardel's fox trot on Broadway can be read not only as the tango's betrayal but as a confirmation of Argentina's imported origins.

Expanding the Context

Heartbreak Tango continues the critical act begun in *Boquitas pintadas:* exposing the tango's lies and truths by juxtaposing them with the false and real values of Hollywood, by reproducing these diverse artifacts in an "analytic" ironic context. Again, to understand how *Boquitas* became *Heartbreak Tango,* the reader has to be conscious of the necessary transformations a text undergoes in a different medium, how relationships within and between texts change. The translator-as-critic must expand the context and take into consideration how a work will be received in other cultures, and therefore his/her own function as mediator between cultures and between past and present. Expanding the context also means understanding the relationship of the work to the author's entire opus – in Puig's case, the significance of Hollywood mythology throughout his writing.

As an interpreter of Latin American literature for North American readers, I had to recognize that the "collective memory" shared by Puig's readers outside of Argentina is not the tango but the mythology of Hollywood. Even the more widely distributed edition published in Spain underwent changes to make the book accessible in the way it had been for Argentine readers. For certain epigraphs, complete stanzas (see epigraphs I and IV) from the tangos were quoted – the one-liners wouldn't have been familiar enough. As in the American English edition, some of Le Pera's tangos were substituted by Homero Manzi's, which, as Puig noted, told stories with more concrete imagery.

An example of Manzi's are the translated lyrics in the epigraph to episode I – more vivid to an American reader than a literal translation of the original tango quotation. Even in the Spanish (Spain) edition, however, the lyrics could not work as *musically,* subliminally, implicitly signifying as in the original. But at the very least they had to serve, as in the English translation, an *explicit thematic* function. Hence Puig chose the tango epigraph to the opening episode of *Heartbreak,* since it underscored the nostalgic theme. "The shadows on the dance floor, this tango brings sad memories to mind. . . " to head episode IV, focused on the principal tragic couple, Nene and J. C., in the revised edition of *Boquitas* published in Spain.

Even though the translated epigraphs strayed semantically and formally away from the originals, they reinstated meaning in a broader sense, restaging the *function* of the original epigraphs, involving both a semantic and formal relationship between the head (epigraph) and the body of the episode.

Puig's participation in the translation process and the larger context of *Boquitas pintadas* within his creative world contribute significantly to the recuperation of meaning in these changes. Discussing the status of self-translation in the works of Samuel Beckett, Brian Fitch observed that the original is no longer necessarily the first work but rather the "sum total of textual material constituted by all the early drafts." (118) Although Beckett is a unique case, this observation applies to some extent to writers such as Puig and Cabrera Infante, who collaborate extensively on the translations of their work, and who even write in English.

Puig's "found objects" – taken from popular mass culture – cover a broad range of possible quotations, some of which appear in his originals. The fact that in the epigraph to episode I one tango can replace another reminds us not so much of translation's inadequacy as of the provisional, makeshift nature of the original. Many other tangos could have been potentially incorporated into the original *Boquitas*. As Borges tentatively concluded in his essay on the versions of Homer, "The concept of a definitive text pertains either to fatigue or to religion." The interchangeability of one tango for another, of a movie tag line for a tango, indicates that what matters here is not the monolithic value of a quoted text but rather the relationship between texts, and between the novel and its reader.

Remote but Intelligible

Like the novelist, the translator has to tinker to find words that he hopes will resonate in the ear of the reader. If the translated title was to fulfill somehow the original title's function, it had to register in the ear of its reader, to suggest nostalgia for a past era, to satirize sentimentality in popular culture, and to anchor the book in its Argentine, or at least Latin American, frame of reference. As is often the case with titles, *Heartbreak Tango* didn't come to us until the last minute, when I had nearly finished the manuscript. The necessity of translating lyrics essential to the plot was the mother of our invention:

Maldito Tango	*Blame That Tango*
en un taller feliz yo trabajaba, nunca senti deseos de bailar	I was happy in the sweatshop, felt no need to dance at all
hasta que un joven que a mi me enamoraba	till the day a gallant wooer came to take me to the hall
llevóme un día con él para tanguear	
fue mi obsesión el tango de aquel día,	My obsession, heartbreak tango,
en que mi alma con ansias se rindió,	plunged my soul to deepest sin
pues al bailar sentí en el corazón	as the music of that tango
que una dulce ilusión nació	set my poor heart all a-spin
. . . la culpa fue de aquel maldito tango,	I will always blame that tango

que mi galán enseñóme a bailar,   and the wooer with his wiles
y que despues hundiéndome en el fango,   once he'd made my heart break
me dio a entender que me iba a   all he told me was good-bye
abandonar

The words *heartbreak tango* come from our translation of *Maldito Tango* – the tango cited in the original episode XI that brings to Fanny's mind what happened between her and the bricklayer Pancho, who seduced and abandoned her; seduction and abandonment is of course the theme of this typically bitter tango. The translation was a *bricoleur*'s find because, simply, it worked, even without the unique form of the tango rhythm, in which the stress of each line falls darkly, downwardly at the end. The English reader had to be aware of the story told, and of the comical, heavy-handed, mechanically rhyming form in which it was told. Since the "Cursed Tango" was to blame for this tale of seduction, I translated its title (literally, "Damn Tango") as "Blame That Tango," a Hollywood resonance inspired in "Put the Blame on Mame," but also evoking a syncopated Latin rhythm, as in "Hold That Tiger." Our intuitive associations here were not random but, on the contrary, relevant to Puig's world. "Put the Blame on Mame" invokes the image of that treasonous femme fatale icon of Puig's first novel, Rita Hayworth, who sings and dances this number in *Gilda*, a 1940s film noir that Puig decided to quote in his following novel, *The Buenos Aires Affair*.

This translated song helped us reconstruct an appropriate context: In terms of theme and mood, it characterized the era, the exaggeratedly "Latin" frame of reference, and a principal theme of the book, disillusionment. We decided to quote different stanzas from it in two epigraphs (IV and IX) to prepare the reader for its appearance in episode XI. These lyrics would become an almost familiar motif – like *"boquitas pintadas"* – epitomizing the book for the reader. Intuitively seeking symmetry, we chose lyrics from "Blame That Tango," the words *heartbreak tango,* for the new book's title. *Heartbreak* resonates with indigenously North American associations, country and western, Elvis Presley's "Heartbreak Hotel" – wrong period but a similar corny effect.

Blame That Tango would have been too light, too frivolous; *Boquitas pintadas,* though corny and silly, does appeal to the nostalgic emotions of the reader. *Heartbreak Tango* is corny, but it does bring to the foreground "heartbreak" (synonymous with disillusionment), and makes *explicit* the tango's presence *implied* "effortlessly" in the original. To further (re)produce the book's coherence, we inscribed the tango in the subheadings for part I and part II. Part I, which recounts the romances of the main characters in the late Thirties, is subtitled *"Boquitas pintadas de rojo carmesí"* ("little lips painted carmine red"); part II, focused upon disillusionment and death, was appropriately subtitled *"Boquitas azules, violaceas, negras"* ("blue, violet, black little lips"). We pondered: What could be the conjunction between "tango" and "lipstick"? And we came up with the obvious, unconsciously inspired perhaps by Fanny's singing along with the tangos: A tango is sung. Part I's subheading became "A tango lingers on true red lips"; part II's, "A tango lingers on blue, violet, black lips." "True red" was a true *trouvaille*—the real name of a Forties lipstick—thanks to my sister Alice's memory.

The creative aspects of this tinkering are self-evident, but it is perhaps necessary to underscore the critical implications. We chose (and to be both a creator and a critic is to choose, to distinguish) to make prominent a song in the book that, though it had been quoted only once, in our interpretation was a potential key, an internally persuasive text. The implied became explicit.

Heartbreak Tango, with *tango* in the title, and the particular details of everyday Argentine life in every page of the text, marks its cultural difference, remaining a "remote" book despite the fact that Puig's humor is made "intelligible." Perhaps more important, *Heartbreak Tango* performs (like *Boquitas*) a critical task, exhibiting the false and real values of popular culture in Argentina by reproducing these textual ruins in an analytic context. The translation responds not only to the author's world, which includes the underlying cinematic texture that unifies all of Puig's novels, but, most urgently, to its potential reader(s).[2]

2. Cinema surfaces not only as a constant referent but as a formal model: As we worked on *The Buenos Aires Affair,* for example, Puig insisted that dialogue appear not in quotation marks but hyphenated, as in screenplays, partly to be "consistent" with the presentation of dialogue in *Rita Hayworth* and in *Heartbreak Tango* (letter MP to SJL, April 15, 1975).

Expanding the Context Further:

From Heartbreak Tango to The

Buenos Aires Affair

The Original Is a First Draft

EARLIER I mentioned the need to view *Boquitas*'s reception in the Hispanic world beyond the River Plate shores, to realize the concessions made in the more widely distributed edition published in Spain to a non-Argentine Spanish reader, less acquainted with the tango lyrics' unique connotations than the *rioplatenses*. By expanding the context further, we discover that even though French and Italian are first cousins of Spanish, the American English edition reproduces the book's rhetorical effects more closely. The "untranslatable" tango has reached a foreign readership through its juxtaposition with other mediating popular forms that have a similar effect upon their consumers; parody in both Americas is produced and received by a camp sensibility shared by urban North and South Americans alike.[1] Parity between Romance languages, on the other hand, often produces subtle distortions. It is easier to transcribe literally, but the same sentence or same phrasing conveys an entirely different spirit. Italo Calvino remarked, in *Translation*, on the disadvantages of translating his work into Spanish or French, as opposed to the "re-creative" advantages of English. (109)

1. As Judith Weiss put it, "It is not inconceivable that the English translation of *Tango* will become a *sine qua non*, like English versions of Borges with explanatory essays. . . . In any case, the changed epigraphs may also be an effective resource given the recent rage of nostalgia for the 1940s and the mixed analyses with which most North Americans are explaining that era of Hollywood." (139)

Manuel Puig was disappointed by the French translator's, or, rather, the French language's incapacity to parody the rhetorical artifices of provincial journalism because of its own formality. He observed that the weakest moment of *Les Mystères de Buenos Aires* was the imaginary interview of Gladys in a women's magazine, in which the main female character fantasizes about her life as a glamorous success story.[2] The corny language of the interview is "normal" in French, Puig noted with exasperation. The same problem had cropped up earlier with *Le plus beau tango du monde.* Concealing cold calculation, Mabel consults a lonely-hearts column in order to talk herself into breaking up with Juan Carlos. Her flowery words appear in French as normal epistolary discourse. The hypocritical Mabel explains that she's fed up with the quarrels she has with her parents over Juan Carlos (which is a lie because, unbeknownst to the parents, the lovers meet secretly in her bedroom), using the following frilly phrase: "my parents' rebukes, rebukes which like each drop of water wear away the stone." (38) The French reader "hears" this florid simile as normal, not exaggerated, rhetoric: *"c'est comme la goutte d'eau sur la pierre, ça finit par m'user."* (44)

The titles of these French translations are, on the other hand, wonderfully resonant. *Le plus beau tango du monde* recalls a tango well known in Europe, and *Les Mystères de Buenos Aires* alludes to the nineteenth-century model of the serial romance, Eugène Sue's melodramatic *Les Mystères de Paris.*

An exhaustive study of the other translations Puig collaborated on (French, Italian, Portuguese) would place the English version in a more panoramic perspective, by revealing the limitations resulting from sameness as well as difference in language and literary traditions, and by exposing the vast repertoire of possible material such as song lyrics, not used in the original and yet relevant to the original. Because of the author's creative collaboration in all these translations, the original becomes an *incomplete* project that continues to be elaborated. We may think that originals can radiate innumerable versions while a translation is one limited version out of many. Collaborations with

2. MP to SJL, letter, February 5, 1975. Also, see Gladys's interview in *The Buenos Aires Affair,* chapter VII, 100–115.

Cabrera Infante and Puig taught me, however, that the translation of one work could have re-creative repercussions on the next translation, and even the next original. The true original could be speculated to be, again, the accumulation of textual material constituted by all the early drafts. Why is the "first" text more original than the "second" when the author's work is "self-translated," as with Beckett, who commuted between French and English, or as with Puig and Cabrera Infante, active collaborators?

Originals and Translations: Mutual Influences in the Creative Act

Changes wrought in the making of *Heartbreak Tango* provoked choices made in *The Buenos Aires Affair* (1973), both original and translation, as well as in the edition of *Boquitas pintadas* published in Spain and in *El Beso de la Mujer Araña* (1976; *Kiss of the Spider Woman,* 1979). *The Buenos Aires Affair,* subtitled a "detective novel," follows *Boquitas* as a formal parody of yet another popular genre, structured by a suspenseful plot centered on an (apparent) crime. Just as Puig chose the serial romance to explore and explode provincial middle-class values in *Boquitas,* so did he choose the model of the detective story to "analyze" the repressive psychosexual causes and consequences of fascism in Argentina. Puig wanted to confront the political violence that marked the Buenos Aires of the 1970s, an atmosphere that he embodies in his two principal characters, Leo, an art critic, and Gladys, an artist. This detective novel, a mock case study of an archetypal sadomasochistic relationship, confirms with parodic precision the nexus Freud first perceived between psychoanalysis and detective work.

Each chapter is headed by a filmic quotation, snippets of dramatic dialogue from mostly American films highlighting iconic stars of the era such as Rita Hayworth and Joan Crawford. Quotations from movie ads, a strategy begun in the translation of *Boquitas,* inspired the epigraphs in *The Buenos Aires Affair.* These dialogues exhibit glamorized models of conduct that, again, contradict or parallel ironically the content/form of each chapter. The "signifier" of each movie quoted is not the phallus but the phallic woman, the lead actress who functions as a prototype. The female star's dilemma – or destiny – in each quote relates to some aspect of the psychodrama in Puig's novel. Precisely because Puig's women have "bought" the messages communicated by the movies, their lives are mediated by these images. Making women the dominant, pivotal figures in his books "was a revolutionary proposition," Puig said in *City 5:* "In a pampas town, to see everything revolving around a feminine figure was quite subversive." (72)

The following interchangeable epigraphs illustrate the continuum between translating and original tinkering:

1) In *Heartbreak Tango,* our translated quotation of dialogue from the Argentine movie *Swan Song,* starring Mecha Ortiz, the Argentine leading lady of the Forties, about the doomed affair between a musician and a socialite, became the epigraph to episode VII. *Swan Song (Canto del cisne)* duplicates the plot of the Hollywood film *Humoresque* (1946), starring Joan Crawford and John Garfield, an unlikely violinist. The punch line here – "To know a soul you must dominate it" – is a corny epigram defining archetypal male-female relationships in which the man must totally possess the woman. It contrasts comically with Juan Carlos's love letters to Nené, which both conceal and reveal insecurity under his macho (cock)iness in telltale misspellings.

Puig decided to use the same quotation, only in Spanish, for chapter XII of the original *The Buenos Aires Affair* – where it takes on more sinister associations. Chapter XII stages the psychopathic crime that Leo is about to perpetrate against Gladys; their passionate affair threatens to lead their dominant male/submissive female role-playing to its final sadomasochistic consequences. But we couldn't repeat this quotation in the English version, so we used a quotation from another American film in Puig's vast repertoire, *Lady Hamilton* (1941), whose punch line is "There is no after." Here the historical figure of Lady Hamilton, played by Vivien Leigh, another glamor icon of the era, now destitute, asserts how her life and hopes ended with the death of her lover, Lord Nelson, played by the equally gorgeous Laurence Olivier. Though this story differs from the plot of *Humoresque/Swan Song,* it shares the theme of a woman's doomed fate. Furthermore, another meaning surfaces in the ironic context of this quotation: Traditional heterosexuality, whose final consequence in Puig's view is sadomasochism, dies – "There is no after." Both "To know a soul. . . " and "There is no after" incisively foreshadow the chapter, but the translation "change" in *Heartbreak* made it possible to dip into an expanded pool of source material. "There is no after" (for male-female roles under patriarchy) enriches the next translation, *The Buenos Aires Affair,* by making explicit one of the original's main implications.

2) Another instance involves reconstructing textual links already connecting the author's originals, between the translations *Heartbreak Tango* and *The Buenos Aires Affair.* Chapter V of the original *Buenos Aires Affair* begins with a quotation from *Dinner at Eight,* starring the legendary Jean Harlow, the glamorous or reckless "dumb" blonde par excellence headed for a tragic destiny. In this episode an anonymous caller (Leo's older woman confidante, a sort of surrogate mother) dares to inform the police of the possibility that Leo may commit a psychopathic crime but fearfully refuses to reveal either Leo's or her name. This chapter serves to heighten the suspense and intensify the sinister atmosphere of the novel.

The original quotation features a comical argument between vulgar sex goddess Jean Harlow and her potbellied husband (played by Wallace Beery), a fraudulent businessman, in which he alludes to his sinister power while she persists in asserting her own, perhaps recklessly. The epigraph suggests a tension between vulnerability and power that develops in the chapter. Puig suggested that we quote from another Jean Harlow classic, *Red Dust.* We had already used the tag line from *Red Dust* in episode II of *Heartbreak* to epitomize the clichéd relationship in which the woman is swept off her feet by a macho stud. In the movie, Clark Gable, despite real-life insecurities, played as always a tough guy whom women couldn't resist. The comic dialogue quoted in *The Buenos Aires Affair* emphasizes not the thrill, however, as in *Heartbreak*'s third episode, but rather the danger the reckless Harlow risks in the middle of the jungle, surrounded by savage beasts:

> Jean Harlow, a platinum blonde in a Chinese prostitute's kimono, at night walks out onto the veranda of white hunter Clark Gable's house, and upon seeing a ferocious tiger, says: "Who are you looking for, alley cat?" The plantation's drunkard thinks the sound of the beast had frightened and awakened her, to which she responds, "I'm not used to sleeping nights anyhow." (65)

Danger is undercut by her obscene comedy, but the ironic play between danger and frivolity serves to highlight the tension created by the banal phone conversation between Leo's confidante and the police officer, and by the danger lurking, that of classic stud Leo turned psychopathic killer.

Both quotations *serve,* in complementary ways, but what is interesting to observe here is the created continuity between *Heartbreak* and *Affair* in English. The same source, *Red Dust,* serves to emphasize both the alienating gaps between men and women in *Heartbreak* and the potentially destructive consequences of that alienation in *The Buenos Aires Affair.*

3) Another of the "adopted" epigraphs in *Heartbreak Tango* (episode XV), the tag line from the movie *Cat People,* blossomed into the first movie narrated by Molina in chapter I of *Kiss of the Spider Woman:* "She was one of the dreaded Cat People/ – doomed to slink and prowl by night. . . /fearing always that a lover's kiss might / change her into a snarling, crawling killer!" (201) In *Heartbreak Tango* this quotation exaggerates the *cattiness* and frustration of Juan Carlos's sister Celina, who, thinking Nené is responsible for Juan Carlos's death, takes petty revenge in this episode. The "cat people" theme deepens in *Kiss of the Spider Woman,* however, into a metaphoric representation of sexual repression and its flip side, violence.

All of Puig's novels are interrelated through a vast network of pop or mass media materials. Like Toto's "revisions" of movie plots, the device that turned into Molina's narratives in *Kiss,* Puig's texts re-create/translate/interpret themselves as well as a broad range of cross-cultural artifacts. The title *The Buenos Aires Affair* obviously did not present any problems in English translation. Indeed, Puig claimed to me that one of the reasons he chose this "Hitchcockian" title was to avoid the complications of *Boquitas.* Even though this was, if anything, a secondary motive, these words *the Buenos Aires affair* are only one more sign of the interdependence of translation and original, and of the pervasive influence practiced by North American culture upon that diverse continent called Latin America.

From Cuba with a Song

Like Puig and Cabrera Infante, Severo Sarduy had grown up adoring the kitsch icons of the American movies: Marlene Dietrich, Doris Day, Rock Hudson, and later James Bond. When referring to my role as his translator, he said in an autobiographical "Chronology": "Later I would meet someone who likes James Bond as much as I do, an American girl who has now finished the English version of *De donde son los cantantes,* called *From Cuba with a Song.* It's about, of course, an emperor of the dynasty of the same name: what a smell of fried rice, eh, Jill!" (26) A joke, of course – *De donde* is *not* about an emperor of the Song Dynasty – but also typical of Sarduy's devious deferrals of referentiality, yielding mirthfully to the pleasures of the text. Affinities with Sarduy were, and still are, the tenuous echoes of shared hyperboles, the free play of sizzling signifiers.

Sarduy's second novella, *De donde son los cantantes,* literally, "from where are the singers," would appear in an anthology featuring the metamorphic theme of transvestism, along with two other novellas of the Sixties by better-known Latin American writers: *El lugar sin límites* (*Hell Has No Limits*) by the Chilean José Donoso and *Zona sagrada* (*Holy Place*) by the Mexican writer Carlos Fuentes. Fuentes convinced E. P. Dutton, Borges's and Puig's publisher, to take on this unconventional project, which also had its incestuous side since Donoso had dedicated *El lugar sin límites* to Rita and Carlos Fuentes. Because these unholy three were neither family sagas nor historical novels about dictators but weird carnivalesque fantasies – and Sarduy was an unknown

—this "package deal" seemed the only way to make these novellas even marginally palatable to commercial publishing. Cabrera Infante predicted in a letter (July 21, 1972) a difficult reception for *De donde:* "The American critic will receive it as an explosion of words and images—maybe the operative word is implosion."

Severo warned me against taking on this extravagant project and wrote, in hyperbolic Cuban mulatta style : ". . . girl, how are you going to deal with the other two novels?. . . Because never [—but never say never—] will you finish, my poor dear, kisses, a spray of caresses. . . . " (June 21, 1970) I translated the three novellas in one year (1970–71).

Transvestism and homosexuality connect these three works, each of whose principal characters cross sexual boundaries. But transvestism also unveils metaphorically a common Latin American experience shared by the three countries represented, a search for cultural identity. In different regions and historical moments, "Latin America" has worn the mask of an Indian, an African, a Spaniard, a Frenchman, and a North American. But where is the real face behind all these masks? Sarduy envisions our sexual identities as cultural products, and sees cultures themselves, particularly in Latin America, as "cross-dressers"; González Echevarría sums up the function of transvestism in Sarduy's work:

> Transvestism is the common denominator in this view of culture and identity, the most visible parts of which are the physical transformations and disfigurements produced by all desire. For Sarduy, to desire is to disfigure, to kill. Cuban and Latin American culture, machismo—everything is a cultural product, including sex roles. (vii)

Fuentes suggested a clever title for the volume: The Baudyville Trio. And Sarduy thought of calling it, in playful irony, TTT2 (= Transgressive Tryptic of Transvestites). But the book's editor decided against these "frivolous" conceits and chose instead what turned out to be a misnomer: *Triple Cross.* The profane image of a transvestite Christ on the Cross in "The Entry of Christ in Havana"—the final scene of Sarduy's novella and one of many sacrilegious moments in these narratives featuring "cross-dressers—inspired the editor to choose *Triple Cross.* This title is confusing not only because the reader's first association is *not* that of a transvestite Christ but mainly because, invoking "double cross," it suggests a spy intrigue. *Triple Cross* was later used, more appropriately, as the title of a best-selling spy novel.

De donde son los cantantes (From Where Are the Singers) quotes a well-known Cuban song, *"El son de la loma,"* the "son" of the hills. *Son* is explicitly a predicate verb here, but implicitly a noun, the generic name of a traditional song form—out of which the cha-cha would later evolve—and also implies a pleasing sound. Songs and poems, Cuban music and the music of the Spanish language, constitute some of the most untranslatable elements in Sarduy's discourse. How to sing along when the original music cannot be heard? His title, an unfinished question without its expected question mark, brings to the (Cuban) reader's mind not only a particular song and its folkloric, historical associations but music's elusive poetry. Like *Boquitas pintadas,* like all good titles, *De donde son los cantantes* is a reigning motif. A whole stanza is quoted at a self-commentative moment when transvestite buffoons Help and Mercy both admit defeat in their search for their idol, Mortal, both denying and recognizing their Cubanness: *"Mamá yo quiero saber/de donde son los cantantes,/que los siento muy galantes/y los quiero conocer."* (111) These words literally mean "Mama I want to know/ where the singers are from/ I find them very gallant/ and I want to meet them," but I translated them, forcing the rhyme and introducing the doubly understood "gay," as

> Mama those singers so gay
> are they from ol' Havana bay?
> oh how I like their rhythm
> oh how I'd like to know them (301)

"From Where Are the Singers" denotes a question without a question mark and, by association, a quest or a series of questions and quests that the narrative poses and leads the reader through: quests that are never resolved, or questions (and answers) that are deferred. In an essay on the tradition of questions in ancient Chinese poetry, the following observation by Eliot Weinberger throws light on Sarduy's open-ended quest(ion):

> A question is the only complete grammatical structure that cannot exist by itself—it must always take us somewhere else, to another sentence or to an unspoken (unspeakable) unknown. It is *the piece of ordinary speech closest to a*

line of poetry [my italics]. Questions, like poems, like sacred formulae, are articulations of desire. The sacred formula: a concentration of power in order to possess what one does not have, become what one is not. The question: to reach the answer, or the unanswerable. Poetry: to find out, or, in Octavio Paz's phrase, "to find the way out". (99)

The "identity" of Cuba appears to be the central quest in Sarduy's novella, structured as a parody of Cuban history by tracing, in three parts, the search for the "Beloved" through three racial components of Cuban civilization (Chinese, African, Hispanic), ending in a hallucinatory version of Fidel's triumphant entry into Havana in 1959. The searchers metamorphose but are always avatars of Help and Mercy, a double configuration of Everyman (or woman). Part I tells of General Mortal's unrequited lust for Lotus Flower, a Chinese transvestite in the infamous Shanghai theater of Havana's Chinatown; part II, the rise and fall of an ambitious black singer, Dolores Rondón, who marries a corrupt politician (she could be an avatar of Beba Longoria in *TTT*); part III, the quest of two devotees of Christ who, setting out in fifteenth-century Spain and ending up in a futuristic twentieth-century Havana, search for the resurrected Beloved. The lecherous General who fails to seduce the Chinese transvestite, Dolores who fails to secure power through her senator, Help and Mercy who seek "Mortal" only to end up with a rotten wooden effigy of Christ: These are failed quests just as Sarduy's diverse representation of what we could define as the Cuban language and culture offers tantalizing glimpses but cannot "portray" Cuba.

The suspended question posed by this work suggests the irrelevance of a dialectic between question and answer, at least where artistic representation is concerned. This suspension also characterizes the problematic categorization of Sarduy's "works" – prose and/or poetry, Zen meditations and/or perverse fantasies – and the defining of the Author, normally identified by a distinct style. In their rich heterogeneity, Sarduy's texts are, of course, identifiable; only Sarduy combines Cuban salsa with jargon stolen from French literary theory. But since his characters' speech leaps from sixteenth to the twentieth century, from Spain to Camagüey or Havana, from Cuban slang to mutilated quotations from classical poets, from popular songs to political rhetoric from Cuban electoral campaigns, from American English advertising propaganda to French insults or German philosophical terms, it is impossible to pinpoint a consistent tone.

The only possible translation of this text, which betrays Authorship and origin, is to reinstate the allusiveness of the quotations, to substitute references, and to translate translations. Or, taking one step further, to reproduce not an idea but an effect. That is, a simulation. Before considering praxis – which hopefully will confirm these general remarks – it would be illuminating to examine Sarduy's literary ideology, or, rather, theory of translation.

Theory: Simulation

Sarduy demythicizes the original in perhaps even more devastating terms than Cabrera Infante's and Puig's fictional betrayals. The original is an imposture, a "bad" copy that – unlike the good copy in Platonic idealism – reproduces not a presence but an absence, a void. In his essay *"La simulación"* (1982) Sarduy traces the continuity of simulation in artistic procedures and esthetics from the baroque period to the twentieth century, as well as from East to West: Simulation inverts not only the represented (as in Picasso's parody of Velázquez's *Meninas*) but "the intent to represent." (106)

Sarduy's essays are fanciful, just as his novels are essay-poems and his poetry prose – always subverting the will to represent. In Sarduy, erudition and imagination go hand in hand, in Borgesian mode, but more directly following Lezama Lima, whose Orientalism, whimsical erudition, and distracted syntax Sarduy has inherited. When his first collection of essays, *Escritos sobre un cuerpo,* was published in 1969, it received a mixed reception in Buenos Aires. Sarduy remarks in his "Chronology,"

> A moron – inspired, it is true, by another – writes in one of those bulletins which proliferate in the world of Books that my criticism is to Criticism what Argentine slang is to Castillian Spanish. Good God, when was I ever interested in Criticism with a capital C, or Castillian! (26)

These essays trace a link between sexuality and writing as supplementary, respectively superseding biological imperatives and the drive for meaning.

In a brief essay titled "Translatio and Religio" (1973) Sarduy places in question the ideology of translation, which presupposes the ideology of an original. If no text is finally the center outside of a given and never completely defined context, the translator becomes a "translator of translations." Taking Oriental philosophies as a practical guide, Sarduy writes in *"La simulación"* that according to Zen Buddhist thought, the world did not begin with a Creator: "In the beginning there is Nothing (wu); Nothing has no name. From nothing One is born; One has no form." (113)

Logocentric Western religion offers the best textual example of the original's problematic presence, the Bible, which exists only as "versions." As Julien Green notes in *Le Langage et Son Double,* in an essay titled "Translation and the Fields of Scripture" (1941), the word *version* – taken for granted in Scriptural discussion, for example, *The King James Version* – presupposes an original interpretation, hence a departure, a displacement. The issue has been complicated further: The closest, or oldest versions are not necessarily the most faithful, some have argued. Green cites the claim that spoken English is closer to spoken Hebrew than Latin – and since the Bible is a collection of tales *told...*

In "Translatio and Religio" Sarduy finds his poetic paradigm for translation in "the art that always precedes all others: painting." (8) Modern painting's response to the revolution of photography was at first to deny representation, to stress abstract expression, in which the subject, the perceiver still figures as center, but no longer objective, now a subjective experimenter. The Abstract Expressionists concerned themselves with the material of painting and how it is manipulated, rather than its referent. A paradoxically more subversive response was found in the American hyperrealism of the Seventies: "No longer a matter of going in the opposite direction from photography, but rather 'paying it back in its own coin,' going in the same direction, *except further and alongside it.*" He continues:

> To achieve, in representing reality, obsessive clarity down to the tiniest, most delirious detail; to go further: shuffling, superimposing the image upon itself, making it *plus vraie que nature,* compulsively meticulous. . . . The photo-realists work from photographs: their paintings condense, expose, contradict photographs: reflections, reflections in the reflections, pores, hairdos painted hair by hair, the reduction of an entire room in the camera's eye. . . .

Sarduy concludes that the translator's "way out," or response to computers that translate (there's sinister humor here: The computer has not taken over – yet – the artist's function), is "to exaggerate a both programmed and parodical precision."

Praxis: With a Song

Translating Sarduy's meticulous tapestries exercises one's capacity for parodic precision not only because a translation needs to sketch precisely what is often more obscure in the original but because the detailed "original" is already a translation, a parody. Sarduy's texts are fraught with mostly intentional misquotations and often unintentional misspellings – editorial distractions, or *"distracciones severianas,"* as Severo remarked in a letter (August 12, 1981) when I asked him to explain why "pullover" in his novel *Maitreya* appeared once as "pullover," another time as "pullover." Sarduy's Cuban Spanish is "contaminated" or enriched by many sources, influenced by years of self-exile in France as well as other linguistic invasions. Perhaps in these "imperfections" Sarduy again follows in Lezama's footsteps; there is much that is playfully and/or unintentionally imprecise in Sarduy's erudition and citations, as when, in *From Cuba with a Song,* he attributes a quotation from Wallace Stevens ("snakes eat toads, bulls eats snakes") to Robert Frost. (265)

In his *misquotations,* be it of classic texts or commonplace phrases, Sarduy favors the notion of translation. When I inquired about the "origins" of two quotations so as to be able to seek out if not the originals at least the published translations, he advised me (June 21, 1970):

> Rewrite the quotations [in *De donde,* 77] from the Bible and from "Electra" not only so as not to have to bother looking for them but out of literary ideology. In *Cobra . . .* I am translating back into French the quotations from Flaubert which before I had translated into Spanish, to end up with a parallel text. This is much more amusing.[1]

Hence the tragic Biblical quotation become "wails of woe, gnashing of teeth, howls that unhinge the earth." (278) Sarduy's writerly advice echoes, and precedes, similar suggestions from Cabrera Infante upon

---

1. Philippe Sollers translated *Cobra* into French in close collaboration with Sarduy.

my inquiry into the sources of *Vista del amanecer en el trópico*. Where the reader is the writer, where translation and writing are parallel, continuous activities, Flaubert's "version" inevitably produces other versions, even in the same language, among which Sarduy's parallel version, standing "alongside" Flaubert's, is a parodic precision. *"De donde son los cantantes"* is and isn't a quotation, and thus is emblematic of Sarduy's rhetorical strategy. The question, already only an indirect question in the original lyrics, no longer appears as a question in Sarduy's title. It makes explicit its elliptical nature by remaining unfinished, even as a question. A double-entendre already implied in the "original" referent or song, it means both "They come/are from the hills" and *"Son* of the Hills." Sarduy uses this paronomasia in (the Cuban) language to introduce a parodic difference between the song and the (mis)quoted lyrics, stressing the pun, which postpones an answer, implying that the simple answer given in the song is not enough – or better, that it inevitably circles back upon itself. "From Where Are the Singers" or "Where the Singers Come From" would not have reproduced the folkloric allusion or the pun on *son*. "From Cuba with a Song" came about in an attempt to reestablish the *effect* of the original (mis)quotation.

The title's elliptic allusiveness provoked translator and consultants to come up with at least one hallucinatory, open-ended alternative: "Cuban Moon Is Smiling." This mysterious phrase – in which the grammatical ellipse recalls the syntax of Chinese English speakers – mentions Cuba, suggests its archetypal tropical moonlight and alludes to the most anthropologically fanciful sector of the book, the Chinese part I, "By the River of Rose Ashes." But this phrase free-floated much too much, without the grounding of a referent; for the publisher it would have exaggerated the already evident opacity of the text itself, as Cabrera Infante forewarned. In that same letter Cabrera Infante comments, after reading the translation,

> Your text is a true texture. . . . My only disagreement is with your keeping some of the names of tropical fruits like *caimitos* and not finding an American equivalent. I think Severo uses it with a pictorial sense that becomes all too exotic (in the word-sense) in your translation. Perhaps berries would have been better. In any case it is a very minor point and some of your ren-

148

derings are really closer to the tour de force than in *TTT* – perhaps due to the fact that Severo is writing a very feminine prose. I particularly liked some of your phrasing, "Rose Ashes becomes a cloud, a baby fawn, *the murmur of the river among its pebbles* [his italics] – much better than the original."

Cabrera Infante's sexist humor shines through – equating Sarduy's gay esthetics with the feminine – but the most interesting revelation is his double standard as a conventional translation critic and a radical self-translator. He advised me to make Sarduy's text more accessible by eliminating foreign words but often insisted upon keeping exotic words and references in translating his own books – and in both cases he was right. "In a Forest of Havana," an exotic misquotation because the forest is really a park, comes from a popular refrain quoted in the Chinese chapter, "In the forest of Havana/a Chinee lost her way . . . " (242). This phrase could suggest by association a labyrinth where one gets lost, and thus a search since one must seek a way out, but such a title might have overtaxed the reader's associative powers.

A list followed, some of the entries inspired in the titles of cha-chas or other Latin tropicalia adopted by the English-speaking world, including an Infantesque suggestion, "Havana for a Night," sung by the self-mocking Mae West: "Havana for a Night" – remember – became a candidate for the title of *La habana para un infante difunto*. The list sprang from an associative thought process, restating the title's origin-less questioning, but reinstating, making explicit the Cuban content, and stressing the presence of song: "Havana Song," "They Sang in Cuba," "They Come from Havana?", "Those Singers from Ol' Havana Bay" (the latter two quotations from the translation of the *"son"*). *Song* and *from* come up again and again, the preposition pointing backwards toward origin. Finally, inspired by James Bond, one of Sarduy's favorite pop figures at that moment, and also inspired in the duel over Cuba between the United States and the Soviet Union, I thought of "From Cuba with Love."

To misquote *From Russia with Love*, a foreign mass culture referent, was not inconsistent with *De donde*, since the book already contained numerous caricaturesque allusions to the invasive civilizations and ideologies that have inexorably shaped Cuban history. In part I, Mortal is momentarily seduced away from Lotus, his Oriental object of desire, by avatars of Help and Mercy dressed as motorcycle molls, their helmets adorned with Fifties iconography: "... color pictures of Elvis Presley, James Dean pins, autographs by Paul Anka, locks of hair from Tab Hunter, Pat Boone's fingerprints, and Rock Hudson's *measurements*." (251) "From Cuba with Love" repeats a cliché, a formulaic dedication pertinent to Sarduy's texts, where commonplaces, the residues of language, are quoted and misquoted. *"De donde son los cantantes,"* a quotation marking the loss of meaning, points to the demise of folklore as the primal source of truth. James Bond movies, self-consciously parodical, mark the demise of another manifestation of popular culture, the spy genre, in part by exaggerating to absurd extremes the genre's technological excess.

Sarduy's playful response to "From Cuba with Love" was prefaced by praise of the baroque extravagance of another Bond film, *Diamonds Are Forever,* whose plot is almost impossible to disentangle:

> Now I don't feel so cheated by not having been the author of *Diamonds Are Forever* which, I agree with you, is divine for its heavy ornamentality, its baroque transvestism, its conceptual labyrinth. Of all the titles you propose I prefer *From Cuba with Love,* simply because it sounds like it will sell and because it evokes the supermacho CIA agent. Now that Cuban journalism insists upon my filiation with that benevolent institution, nothing could be more opportune. (Jan. 4, 1972)

Sarduy's concern here, like his publisher's, includes the pragmatic, but the truth is that no title would have turned Sarduy's "weavings" into a mass-marketable product.

"Diamonds are forever," a hyperbolic cliché that becomes visualized in the Bond superproduction, brings out comments by Sarduy that throw light upon the relationship between *De donde* and *From Cuba.* The first meeting point is the baroque strain in twentieth-century pop culture: How better, indeed, to respond to the complexities and contradictions of modern life, in which technology harnessed for progress threatens to annihilate humanity, than through "conceptual labyrinths" like Bond movies and Sarduy novels. The second crossroads where translations and original meet is political: Just as *De donde* ends in parodic homage to *the* turning point in Cuban history, turning Fidel's entry into Havana into Christ's road to a futuristic Calvary, the allusion to *From Russian with Love* responds to the Stalinist turning of Cuban politics in the Seventies, in which it became a policy to discredit Cuba's exiled intelligent(c)ia.

An Answer to a Question?

From Cuba with Love made its way to *From Cuba with a Song* to signal more clearly the text's poetic function as a song, and its Cubanity, making explicit what was implied in the original title. Though not a grammatical ellipsis like the original, this title could also be an incomplete answer to a suspended question, a fragment of a sentence that in this case might be "They come from Cuba with a song." It completes the original half-sentence: "The singers are from... Cuba with a song" not in a linear but in a circular way, *from* the syntactic link both posing and responding to the enigma of origin. In translation the enigma becomes explicit, providing an answer that still remains an enigma: Who or what is from Cuba with a song and what does it *mean* to be from Cuba?

Sarduy plays upon the identity crisis of the Cuban exile within a larger philosophical framework of centerlessness, and from the perspective of Ibero-America's heterogeneity: To be Cuban is to be always in exile. He denies the dichotomy between exile and home as he does between translation and original – equating exile and translation – and, finally, between self and other. Sarduy remarks to interviewer Danubio Torres Fierro in *Memoria Plural:* "I would say: there is no nostalgia, no memory, no image of time passing, simply because I've never left Cuba. I, another I, the other I, am here – there. ... Memory has no place, or rather constitutes the place of origin, the maternal tongue." (249) Sarduy questions the "mother tongue," "origin," "one's own language," which is perhaps "the most displaced, the most alienated of all," as Paul de Man writes in his exegesis of Benjamin's "Task of the Translator." (92)

The "task of the translator" is never ended. "Song" expresses both translation's (writing's) metaphoric attempt and its literal failure to be primary, to signify. It functions as an unmistakable emblem of the book – a song, or words as music – and at the same time metaphorically – or better, metonymically – speaks of an ever-widening circle of signifiers deferring signification.

The Mysterious Orient

Like many *trouvailles,* the title came about as an intuitive mimetic response: bringing forth the (substantive) *son* implied in the original. It is not entirely in jest that Sarduy claims the "supplementary" reference to the Song Dynasty. The mysterious Orient enters apocryphally, or at least hyperbolically, as one of the three fundamental Cuban cultures, hence the impulse behind "Cuban Moon Is Smiling" finally had its way! Culture is the product of a series of displacements and errors: Columbus, whose texts are quoted in the last section, thought that the Caribbean islands were part of India and Japan; the Spaniard in the first part chases a transvestite he mistakes for a gorgeous Chinese vedette.

Havana's Chinatown, and especially the notorious Shanghai Theater, above all emblematize a disfigured, erroneous, or postponed identity in *De donde.* The Chinese transvestite actress who seduces the General with her fleeting (dis)appearance is the crossroads of many polyvalences: sexual and cultural identity, the endless slippage of writing. One Cuban scholar, José Arrom, reacted indignantly to Sarduy's omission of the pre-Columbian Taino component of Cuban history, which is, anthropologically, more significant to Cuba's racial make-up than the Chinese immigration to the Americas in the aftermath of the Boxer revolt. Sarduy does not pursue, however, an originary prehistory but rather the text History, an endless series of misinterpretations, of translations.

The Eastern world – particularly India – and its philosophies, which dethrone the rational subject and offer alternative cosmogonies to Western logocentrism, were to become increasingly prominent in Sarduy's writings, particularly his next two novels, *Cobra* and *Maitreya.* The Orient, the other side of the mirror, appears already in *De donde* as a referent but, more precisely, as a parodic mirror: Cuba's enigmatic identity is exemplified in the fugitive convergence of the Hispanic General and the inscrutable transvestite whose signals he fails to decode.

"From Cuba with a Song," a signatory formula, could be the signature of one who dedicates a book to another, but whose? The Author's dethroning is restated, stressed *even further* in English, the language of displacement shared by exiles from all corners of the world. The translation's title seems to answer the "original" question, to serve as a response – as all translation should – to a previous text, making explicit the implied. At the same time, since a question's meaning is its possible true answers, both titles are "suspended thoughts."[2] *From Cuba with a Song* responds by extending the mystery, responding – like the original title – as neither question nor answer but from the void of language's irreducible polyvalence.

2. A question is a "suspended thought": "The meaning of a question [according to linguists] is all its possible answers – or all its true answers." (Weinberger, 98)

Between Text(ure)s: Petit
Ensemble Caravaggesque

*Work on good prose has three steps: a musical stage when it
is composed, an architectonic one when it is built, and a tex-
tile one when it is woven.*

WALTER BENJAMIN

S ARDUY'S "treasonous" reproductions recycle
rather than break with their model. The original is already a subversion, he says in *"La simulación";* the "copy" reminds us of the original's
savagery. Baroque art follows its classical models: Velázquez's dwarfs
exaggerate the figural asymmetries that even classical painting, intentionally or not, often conveys. Boucher's neoclassical portrait of "Madame Bergeret" is perfect except that she looks either like a precocious
little girl dressed as a great lady or an aristocratic dwarf.

To dramatize the ongoing dialogue in and between *Cobra* and its
translation I have chosen a passage whose model is pictorial, literally
"visible," a paragraph from the chapter *"Enana Blanca"* ("White
Dwarf"), subtitled in original and translation *"Petit Ensemble Caravaggesque":*

> *Eran enanas, pero no para tanto.*
> *El relato que precede, como todos los de la infundiosa Señora, adolece de la
> hipérbole tapageuse, el rococó abracadrabante y la exageración sin coto. Eran
> enanas, sí, pero como cualquier enano. Tenía, por ejemplo, la Señora, las propor-
> ciones—"y también la compostura y majestad!"—de la azafata de una infanta
> prognática parada junto a un galgo que pisa un pajecillo y contemplando a los
> monarcas que posan. En cuanto a Cobrita, digamos que era exactamente como una
> niña albina, coronada y raquítica, que atraviesa el desfile de una compañía de ar-
> cabuceros tironeada por un fámulo y con un pollo muerto amarrado a la cintura.*
> (47–48)

Here Sarduy flaunts the artificiality of his characters, La Señora and Cobra (now Cobrita), who have undergone "reductionist" metamorphoses. They are not anchored in real life but translated from paintings, versions of iconic figures by Rembrandt and Velázquez – masters of realism under the aegis of Caravaggio.

The narrator sets out to describe in colloquial, "realist" language the characters, claiming that the previous description was a big "rococo" lie. But he then proceeds through even more artificial simili, in a more archaic, rhetorical Spanish, to describe them. The text carries nonreferentiality to its extremes by alluding only obliquely to the paintings. The allusions to the long-nosed princess's attendant (with whom La Señora is compared) and to the spotlighted figure of a bizarre little girl (with whom Cobrita is compared) presuppose a reader familiar with at least two chestnuts of pictorial culture, popularly known as *Las Meninas* (1656) and *La Ronde de Nuit* (1642), or *The Night Watch*.[1]

The allusions are further obscured by the narrator's "Caravaggesque" deformations, underscoring metonymically certain minor details that metamorphose even further in translation: The page stepping on the greyhound is not the first, nor perhaps even the last detail viewers of *Las Meninas* will normally notice. Sarduy practices here what he calls "Caravaggismo": The "chiaroscuro" technique in which the "brutal" projection of light serves as a condensing procedure to catch the eye, making it concentrate on one of the figures in each painting. In *La simulación* he describes how "Caravaggismo" focuses on

> a part of the body, or one of its metonyms. . . . The rest of the body – paradoxically the rest, the remains – is relegated to a distant, anonymous zone, excluded from representation and desire. . . (57)

Elsewhere in *La simulación* Sarduy describes the effect of this "copy":

> it revives the revenge of the model, rescuing its iconoclastic energy; the irreverent copy both subverts classical figuration and awakens, provokes the blasphemy already contained in it: the barely hidden teratology of the Meninas. . . the twisted faces of Rembrandt. . . (123; my translation)

1. *Las Meninas* was originally called, descriptively, *"La familia de Felipe II"* (since 1666). It would have been heresy to refer to this royal family portrait as *"Las meninas"* – first introduced by Pedro de Madrazo in his 1843 Catalogue. See *El Prado Básico,* ed. J. Rogelio Buendia (Madrid: Silex, 1982), 222.

An Irreverent Copy

Not only the details Sarduy selects, but also the manner in which he describes them produces a "metonymical dismemberment." Rembrandt's chubby looking little girl, or deformed dwarf, becomes *"una niña albina, coronada y raquítica."* *Raquítica* denotes "rickettsial," deformed in the sense of feeble, suffering from malnutrition. Like Flaubert, Sarduy has said that he is a realistic writer and just copies what he sees. "She's raquítica, that is, small, deformed, in relation to the men, the figures surrounding her," he responded to my query. He translates what he sees in the frame into yet another context, language. The result is an "irreverent copy" that reminds the reader of the original's distortion of classical figuration: Is she a little girl, someone's daughter, or some fantastic, dwarflike presence? André Malraux has spoken of the chicken or duck tied to her waist as the intrusion of the fantastic, the inexplicable in realist painting – or does this dead bird (possibly a rooster?) symbolize metonymically the painting's subject matter, the militia company of Captain Frans Banning Cocq?

Sarduy's "copy" establishes immediately a distance through the precious French subtitle, which announces a foreign perspective upon the Spanish text and the supposed Italian pictorial model. He irreverently intermingles colloquial vulgarisms with an archaic Spanish *("y también la compostura y majestad")* appropriate to the baroque iconography but creating a blasphemous effect by equating classical figures with his macaronic marionettes. His irreverence recalls the underlying irreverence of the original and its original. Velázquez's models were the noble yet prognathic Hapsburgs: Reality is monstrous. Rembrandt's supposed group portrait of the respectable, bourgeois voluntary militia company of Delft undermined its own official function by highlighting a phantasmal, marginal figure, decentering the viewer's attention onto a grotesque detail.

The Translation

First, the rough draft (the composite of mine and a graduate student's):
"Petit Ensemble Caravaggesque"
["Little Caravaggesque Ensemble"]

                              [only to a certain extent]
  1) They were dwarfs, but [let's not overdo it].

                                            [insidious Lady]
  2) The preceding story, like all stories of the [fibbing Madam], suffers
  from [boisterous, swashbuckling   abracadabra] [blustering] hyperbole,
  [voodooing] rococo and boundless exaggeration.

  [Oh yes, they were female dwarfs, but just like any other male ones.]
  3) [Yes, they were dwarfs but like any old dwarfs.]

            [Lady]   [as well as the majesty and
  4) The [Madam], for example, had the proportions –
  composure of a salient jawed infanta's chamber maid]   – of
  the lady-in-waiting of a prognathic princess standing beside a page who
  steps on a greyhound, watching the monarchs pose.
  5) As to Cobrita [little Cobra], let us say that she was exactly
                  [rickettsia]   [parade, round]
  like a crowned and [rickety] albino girl crossing the [march] of a [militia
  company, company of musketeers]   [carrying] [harquebuse company],
  pulled along by a servant and [with] a dead chicken tied to her waist.

Final draft:

                        "Petit Ensemble Caravaggesque"

  1) They were dwarfs, but let's not overdo it.
  2) The preceding tale, like all the insidious Madam's stories, suffers
  from swashbuckling hyperbole, abracadabra rococo and boundless exaggeration. 3) Yes, they were dwarfs, but like any old dwarfs. 4) The
  Madam, for example, had the proportions – "and also the poise and
  majesty!" – of a prognathic infanta's lady-in-waiting standing beside a
  page who steps on a greyhound, watching the monarchs pose. 5) As to
  Cobrita, let us say that she was exactly like a crowned and rickety albino
  girl, crossing a company of musketeers on their nightwatch, pulled along
  by a servant and carrying a dead chicken tied to her waist. (*Cobra*, 29)

"Petit Ensemble Caravaggesque" serves the same precious effect in English as in Spanish. *Cobra* presupposes a "hypothetical" reader whose
knowledge includes French as well as the highlights of art history.
French, the language of Sarduy's exile, and traditionally the language
of "culture" for Latin America, constantly invades his discourse, often
as Gallicisms already accepted into the Spanish language.
  Sentence 1 is spoken, and slightly sarcastically, to set off the rhetori-

cal bombast and archaic vocabulary that follow. Sarduy's humor is based also on the juxtapositions of verbal contradiction between "smallness" (*enanas*) and "exaggeration" (*para tanto* = so *much*); hence "overdo it" is more comical than the more modified "to a certain extent."

Sentence 2: So as not to repeat "stories" (not repeated in the Spanish either) "tale" came in not only as an appropriately archaic word but also to pinpoint the Señora's exaggerated tale-telling. Repetitions are weak unless they serve an intentional emphatic effect, as with "dwarfs" in the next sentence. The more literary "insidious" followed *infundiosa*, more rhetorical than its more common synonym *mentirosa*, or "fibbing."

The rococo adjectives *tapageuse, abracadabrante, sin coto* demanded recherché responses. The Gallicism *tapaguese*, meaning "rowdy," "flashy," and Sarduy's invented "abracadabrante" provided an artificial note of exaggeration. "Rococo abracadabrante" contains anagrammatically—as occurs throughout the book—the word *Cobra*, hence the equally neologistic transformation of abracadabra into an adjective: "abracadabra rococo." What would suggest rowdy and flashy in an archaic, resounding form? "Swashbuckling" came up in association with the image of Rembrandt's militia company, but evoked as much by Sarduy's seventeenth-century words as by their referents. Vaguely onomatopoeic, "swashbuckling" reinstates the opacity, the intentional sonority of Sarduy's language, and suggests pirates or musketeers—archaic, rowdy, flashy figures familiar to English readers. It announces the Rembrandt image, whose innovation consisted not only in the mysterious detail of the dwarf and servant, but in going beyond the constraints of classical portraiture by presenting the characters in action, brandishing swords.

"Swashbuckling hyperbole" resonates like "hiperbole tapageuse" because of its slight alliteration, the fricative *b* replacing the function of the fricative *p*. "Boundless" helps to round out the alliterative series of *b*s in "swashbuckling, hyperbole, abracadabra."

Sentence 3: The sexual difference marked in the Spanish *enana-enano* underscores the fact that these characters are transvestites, females that are "really" male, and works smoothly in Spanish because all nouns are gender-identified. In English the distinction becomes stylistically awkward, forcing the writer to make a choice. The *explicit* meaning of the Spanish sentence, in which the masculine *cualquier enano* indicates the species "dwarf," does come out in the final English version: "They [specifically] were dwarfs but like any old dwarf [generically]." The implied female-male duality enunciated explicitly as Spanish grammar allows is also implied in English, but by association rather than through the concrete evocation of the words themselves. When we see in English "any old dwarf" we do think of the word *dwarf* as "male," and as representing the neutral category. And since we already know from the context that Señora and Cobra are "female," i.e., transvestites, we recognize the implied play on the characters' sexual ambiguity.

But again, translation is an act of choosing where the emphases lie, which meaning is most urgent. In this passage of the chapter "White Dwarf," the main point is not the characters' sex but their dwarflike dimensions.

Why Señora into Madam? It is more difficult to translate, to communicate *pendejo,* literally "pubic hair" but figuratively meaning in popular speech "jerk," than a multilevel wordplay. Everyday words like the address *señora,* charged with associations, emotions, even smells, are the most ineffable. *Señora* can mean simply "missus," as in Bioy Casares's novel *Dormir al sol* (1973), which I translated into *Asleep in the Sun* (1978). Here Lucio, the protagonist, is a simple lower-middle-class clockmaker who refers to his wife as *mi señora,* the closest equivalent in American idiom being the homey expression "the missus." But *Señora,* can more formally signify "Madam," or in another, religious context, "Lady": *Nuestra Señora,* the Virgin, translates as "Our Lady." In Sarduy's tale all these associations resound: the *Señora,* the "Procuress" (5) runs the "Lyrical Theater of Dolls" (chapter 1), or "lyrical bawdyhouse" (4), in which Cobra is the best "doll." Most readers of Sarduy would probably know what *Señora* means; its exotic otherness, its immediate mystery and opacity could suggest the everyday missus, the formal but ironical address to a Lady, and the unmentionable Procuress.

Lady seemed too polite, demanding too much of the reader to fill it in with the appropriate irony. Madam finally seemed to the most humorous, the most suggestive in English. It emphasizes the brothel connotation, with the added advantage that it's a slightly archaic English word contaminated by the French *Madame*. French continually contaminates, invades the mythic purity of Castillian in Sarduy's Cubanese; American English can reflect similar "impurities."

Sentence 4: A precarious balance between elegance and vulgarity, archaic and colloquial, must be maintained throughout: "Poise and majesty" produces an ascending sequence of pomposity, like *majestad y compostura* from shorter to longer word. "Prognathic" – one of those many Latinate terms that are more vivid in Spanish than in English – is appropriately specific and recherché here, neater than "salient-jawed." While "princess" would have provided alliteration, *infanta* locates the allusion more precisely in Velázquez's Hapsburgian court.

Since the discussion of a sentence could extend *ad infinitum,* I will take up only two final details in sentence 5: *raquítica* into "rickety," and *el desfile de una compañía de arcabuceros* into "a company of musketeers on their nightwatch."

In exacerbating and eroding precision Sarduy practices a "Caravaggesque" translation upon Rembrandt's militia company by selecting and describing R's mystery dwarf "exactly" as *"raquítica."* His version of this figure becomes Cobrita, in turn a reduction of Cobra. Cobra, the supposed signifier, can never be approached directly but only through a chain of signifiers that end up "circumscribing the absent signifier." *She* is indeed dethroned in the multiple guise of Cobrita, Sarduy's *niña raquítica,* and Rembrandt's mysterious dwarf her(?)self. All these figures progress metonymically, tracing an orbit around an absence that Rembrandt already locates at the center of his original. But Sarduy's translation of this pictorial figure already comes out of language's polyvalence: *Raquítica,* while formally denoting "rickets," mainly a child's disease, informally connotes "feeble," "frail," "deformed." Though it is not farfetched to suppose that a child in cold, damp Delft suffered from malnutrition, a lack of sunlight, and Vitamin D, why didn't Sarduy – not knowing if Rembrandt's little girl looked unhealthy only to his twentieth-century eyes – use a more general term? *Raquítica* has the vivid virtue of specificity and yet is colloquially vague, and Sarduy perceived the figure, possibly a healthy little girl in Rembrandt's eyes, as a sickly little monster, an interpretation supported by a metonymic chain in which the dead chicken tied to her waist could possibly symbolize her sickliness.

Raquítica produced in English either the technical, specific "rickett-sial" or the colloquial, polyvalent "rickety," also referring to the effects of rickets but suggesting something—less commonly some*one*—feeble and frail, like a rickety ladder. The betrayal, the impressionism of Sarduy's term becomes even more explicit in "rickety," even more distant from the chubby little image. And yet what translation would have been more faithful, more self-effacing? Translation inevitably marks its violent transit, often even more so when replacing a signifier with its "literal" equivalent.

Though Rembrandt's painting is a well-known classic, Sarduy's allusion to it, needless to say, obliges the reader to guess. That he doesn't mention the title, however, is perhaps a faithful translation: The "original" title itself was invented long after the painter's death. Before the nineteenth century, titles were rarely assigned to paintings; their spectators already knew the story, be it mythology or everyday events, told by the painting. And though this painting has been popularly known for a century or two as *The Night Watch* or in Spanish *Ronda de noche*—hence the literal translation alternative "round"—its proper "original" title would have been the already mentioned *The Shooting Company of Captain Frans Banning Cocq*. Hence Sarduy's obscurity reflects *faithfully* the painting's effect on any "reader" outside of Rembrandt's immediate context.

But he compensates with a clear clue by describing *"desfile de una compañía de arcabuceros"*; Rembrandt did represent the company in an *action* portrait, a novelty that marks the painting's place in history. Where the self-effacing translation of *raquítica* into "rickety" did violence, made explicit writing's treason, here I did violence by "adapting" the text in English. I replaced *desfile* with the distant (though closer to the original's source, itself already a misnomer) "nightwatch," making up perhaps for the greater distance Sarduy's English reader has to travel in order to gain entrance to a baroque repertory of images with which his Spanish reader is more at home.

Although muskets and harquebuses are different weapons, the musket not yet invented in Rembrandt's times, the more common word "musketeers" seemed preferable since it more dramatically evokes the image that *arcabucero* does for today's Spanish reader. To "us" Rembrandt's figures *look like* Dumas's Musketeers. "Nightwatch," "musketeers," are parodic precisions that at the same time mistranslate like the original, and its source.

Baroque Bricoleur

The translator/writer makes use of the tools available, gives old materials a new life. What was important to underscore in the translation of *"Petit Ensemble Caravaggesque,"* as the Caravaggesque presence suggests, was the dialogue with baroque art and rhetoric. But what happens to the many misquotations of classic baroque texts in *Cobra,* so familiar to Spanish readers, so alien in English?

During an orgy scene Sarduy alludes to a much-quoted verse in popular lore of the great baroque poet Luis de Góngora, a text from the *Soledades* (a seminal influence on Lezama), which, like Puig's tangos, loses its resonance in literal translation. Sarduy parodically degrades *"a batallas de amor, campos de plumas,"* literally "for battles of love, fields of feathers," into an ecstatic exclamation uttered in the "Lyrical Theater of Dolls." The famous quotation metamorphoses into *"a pachanga de amor, felpa de vino"* (22): "for wild love orgies, wine felt cushions." The elliptical *felpa* indicates metonymically "cushion"; *pachanga,* a dance, in Cuban connotes "the good life," hence this liberal transposition. Sarduy's homage and burlesque subversion, again as in the Caravaggesque passage, reflects an indirection already effective in the original. In the repressive sixteenth–century inquisitorial society to which he was subject, Góngora had to write of sexual love, that antisocial impulse, in euphuistic euphemisms. Sarduy maintains here the syntax's flowery inverted indirection, but in more liberated times, and in exile from the repressive Cuba of the late Sixties and the Seventies, he takes the liberty to add a more obscene touch.

The unimaginative route was to seek out a translation of Góngora to then misquote it; hadn't Sarduy already advised against such futile fidelities? The more interesting hypothesis was to seek out in the English language a kindred text within the rich baroque tradition that extends from Shakespeare and Donne to the Victorian pre-Raphaelites such as

Swinburne. Like Quevedo and Góngora, the pre-Raphaelites rebelled against a repressive milieu. *Bartlett's Familiar Quotations* provided me with a verse by Swinburne – yes, Swinburne again – that euphemized the birth of desire: "And Venus rose red out of wine." Though not anywhere as familiar to Americans as Góngora's verse is to Spanish readers, it certainly struck a comic note. And I misquoted it, "inserting" the more obscene "Priapus," following Sarduy's phallic obsession and displacing the feminine Venus: "And Priapus rose red out of wine." (11) *Penis* would have been a too-obvious rhymed substitute for *Venus;* a touch of recherché formality seemed necessary for the humor.

Another diachronically more appropriate choice "arose" from the pages of Shakespeare's *Antony and Cleopatra:* "Oh, withered is the garland of war,/the soldier's pole is fallen," which I vaulted into "Oh, blooming is the garland of love/the lover's pole is rising." But the epigrammatic precision of Swinburne's verse worked best, as Sarduy remarked in a letter (April 18, 1973): "I like the quotation from Swinburne and I think that, as a subterranean reference, it must work better for an English reader than Góngora; besides, it's funny."

Part IV:

Words Are Never the Same

> *Truly, that we might not varie from the sense of that which we had translated before, if the word signified the same thing in both places (for there bee some wordes that bee not of the same sense euery where) we were especially carefull, and made a conscience, according to our duetie.*
>
> RECORDS OF THE ENGLISH BIBLE

Cositas Are Not Things

THE TITLE *The Subversive Scribe* and what follows – with an ironic smile underneath – is meant to jolt the reader out of a comfortable (or uncomfortable) view of translations as secondary, as faint shadows of primary, vivid but lost, originals. Originals and translations, acts of communication, both fail and succeed, both fulfill and subvert the drive to communicate. The word aspires to be the same, to be as complete as its object (be it another word or a primal reality), but is always, to greater or lesser extent, a fragment, an approximation. To dramatize this I have purposely focused on writers and writing that speak explicitly of the original's self-betrayal. More significantly and prior to this written meditation, I gravitated toward such writers and writing.

The Subversive Scribe also both succeeds and fails: The reader may agree that the translations of these writers are continuations of the original's creative process, and that these translations (and their discussion) perform a critical act as well, but such may not be the case with all translations and translation discussions. In all honesty, I can only speak for my own experience and hope that others find familiar repercussions, though the textual journeys they take may lead them down different paths.

Perhaps translations, like originals, ultimately subvert *form* more than *meaning,* despite our modernist notion that form *is* meaning. Just as "reality" has one form, and language another, so does *Boquitas pintadas* have one form, and *Heartbreak Tango* another. By substituting movie tag lines for tangos, we changed the medium but sustained the message, the function that the original tangos had served for the reader. What occurs in translation is a shift of the relationship between form and meaning, different combinations that produce different emphases. But the communicating vessel survives in its progressive afterlives.

The most common everyday words somehow lose their nuances, their fringes of affective or even sensory associations in foreign subtitles. To stress their ineffability, to mark the distance between the most obvious equivalents, I can only propose a few more illustrations. *Cosa* is "thing" but *Tres tristes tigres* and *Three Trapped Tigers* show how *cosas* or *cositas* are and aren't things or little things.

The (s)exploitative atmosphere of pre–Castro Cuba, an ideological subtext of *Tres tristes tigres,* becomes even more (s)explicit, as Lori Chamberlain observes, in *Three Trapped Tigers.* A deliberate textual and sexual elaboration occurs at the very beginning of the section called *"Los Debutantes."* Even though "debutants" is one of the meanings in Cabrera Infante's exploration of the relations between English and Cuban Spanish, this chapter was renamed in English "The Beginners," since *debutantes* in colloquial Spanish radiates more meanings than its more specific, more limited colloquial English cognate.

The narrator of the book's first anecdote is an unnamed little girl who becomes, possibly, the mysterious unnamed woman on the psychiatrist's couch, and who may be the "absent center" of the book, Laura Díaz, the woman loved by both Cué and Silvestre. The little girl tells a tale of small-town voyeurism, in which she and her girlfriend Aurelita would huddle under a truck to watch a young woman, Petra, and her boyfriend "make out" on Petra's porch. But the little girl never tells (to the townspeople or to the reader) what exactly she and Aurelita were doing under the truck as they watched. The Spanish version is more modest than the English version, as Chamberlain rightly notes, and in these parallel tales of Petra's intercourse with her boyfriend and of the two girls' mutual masturbation "leaves the details of the story to the reader's imagination. The English version does not." (198)

The original *"Lo que no le dijimos nunca a nadie fue que nosotras tambien hacíamos cositas debajo del camión"* (23) literally says, "But what we never told anyone was that we too did things under the truck." In *Three Trapped Tigers* this became "But what we never told anyone was that we too used to play with each other's things under the truck." (11) Chamberlain presumes that this "additional material" (199) cannot be attributed solely to the translator's imagination, though in this case as in others, "imagination" did intervene, both translator's and author's. Why? Maybe because even though "things" is a vague euphemism of equal weight in both languages, in English it is more neuter: In Spanish every word has a sex, and *cositas* is feminine. So is *la muerte,* "death," with which sex has been so intimately connected in Western thought: Sex and death lead us to the unknown, to the frightening void.

La Cosa, "Death" and/or the "Vagina" (Hell), make explicit the implicit: *Cosita* is vague and yet disturbingly feminine. Cabrera Infante writes in *Infante's Inferno* that *vaina,* meaning "thing" in street language, shares its etymology with *vagina,* both words denoting "sheath."[1] The vagina's metaphoricity, its otherness, is experienced through male eyes in both *TTT* and *Inferno.* At the end of *Infante's Inferno* this "undecidable" form becomes oxymoronically an infinite claustrophobic space: It is the crossroads of the infinite and the finite, of sex (life) and neutrality (death). The vagina is both decisive (the place of birth) and the undecidable. Where am I? despairs the lonely "Infante" inside the womb or the bowels of the earth on the last pages of *Inferno.*

The supplementariness of *cositas,* perhaps more than the translator's or writer's "imagination," activates the translation's transgressive "things." The potent(ial) meaning of *cosita* in *"Los debutantes"* is something sexual, sex, the sex. The affective and effective diminutive in the Spanish weaves an infantile but also intimate note into the vagueness of "thing." This implied sexualness, which the grammar of the Spanish language articulates, is literally neutralized by English grammar. The translator(s), attempting to be true to language's effects as well as to literariness, chose to reinstate, through this so-called liberty, the underlying sexual "thrust" central to the beginnings of these beginners.

---

1. *Infante's Inferno,* 320. Jacques Derrida, in "Living On: Border Lines," describes the vagina as emblematic of undecidable borders: In "the inward refolding of *la gaine*" (vaina, sheath, girdle), outside becomes inside. The outer edge is reapplied inversely "to the inside of a form where the outside then opens a pocket." (137)

Where the exchange will never be exact, such "additional material" attempts to maintain the "economy of translation."[2]

2. In "Roundtable on Translation" (154–155), Derrida views the problem of translating from French to English, "sexed personal pronouns with unsexed ones," as one that threatens to upset the "economy of translation." Besides substituting one word (and gender) for another, genderless one – *she* or *he* for *it* – the translator would have to add a note of explanation, imposing another kind of discourse – gloss, warning, commentary, analysis – that is not the discourse of translation.

Writing, Translation, Displacement

> *The concept of the definitive text belongs to the realm of religion, or fatigue.*
>
> BORGES, "SOME VERSIONS OF HOMER"

A *leitmotif* of this odyssey into the underworld of translation has been the exile of the text, which takes on a critical signification in Latin America, where intellectuals have often been political exiles, from Argentina's Esteban Echeverría and Cuba's José Martí to today's many refugees from the continent's embattled political fronts.

That *Cobra* reflected Sarduy's experience of exile is clear enough: Cuba is no longer the "painted backdrop" of his metamorphic characters' quests but exists only in spicy Cuban phrases and Lezamesque periphrasis, or in the metaphoric relationship between Cuban exile and events in the East, where exiled Tibetan monks yearn for their homeland, conquered by Communist China. From Western Europe the plot works its way to Morocco, where Cobra seeks a manifold "conversion" that is not only sexual. The deformations of characters and places reflect the West's desire to appropriate, to become the East, as well as the East's desire to appropriate the West. From a psychoanalytical perspective, these deformations obey a wish to die in order to live, to become something else. The text ultimately communicates these disfigurements and displacements through its opaque, masking rhetoric, which undermines the myth of an innocent transparent speech.

If we can consider translation and original writing as equally "devious" rhetorical acts, I would like to expand the frame, taking into consideration the psychic as well as the rhetorical process of displacement to suggest how "words are never the same."

171

Writing

"Displacement and misplacement are this century's commonplace," Joseph Brodsky writes in "This Condition We Call Exile." Severo Sarduy engraves in his writing a double sense of displacement, his physical exile in France and the already displaced identity of his Cuban origins, inspired by Lezama, who once claimed that to be Cuban is to feel foreign. Like Lezama, Sarduy responds to the absence of a primordial nature by rewriting the world with what Lezama has called the "invincible joy of the reconstructed image."

Sarduy's novel/prose poem *Maitreya* (1978) continues the voyage from West to East begun in *Cobra,* following, as Jerome Charyn observed in the *New York Times* (March 16, 1975), the "ultimate mutability of all human landscapes." *Maitreya* attempts to represent the ineffable unrepresentability of mystical experience, of the quest for Maitreya, the prophesied Buddha of love and compassion. Like Cobra, the "protagonist" of *Maitreya,* Louis Leng, a Cuban Chinese cook stolen from Lezama's *Paradiso,* becomes a string of avatars, successive reincarnations of the Buddha. The immanent, passive wait for Maitreya becomes in the process of the writing (and reading) an imminent, active search.

Politics and history appear, if veiled, as motivating forces in all Sarduy's narratives. *Maitreya* begins with the Chinese invasion of Tibet, foreshadowing the Cuban revolution in hindsight. Desire again leads to a voyage, now a constant displacement of scenes that continues in Sagua la Grande, Cuba, where there is a Cuban-Chinese colony, in Miami's "Little Havana," in New York, where Leng sets up a restaurant, and ends apocalyptically in Iran. The novel parodies History's cycles, beginning with the destruction of a religious society by troops mobilized by Western ideology and ending with a religious revolution to purge the East of Western ways.

At first glance it might seem an unnecessary complication for Sarduy to explore a possible Cuban identity within the iconography of Buddhism, so foreign—it would seem—to Spanish America. But, apart from satirizing the crossfire in recent Eastern and Western history, Sarduy too is attempting a revolution to purge Latin American fiction of Western doctrines and practices, among them, the obsession with identity.

Whether because of his Cuban hybrid origins or because of the loss of a theosophical center in Western thought, Sarduy has found a translation of his estrangement in the scenario and beliefs of the impenetrable East. *Translatio,* "metaphor" in Latin, was used as a political term in the Middle Ages to designate the westward movement from Greece to Rome. Sarduy participates in the modern movement eastward, "translating" back to the imagined origins, to India where he claims he was able to perceive most fully that void from which Western man takes flight, in horror. An inverted Columbus, Sarduy approaches the East (or is it the West?) from the opposite direction, confirming what Gustave Flaubert, another *voyageur sur la terre,* has written:

> Don't we, at bottom, feel just as Chinese or English as French? Aren't all our dreams of foreign places? As children we long to live in a land of parrots and candied dates, we're nurtured on Byron and Virgil, on rainy days we yearn for the Orient, or we want to go and make our fortunes in India, or grow sugarcane in America (87–88)

Like Flaubert in *Salammbô,* Sarduy inevitably "translates" the non-Occidental experience. His way, as he has said, is the opposite of the blank canvas, of the minimalist haiku. Rather than imitating literally, he represents the void in his terms, explained to journalist Francisco Rivera as "saturation, proliferation, the uncontrollable spilling of signs, filling the page to the point that there's not a space, not even a crack left for the subject." (6) The subject, in at least two senses, disappears. The baroque hyperbole, displacing the Buddhist metaphor of the void, compensates for a lack. Indian temples swarming with copulating figures find their double in the sensuous cornucopia of baroque churches.[1] The immediate source of Sarduy's rootless proliferations is

---

1. André Malraux, and Lydia Cabrera, "anthropoet" of Afro-Cuban culture, reached such analogies before Sarduy. Malraux speaks (also from a Western perspective) of similarities between Asiatic and Western baroque art: "The human form, in later days to implement the divagations of baroque, served as a pretext for that thoroughly anti-Gothic style, the 'orchidaceous style,' which underlies all Asiatic art, from the luxuriance of India to the ornate majesty of the T'ang period. It is a system of lines which is not the closed system of the medieval angles in the West and that of Wei art, nor even the system, no less closed, of our classical

Lezama's "rhetoric of the simile" in which, Rodríguez Monegal writes, "comparisons leap from one analogy to another, infinitely approaching a third unknown point." (529)

This sliding rhetoric can also be compared to the process of displacement, defined by Freud as the oneiric process of "indirect representation" but also connoting, in rhetoric, metonymy. Displacement refers to the form of censorship that takes place when the affective focus of a dream – too intense to be represented directly – is displaced onto objects or words of lesser emotional importance. A simple example would be the representation of one's father (or some authority figure) in a dream as a policeman giving out a ticket. By masking the referent, displacement shifts the dreamer's focus away from the unrepresented story of the father onto the representation, the policeman.

Jacques Lacan, Freud's French interpreter, delved into representation and the *language* of the unconscious and came up with the nexus between dream processes and rhetorical operations, defining condensation as a metaphoric process, and displacement as metonymy. The rhetorical figure of metonymy operates by supplanting a displaced sign with a term that could be its logical product but whose meaning is not necessarily connected to the original term. "The crown" represents metonymically "the monarchy" but referents *crown* and *monarchy* remain independent of each other. Metonymy *displaces* an original, latent term with a lateral term, thus approaching but never reaching the total sense of the original, which always remains to be recovered.

Translation does not *intentionally* conceal meaning like psychic displacement. And rhetorical displacement, or metonymy, functions on the level of signifiers only, whereas translation is a communication process that seeks the connection between signified and signifier. However, the *effects* of these processes are similar, since translation does produce a rift between words and meanings.[2] If Lacan translated

---

arts; but a free play of arabesques in which the human body becomes a tulip, fingers are elongated and melt into the air like the flying forms of Baroque." (*The Voices of Silence: Man and his Art,* tr. Stuart Gilbert, [N.Y.: Doubleday & Co., 1956,] 170–171.) Upon visiting Java in the 1920s to study the temple of Borobudur, Cabrera discovered, "suddenly one of the reliefs looked to me like a Cuban mulatta with a basket of fruit on her head." ("A Conversation with Lydia Cabrera," by S.J. Levine, *Review* 31 [New York, 1982], 14.)

2. See C. McDonald, ed. *The Ear of the Other,* pp. 94–98, for Freud's use of *Ubersetzung* (translation) to mean both the "faults" or repression that occur in all "translation processes"

Freud's processes into rhetorical terms, it was Freud himself who first used the metaphor *translation* to define dreams, or the dream-content:

> The dream-thoughts and the dream-content are presented to us like two versions of the same subject-matter in two different languages. Or, more properly, the dream-content seems like a transcript of the dream-thoughts into another mode of expression, whose characters and syntactic laws it is our business to discover by comparing the original and the translation. (277)

The notion of an original remains sacred here, though Freud admits its ineffability in the slippery sphere of the psyche; he also still has faith in metaphor, in the possibility of describing the dream processes in other more accessible terms.

Between writing and referent, translation and original, Paul de Man speaks more skeptically of a "metonymic, successive pattern" rather than a "metaphorical unifying pattern in which things become one by resemblance. They *do not match* each other, they *follow* each other; they are already metonyms, not metaphors." (90) Perhaps he had the last (though never final) word on metaphor's failure in "Conclusions: The Task of the Translator," where he concluded that writing never succeeds in being metaphor, it can only be *metonymy*, "fragmented" in relation to the *reine Sprache* as every translation is fragmented in relation to the original.

Translation

What has made me most conscious of the metonymical motion in any literary translation is the urge to *fragment* certain terms that recur (like obsessions) rigorously, intentionally throughout a work, into diverse synonyms of lesser or lateral significance.[3] *Maitreya* provided an explicit example, the consistent appearance of the word *desplazamiento*, "displacement," or more frequently as a verb, *desplazar* or *desplazarse*.

(e.g., symptoms, dreams, the analyst's interpretation) and the processes themselves.
3. See also Michael Riffaterre: "Transposing presuppositions will mean either making the implicit explicit or a lateral displacement whereby the semiotic detour, a figurative form of phrase... will be replaced by a metonym of the representation that was blocking the way." (101)

The obsessive repetition of this vocable brought out the strategy of displacement in the original; that the term appears mostly in its verbal form stresses its definition as movement, approaching or moving away from a focal point, like translation.

The accumulations and substitutions of images in *Maitreya* – sea conches that turn abruptly into skulls, fleshy mushrooms into bulbous phalluses – speak of rhetorical displacements and cultural metamorphoses. The conch shell signals one of many affinities between East and West Indies; of magical significance in Afro-Cuban rituals, as in the "Dolores Rondon" chapter of *From Cuba with a Song,* the conch shell here becomes that of dharma, a symbol of one of the Buddha's eight blessings.

Displacement can also be observed in the vacillating, swerving story line in which supremely mystical or lyrical moments unexpectedly disintegrate into vulgar, trivial, comic scenes to then slip back again into a spiritual register. As Sarduy once remarked, *Maitreya* is a "spicier" version of Hermann Hesse's *Siddhartha,* debunking this other Westerner's solemn reverence for Eastern mysticism. The longed-for Buddha Maitreya appears as a child who disappears and then reappears as a transvestite – a kind of Siddhartha in drag, dragging out of the closet Hermann Hesse's sublimated homosexuality – and then again as a macho man, as an obese diva and so on. The subject, everyone and no one, Sarduy commented to Rivera, is expelled: "The I is no longer a monolith but a crossroads, a series of ephemeral, unconnected elements." (6) Sarduy perceives a unity behind cultural diversity; the *bricoleur* joins fragments to create the illusion of a monolith, be it a protagonist or a novel, to expose at the same time its fragmentation.

Translation, upon fragmenting that self-conscious illusion to create yet another illusion, exposes, parodies the creative process of the "original," a process of conversions and of apparent disconnections. *Desplazamiento* or *desplazar* always connotes something slightly different in each new usage – to travel, to move, to shift, to dislodge, to move in an indirect, swerving motion, to discard. These synonyms displace their center, a word that already means moving away from or toward a center, an infinitely displaced subject. What in the original is implicitly fragmented, a collage of synonyms, becomes explicit in the

English translation, where even the literal translation, "displace-ment," "displaced," "to displace," will suggest lateral connotations. Describing a journey to the mountains in search of paintable panora-mas (thinly disguising his own journeys to the East in search of the void he will adorn with baroque images), Sarduy's narrator writes: *"los desplazamientos de prospección pictórica de Iluminada,"* implying the latent content of journey or voyage in *desplazamiento.* (55) Or, when describing Lady Tremendous, the fat diva, roller-skating down Fifth Avenue toward Washington Square Park, he has her *desplazarse en zig-zag,* move and/or displace volumes of air in a zigzag *indirect motion:* Her detours are also language's detours.

Among these detours is the literal translation, "displacement" or "displace" in English, which in any case would not fit into these partic-ular contexts. To displace in English is more precise, less diffuse, less colloquial than *desplazar* (or *desplazarse*) in Spanish. We encounter again the well-known problem of the different relationships that En-glish and Spanish have with the "original" language, Latin, which has served as the basis of diverse "parodies," that is, Italian, Portuguese, Spanish, French, English.

In English, two of the more generally accepted meanings of *displace* are (according to the *Random House Dictionary*) 1) to move or put out of the usual or proper place, and 2) to take the place of, supplant. (The *OED* adds: to displace a sovereign or leader.) Thus *displace* works fairly well in the translation of the following: "Behind the door, dupli-cating its painted image and as if displacing the door forward, turning it around to show its other, wooden side, a monk appeared embracing a mongoose." (33) As the monk is opening the door and moving it forward he replaces one image, his effigy or double – of possible mys-tical significance – with the blank, trivial side of the door, an absence of imagery. This supposed physical displacement (appearing *as* a simile) is a metonymic action.

Upon displacing the "real" object of the subject's desire toward something insignificant, metonymy represents the "lack of being" that elicits desire. Desire, the latent content of the search for Maitreya, the Beloved Buddha of the future, motivates the "journey," the move-ment of images, the plot. A dead lama will be reborn as Maitreya, repeatedly "translated" into an Other who becomes the object of desire and the place of the word. But the Other (a series of metamorphosing characters or "actants") also always desires Maitreya; desire is always mediated, its object always deferred. Upon opening the door, analogically "as if displacing it," the monk appears embracing not the object of his desire, Maitreya, but a mongoose, another deployment that covers, discovers the significant, signifying absence that is Maitreya.

The choice of "displacing" here brings in both the action and the psychoanalytic/rhetorical connotation in the original, but the colloquial ease of *desplazando* is sacrificed: "Moving" it forward would sound more casual in English. As with the translation "Illuminated's pictorial travels" (37) – which expresses the implicit meaning of *desplazamiento,* the literal and metonymic voyage of images, the carrying over of landscape into painting – *desplazamiento* is always displaced.

I would like to mention one more meaning of *displace* in English that is "diluted" when translated in the opposite direction, into Spanish. This is actually the first meaning of *displace* listed in *Random House* (though not in the *OED*): "to compel (a person or persons) to leave home, country, etc." The expression "displaced person" has a particular sense in English that in Spanish corresponds to *(refugiado)* "refugee" or *(exilado)* "exile." Perhaps in this case the English translation is closer to the displaced "subject" of the original. The translation exposes the text's exile, supplanting its language, displacing the original's identity again toward the future, or toward an unknown third point.

Within this web of connections, displacement, that is, writing or translation, is the refugee's refuge, the "native" land of the expatriate. Thus the verbs "to displace," "to travel," "to zigzag," "to move" lead us to both exile and home; they both differ from and repeat *desplazar.* The translation continues the double activity of diversification and repetition that constitutes the metonymic voyage of writing. Sarduy's surprising analogies, sprouting from Lezama Lima's *sobresaltos* (shocks or jolts), in turn born upon Lautréamont's dissection table, and reincarnating Erik Satie's sati(e)ric "sudden visitations," are reborn, we can only aspire, in Translation.

La criba de la escriba, or The Riddle/Crib of the (female and Hebrew) Scribe:[4]

In a Chinese restaurant in Paris (Severo's favorite, Le Canton, right off St. Germain des Pres), surrounded by translucent screens and decorative gold grids depicting archetypal Orientalia, Severo and I talked about the many sievelike images, screens, and grids within the dense yet riddled texture of his verbal tapestries. Sarduy's readers (and translators) are induced by such "palimpsests" to read between the cracks, glimpsing in these intermittent absences the fragmented presences of other texts, other words.

Wondering about the significance of the repeated verb *acribillar* (in *Maitreya*), meaning, literally, "to riddle with holes," led to this spreading branch of our meandering conversation, but also to etymological dictionaries.[5] Translating *Acribillar* as "Riddle" turned out to be a double miracle of fidelity, semantically and mimetically, the letters *r, i, l* trilling and glittering in both words. *Criba* from the Latin *cribellare,* from *cribellum,* comes from the diminutive of *cribrum,* whence comes also "riddle."

Riddle means puzzling or dark utterance, enigma, from the Old English *raedels,* opinion, and from *raedan* (read or rede), meaning to think, to conjecture upon the significance of, as in to read a riddle, or a dream—and meaning also to interpret aloud or silently. *Riddle* as a verb means to speak in riddles but also to solve a riddle, thus meaning itself and the opposite: To speak in a riddle is to perpetrate a riddle; to solve it is to dis-solve it. Or to destroy it, to riddle it with bullets, so to speak. *Riddle* has multiple origins: In Late Old English, from German and Indo-European, *hriddel* means "coarse-meshed sieve." But *riddle* also shares Greek and Latin etymologies with *crisis,* from the Greek *kri-* and *-xrain* (clean, pure, hence sift through a sieve) and *krinein* (to decide), evolving into the Latin *cribrum* and *discrimen* (to discriminate). To sup-

4. *Escriba* designates "scribe" as well as Doctor and interpreter of Hebrew law. (*Pequeño Larousse Ilustrado,* 1966.)
5. For example: *"Una cúspide brumosa, con ramas amaneradas, de ciruelo seco, fue motivo persistente en los ejercicios de canevá que* acribillaron *infantas apócrifas de la corte austríaca."* (76) Which became in English: "A misted cusp of dried plum-wood with mannered branches was a persistent motif in the *riddled* canvas tapestry embroidered by apocryphal princesses of the Austrian Court." (56)

plement the grid, the woven screen of this etymological labyrinth, the word *crisis* recalls decision, judgment. In its primary acceptation *crisis* denotes first a turning point in a disease and, by extension, a vital or decisive stage in events; out of *crisis* comes *criticism*.[6]

Riddle means literally *acribillar* and more – in parodic precision – serving the numerous grids, enigmas, and readings that riddle Sarduy's text. *Riddle* adds meaning, or more precisely makes the implicit in *acribillar* explicit, excavating the subtext, deciding the undecidable, inscribing a critical difference.

6. The *OED* is also my guide here, *The Shorter Oxford English Dictionary*, rev. & ed. C. T. Onions (Oxford: Clarendon Press, 1959). Dis-criminate brings in the association with crime as a social disease, upon which judgment, discrimination, must be passed.

Epilog: Traduttora, Traditora

Don't write, translate, and you will earn an honorable living.

STENDHAL'S ADVICE TO WOMEN

THE EPILOG to *Infante's Inferno*, "Movies Must Have an End," (*Havana* recuperated in the mimetic *Have an End*) ends with the narrator's "rebirth" after his anguished fall into a boundless vagina, with a copy of Jules Verne's *Voyage to the Center of the Earth* as his sole guide and companion. In this epilog I would like to briefly ponder the feminized translator, traitor: me as self-betrayer fallen under the spell of male discourse, translating books that speak of woman as the often treacherous or betrayed other, as well as subversive scribe, "transcreating" writing that stretches the boundaries of patriarchal discourse.

Woman is Other, either idealized or degraded in most writing by men, and sometimes – despite themselves – in writing by women writers. Sarduy's "female" characters in *Maitreya* are monstrous obese transvestites. Puig's women, often his central characters it is true, are mostly either repressed and/or bitchy women under the sway of patriarchy. He satirically exposes their repression but identifies with and does not take them beyond their phallocentrism. *Three Trapped Tigers* begins, after the emcee's introduction, with a duplicitous tale told by a little girl and ends with the senseless ravings of a madwoman in a park, a kind of grotesque Molly Bloom. *Infante's Inferno* also speaks of women betrayed or women betrayers. Cabrera Infante often emphasizes the individuality of women, as Puig does, but even though La Estrella is the supreme artist she is also a monstrous black whale.

Woman embodies language's slippery strategies. A woman is like a translation: unfaithful if beautiful. But as the madwoman says at the very end of *TTT,* I "cant go no further." I can only question the belief system that uses these terms to define woman and translation.

What drew me as a translator to these writers was the playful, creative possibility of self-betrayal, of re-creating (in) language. Flaubert claimed that the stage of writing he enjoyed most was sculpting the sentence; for the translator, sculpting the sentence is *the* creative part. The Zukovskys rejoiced in the textual pleasure of their mimetic translation of Catullus, a betrayal repeating in perhaps the most faithful, obsessive manner Lesbia's betrayal, the generating spark of Catullus's poem. As the Amazon betrays the narrator in the penultimate chapter of *Infante's Inferno,* my "betrayal" (in conspiracy with "himself") also obeys a subversive pleasure and a logic already posited by and motivating the original, in which words may reflect reality but mostly they produce more words.

More mainstream writers such as García Márquez and Vargas Llosa have taken on public roles as political spokesmen, as dissidents. But the relatively marginalized Puig, Sarduy, and Cabrera Infante express dissidence in perhaps more corrosive, radical ways, digging into the root ·(route) of hypocrisy, into language, the very matter in which consciousness is inscribed. *Marginality* and *dissidence* are words that have been used to define the feminine role in history and culture. Julia Kristeva sees woman's inevitable marginality as an advantage; she aligns woman with the artist, particularly with avant-garde artists. But once in the realm of verbal discourse, whether or not we are dissident, we all usually have to use the so-called patriarchal code, even though our intention is to question or to make it over. "Mother tongue" is a deceptive metaphor: Mother gives or teaches us father's tongue. If, as Domna Stanton has stated, the feminist's and/or dissident's principal recourse is to expose somehow language's "phallic intentionality" (107), nonfeminist Puig, Cabrera Infante, and Sarduy undermine such an intentionality – intentionally or not.

Hitchcock offers a striking example of a misogynist whose works nonetheless reflect a sympathetic attitude toward and even an identification with women. In an analysis of his film *Blackmail,* Tania Modleski shows how Hitchcock's depiction of a victimized woman and of the "male solidarity" that casts suspicion on her "entails a covert acknowledgment of women's feelings of rage, helplessness, victimization, oppression, feelings that the female spectator may readily tap into." (311) Hitchcock repeatedly exposes in his films the ineffectiveness and hence his distrust and "fear of the forces of the law," which often places him "in a sympathetic relation to his outlaw heroines." (311)

Unlike Hitchcock's outlaw heroines, I do not pretend to plead "not guilty." Though I have translated perverse stories by Silvina Ocampo, ironic folk tales by Lydia Cabrera, prose poems of despair by Alejandra Pizarnik, and even a children's story by Clarice Lispector, my main work as a translator has been as handmaiden to the discourse of male writers. But what is really the problematic issue here is this catchword *handmaiden,* the gender-identified term and role that has been assigned to translators, male or female.

In a piece titled *"Traduire, dit-elle,"* Albert Bensoussan (*TTT*'s French translator) wrote playfully and poignantly:

> *Le traducteur subit, soumis, subjugué. Femelle, même s'il est parfois amazone. Pris, prisonnier, enferré, enserré. Ne s'appartient plus. Aliené, absorbé, ravi et depossèdé de sa parole propre. Parole de l'autre, l'auteur, la hauteur. Le traducteur est inférieur, postérieur, postsynchronisé. Le traducteur rend en son langage l'auteur publiable, mais il est oubliable. L'auteur s'ouvre, le traducteur se ferme, le premier s'éclot, le second se clot. L'auteur se crée, le traducteur secret.*
>
> *Le traducteur n'est que voix de passage.* (71)

None of these Borgesian games about translation being "a more advanced stage." The translator is secondary, enslaved, nay raped by another's words; the translator does not belong to himself but is alienated from his own language; the author creates himself, the translator remains secret. The translator is only a voice of passage. The translator is female, even if she is sometimes a male.

If somehow we learn to de-sex the original vis-à-vis its translation, particularly in our postmodern age, when originality has been all but exhausted, if we recognize the borderlessness or at least continuity between translation and original, then perhaps we can begin to see the translator in another light, no longer bearing the stigma of servant, of handmaiden. Translation, saddling the scholarly and the creative, can be a route through which a writer/translator may seek to reconcile fragments: fragments of texts, of language, of oneself. From a readerly perspective, translation is an act of interpretation. From a writerly one (for this now visible invisible scribe), it has been a (w)rite of passage.

Deferral, diffuseness, openness are some of the terms that have been used to approach uniquely feminine (subversive) writing, such as Gertrude Stein's radical reinventions of prose or Clarice Lispector's representations of an idealized feminine voice. These same terms could also apply to the narrative interruptus of Laurence Sterne, or to the inventions of Borges's Argentine guru Macedonio Fernández, of Lezama Lima, Sarduy, and Cabrera Infante. While Cabrera Infante treats woman as other, often misogynistically, he rejects historical discourse in favor of hysterical chatter; he empathizes with (as well as fears) the Amazon. Like Puig, he turned from his father's ethos and adopted his mother's love of the cinema. The Infante reborn as a writer parodies the father tongue; *Infante's Inferno* is a chatty, gossipy book. A bumbling Don Juan's jaded talk, the silly verbal fireworks of Cuban male *relajo* defy the codes of formal speech. The narrator of this book – which is really a chain of anecdotes – reincarnates finally his mother, the storyteller, the digresser, the pleasure seeker seeking pleasure only in the telling.[1]

1. Carol Maier speaks of bringing out a similar subversive thread in her translations of poems by Octavio Armand, which express male rage against a "strong" mother but also implicit admiration. As a woman translator, Maier speaks both through and against the translation but at the same time approaches the "strong, articulate female whose lack" these poems "both created and lamented." ("A Woman in Translation, Reflecting," *Translation Review*, 17, 1985, 7.)

Bibliography[1]

ADORNO, THEODOR. "The Fetish Character in Music and Regression of Listening," *The Essential Frankfurt Reader*. New York: The Continuum Publishing Co., 1980.

BARTH, JOHN. "The Literature of Exhaustion," *Atlantic* (August 1967).

——— "The Literature of Replenishment," *Atlantic* (January 1980).

BASNETT-MCGUIRE, Susan. *Translation Studies*. London & New York: Methuen, 1980.

BENSOUSSAN, ALBERT. "Traduire, dit-elle," *L'Envers du Miroir*, no. 1 (Autumn 1982).

BLANCHOT, MAURICE, cited in "Roundtable on Translation," in Christie V. MacDonald (ed.), *The Ear of the Other: Otobiography, Transference, Translation: Texts and Discussions with Jacques Derrida*, trans. Peggy Kamuf. New York: Schocken Books, 1985.

BORGES, JORGE LUIS. "Las versiones homéricas," *Discusión* (Buenos Aires, Emecé Editores, 1964).

——— *Labyrinths*. New York: New Directions, 1962.

BORINSKY, ALICIA. "Castration: Artifices: Notes on the Writing of Manuel Puig," *The Georgia Review*, vol. XXIX, no. 1 (Spring 1975).

BRODSKY, JOSEPH. "This Condition We Call Exile," *The New York Review of Books* (January 21, 1988).

CABRERA INFANTE, G. *Tres tristes tigres*. Barcelona: Seix Barral, 1967.

——— *Three Trapped Tigers*, trans. Donald Gardner and Suzanne Jill Levine in collaboration with the author. New York: Harper & Row, 1971.

——— *Un oficio del siglo veinte*, 2d ed. Barcelona: Seix Barral, 1973.

——— *Vista del amanecer en el trópico*. Barcelona: Seix Barral, 1974.

——— *View of Dawn in the Tropics*, trans. S.J. Levine. New York: Harper & Row, 1978.

——— *Exorcismos de esti(l)o*. Barcelona: Seix Barral, 1976; For "Exorcising a Sty(le)," see *Review* (New York, 1974), 61–62.

——— *Infante's Inferno*, trans. S.J. Levine with the author. New York: Harper & Row, 1984.

——— *La habana para un infante difunto*. Barcelona: Seix Barral, 1979.

——— "Horror Kirie," *Liminar* (Tenerife, Islas Canarias, Sept.–Oct. 1979).

——— "Interview: The Art of Fiction," by Alfred MacAdam, *Paris Review*, 97 (New York, Spring 1983).

CALVINO, ITALO. "Statement on Translation (June 1982 conference in Rome),"

---

1. except for works fully cited in footnotes.

Translation: special issue on The Italian Book in America (New York: Columbia University, 1986).

CHAMBERLAIN, LORI. "The Language of the Mirror: Guillermo Cabrera Infante's *Tres tristes tigres,*" in *Translation as Poetics in Postmodern Writing,* dissertation ms., UCLA, 1984.

CHARBONNIER, GEORGES. *Entretiens avec Jorge Luis Borges.* Paris: Gallimard, 1967.

CHIAMPI, IRLEMAR. "Lezama Lima: la imagen posible," *Revista de la Universidad de Mexico,* no. 13 (May 1982).

DE MAN, PAUL. "Conclusions: Benjamin's "Task of the Translator," *The Resistance to Theory.* Minneapolis: University of Minnesota Press, 1986.

DERRIDA, JACQUES. "Living On: Border Lines," trans. James Hulbert, *Deconstruction & Criticism.* New York: Seabury Press, 1979.

DONOSO, JOSÉ. *El lugar sin límites,* Mexico, Joaquin Mortiz, 1966; *Hell Has No Limits,* in *Triple Cross,* trans. S.J. Levine. New York: Dutton, 1972.

DUBOIS, J. et al. *A General Rhetoric,* trans. Paul Burrell and Edgar M. Slotkin. Baltimore: The Johns Hopkins University Press, 1981.

EAGLETON, TERRY. *Literary Theory: An Introduction.* Oxford: Basil Blackwell, 1983.

ECO, UMBERTO. *Postscript to The Name of the Rose,* trans. William Weaver. San Diego: Harcourt Brace Jovanovich, 1984.

FITCH, BRIAN T. "The Status of Self-Translation," *Texte* 4 (Toronto, 1985).

FOSTER, DAVID. "The Demythification of B.A.," *Alternative Voices: in the Contemporary Latin American Narrative.* Columbia: University of Missouri Press, 1985.

FREUD, SIGMUND. *Wit and Its Relation to the Unconscious,* trans. James Strachey. New York: W.W. Norton & Co., 1963.

——— "The Dream-Work," chapter VI of *The Interpretation of Dreams,* from *The Standard Edition of the Complete Psychological Works of Sigmund Freud,* vol. IV, trans. James Strachey in collaboration with Anna Freud. London: The Hogarth Press & the Institute of Psychoanalysis, 1900.

FRYE, NORTHROP (ed.). *The Harper Handbook to Literature.* New York: Harper & Row, 1985.

GASS, WILLIAM. "The First Seven Pages of the Boom," *Latin American Literary Review,* vol. XV, no. 29 (Pittsburgh, Jan.—June 1987).

GONZÁLEZ ECHEVARRÍA, R. "Prologue," *Maitreya,* trans. S.J. Levine. New Hampshire: Ediciones del Norte, 1987.

GREEN, JULIEN. "My First Book in English," *Le Langage et Son Double.* Paris: Editions de la Difference, 1985, 216–231.

GUIBERT, RITA. "Interview: Cabrera Infante," *Seven Voices.* New York: Knopf, 1972.

HALLIWELL, LESLIE. *Halliwell's Filmgoer's Companion.* New York: Avon Books, 1971.

HEMINGWAY, ERNEST. *Green Hills of Africa.* New York: Scribner, 1935.

HUTCHEON, LINDA. "Encoding and Decoding," *A Theory of Parody.* New York & London: Methuen, 1985.

JAKOBSON, ROMAN. "The Linguistic Aspects of Translation," in Reuben Brower (ed.), *On Translation.* Cambridge: Harvard University Press, 1965, 232–238.

JUMP, STEVE. "Guest Novelist Is Off and Punning at OU Conference," *The Norman (Okla.) Transcript* (March 28, 1987).

KENNEDY, WILLIAM. "Island of Luminous Artifact," *Review 25/26* (New York, 1979).

KERR, LUCILLE. *Suspended Fictions: Reading Novels by Manuel Puig*. Chicago: University of Illinois Press, 1987.

KRISTEVA, JULIA. "Women's Time," *Signs* 7 (1981).

LACAN, JACQUES. "Metaphor and Metonymy (I)," *Le Seminaire*, livre III, *Les Psychoses* (1955–1956). Paris: Editions du Seuil, 1981.

LEFEVERE, ANDRÉ. "Translations and Other Ways in Which One Literature Refracts Another," *Symposium: On Translation*, vol. XXXVIII, no. 2 (Summer 1984).

LEWIS, PHILIP E. "The Measure of Translation Effects," in Joseph F. Graham (ed.), *Difference in Translation*. Ithaca & London: Cornell University Press, 1985.

LEZAMA LIMA, JOSÉ. *La expresión americana*. Santiago de Chile: Editorial Universitaria, 1969.

———— *Oppiano Licario*. Mexico: Ediciones Era, 1977.

———— "Confluencias," *Mariel* (New York, Spring 1983).

MAIER, CAROL. "Some Thoughts on Translations, Imagination and (Un)academic Activity," *Translation Review*, 6 (Winter 1986).

MALRAUX, ANDRÉ. *The Voices of Silence: Man & His Art*, trans. Stuart Gilbert. New York: Doubleday & Co., 1956.

MANN, PAUL. "Translating Zukovsky's Catullus," *Translation Review*, 21–22 (The University of Texas at Dallas, 1986), 3–9.

MEDDEB, A. "La palimpseste du bilingue," *Du Bilinguisme*. Paris: Editions Denöel, 1985.

MENCKEN, H. L. *The American Language*, 4th ed. New York: Alfred A. Knopf, 1957.

MODLESKI, TANIA. "Rape versus Mans/laughter: Hitchcock's *Blackmail* and Feminist Interpretation," *PMLA* vol. 102, no. 3 (May 1987).

NELSON, ARDIS. *Cabrera Infante in the Menippean Tradition*. Newark, Delaware: Juan de la Cuesta Hispanic Monographs, 1983.

PÉREZ FIRMAT, GUSTAVO. *The Cuban Condition: Translation and Identity in Modern Cuban Literature*. Cambridge: Cambridge University Press, 1989.

PÉREZ RIVERA, FRANCISCO. "Budismo y Barroco en Severo Sarduy" (an interview), *Linden Lane Magazine* (Princeton, Jan.–March 1983).

POGGIOLI, RENATO. "The Added Artificer," in R. A. Brower (ed.), *On Translation*.

POLLARD, ALFRED W. (ed.). "Preface to the Version of 1611," *Records of The English Bible*. London: Oxford University Press, 1911, 374.

PUIG, MANUEL. *La traición de Rita Hayworth*. Buenos Aires: Jorge Alvarez, 1967.

———— *Betrayed by Rita Hayworth*, trans. S.J. Levine. New York: E.P. Dutton, 1971.

———— *Boquitas pintadas*. Buenos Aires: Editorial Sudamericana, 1968.

———— *Heartbreak Tango*, trans. S.J. Levine. New York: E.P. Dutton, 1973.

———— *Le Plus Beau Tango du Monde*, trans. Laure Guille-Bataillon. Paris: Editions Denöel, 1972.

———— *The Buenos Aires Affair*. Buenos Aires: Editorial Sudamericana, 1973.

———— *The Buenos Aires Affair*. New York: E.P. Dutton, 1976.

———— and S.J. Levine. "Author and Translator: A Discussion of *Heartbreak Tango*,"

Translation. New York: Columbia University Press, 1974.
———— "Interview," _City 5_ (New York, CUNY, Winter 1976–77).
REDFERN, WALTER. _Puns_. Oxford: Basil Blackwell Pub., 1984.
RIFFATERRE, MICHAEL. "Translating Suppositions on the Semiotics of Literary Translation," _Texte 4_ (Toronto 1985), 99–109.
RÍOS, JULIÁN. "Auto da Fenix," trans. S. J. Levine, _The Review of Contemporary Fiction,_ vol. VI, no. 1 (Illinois, Spring 1986). 187–197.
———— "Entrevista con Guillermo Cabrera Infante," _Espiral_ 51 (Madrid, 1980).
RISSET, JACQUELINE. "Joyce Translates Joyce," in E. S. Shaffer (ed.), _Comparative Literature: An Annual Journal_ (New York and London, Cambridge University Press, 1984), 6–11.
RODRÍGUEZ MONEGAL, EMIR (ed.), _Noticias secretas y públicas de America_. Barcelona: Tusquets, 1984.
———— "GCI: La novela como autobiografia total," _Revista Iberoamericana,_ 116–117 (1981), 265–272.
———— "Vista del amanecer en el trópico," _Plural_ (Mexico, May 1975).
———— _Borges: A Literary Biography_. New York: E. P. Dutton, 1978.
———— and Alastair Reid (eds.), _Borges: A Reader_. New York: E. P. Dutton, 1981.
———— "Paradiso: una silogística del sobresalto," _Revista Iberoamericana,_ nos. 92–93 (Pittsburgh, 1975).
SARDUY, SEVERO. _De donde son los cantantes_. Mexico: Joaquin Mortiz, 1967.
———— _From Cuba with a Song,_ in _Triple Cross_. New York: E. P. Dutton, 1972.
———— _Cobra_. Buenos Aires: Editorial Sudamericana, 1973.
———— _Cobra,_ trans. S. J. Levine. New York: E. P. Dutton, 1975.
———— "Cobra," _Review 72_ (New York, Fall 1972), 37–40.
———— "El barroco y el neobarroco," in Cesar Fernández Moreno (ed.), _América Latina en su Literatura_. Mexico: Siglo XXI Editores, 1972.
———— "Chronology," _Review 72_ (New York, Fall 1972).
———— "Translatio and Religio," trans. S. J. Levine, _Fiction,_ vol. 4, no. 1 (New York, 1975).
———— _Maitreya_. Barcelona: Seix Barral, 1978.
———— _Maitreya,_ trans. S. J. Levine. Hanover, N.H.: Ediciones del Norte, 1987.
———— _La simulación_. Caracas: Monte Avila Editores, 1982.
STANTON, DOMNA. "The Fiction of _Preciosité_ and the Fear of Women," _Yale French Studies,_ no. 62 (1981).
STEEGMULLER, FRANCIS (ed. and trans.), _The Letters of Gustave Flaubert 1830–1857,_ vol. I. Cambridge: Harvard University Press, 1980.
GEORGE STEINER. _After Babel_. New York and London: Oxford University Press, 1975.
———— _Antigones_. New York: Oxford University Press, 1984.
SULLIVAN, J. P., trans. and intro. _The Satyricon_. Middlesex, England: Penguin Classics, 1969.
TODOROV, TZVETAN. _Mikhail Bakhtin: The Dialogical Principle_. Minneapolis: University of Minnesota Press, 1984.
TOMLINSON, CHARLES, quoted by E. S. Shaffer (ed.), "Introduction," _Comparative Literature: An Annual Journal_.

TORRES FIERRO, DANUBIO. *Memoria plural: Entrevistas a escritores latinoamericanos*. Buenos Aires: Editorial Sudamericana, 1986.

TOURY, GIDEON. *In Search of a Theory of Translation*. Jerusalem, Israel: Porter Institute, 1980.

UPDIKE, JOHN. "Infante Terrible," *The New Yorker* (Jan. 29, 1972).

VALESIO, PAOLO. "The Virtues of Traducement: Sketch of a Theory of Translation," *Semiotica* 18:1 (The Hague: Mouton Publishers, 1976).

WEINBERGER, ELIOT. "What Were the Questions?" *Sulfur* (Ypsilanti: Eastern Michigan University, 1986).

WEISS, JUDITH. "Dynamic Correlations in *Heartbreak Tango*," *Latin American Literary Review* (Pittsburgh, Fall–Winter 1974).

ZUKOVSKY, CELIA AND LOUIS, trans. *Catullus* (Gai Valeri Catulli Veronensis Liber). London: Cape Goliard Press, 1969.

Index of Names

Suzanne Jill Levine is professor and chair of Latin American and Iberian Studies at the University of California at Santa Barbara. She was born and raised in New York City, received her B.A. degree from Vassar College, her M.A. from Columbia University, and her Ph.D. from New York University. In 1989, Ms. Levine was awarded the PEN West Elinor D. Randall prize for literary translation for her translation of Adolfo Bioy Casares's *The Adventures of a Photographer in La Plata*. Ms. Levine currently serves on the advisory board of Graywolf Press for its Latin American literature series, *Palabra Sur*.

This book was designed by Tree Swenson.

It was set in Bembo type by The Typeworks

and manufactured by Edwards Brothers on acid-free paper.